DAV
GILLANDERS
'I do all the talking!'

David Gillanders

talking to Jack Davidson

Http://www.fast-print.net/bookshop

DAVID GILLANDERS
'I do all the talking!'

All research, design work and typesetting by

Jack Davidson
www.J777AWD.co.uk

A catalogue record for this book is available from the British Library

ISBN 978-178456-641-8

First published 2019 by
FASTPRINT PUBLISHING
Peterborough, UK.

DAVID GILLANDERS

'I do all the talking!'

**The
LIFE STORY OF
DAVID GILLANDERS,
CHAMPION RALLY DRIVER**

~ A True Lifetime of Adventure ~

Incredible stories of fun and drama

**FOREWORD by
MALCOLM WILSON, OBE**

With contributions from:

Ross Baird
John Bennie
Simon Mervyn Cobb
John Davenport
Howard Davies
Nicky Grist
Gordon Hutcheon
Graham Neish
Ken Rees
Campbell Roy
Bob Wilson

FIRST EDITION PRINT 2019

DISCLAIMER

Whilst every effort has been made to ensure the accuracy of the information contained in this book, the author or the publisher cannot be held responsible for any errors or omissions.

The author reserves the right to make any changes to the information in this publication without notice. Any such changes shall be made at the time of the next reprint, providing the corrected information is supplied in good faith and with due substantiation.

The author and the publisher do not give any warranty as to the ownership of the copyright of any contributors' material forming part of this book and do not accept any liability for any direct, indirect, incidental or any consequential losses arising out of or from the infringement of any third party rights in relation to any material in this publication.

Every possible effort has been made to identify the photographers to provide due credit, and also to seek permission to use any such photographs, but where it has not been possible, the author and publisher wish to thank the relevant individuals in grateful anticipation that permission would actually be granted.

CORRECTIONS

The author and the publisher hereby offer to make any corrections and/or changes to the content of this publication should any incorrect and/or inaccurate information be erroneously published. Such corrections and/or changes shall be made effective at the time of the next reprint.
Contact: jack.davidson@J777AWD.co.uk

Front Cover Main Image:

Flying High © William Brown

Contact:

  jack.davidson@J777AWD.co.uk

  Jack Davidson

The Mini Cooper S
Photograph: Ken McEwen

The Volvo 240T

Photograph: Jack Davidson

The MG Metro 6R4
Photograph: Jim Sutherland

The Ford Escort RS Cosworth
Photograph: Jim Sutherland

CONTENTS

Foreword   11
Preface   16
Dedications   17
Acknowledgements   18
1   INTRODUCTION   19
2   BORN TO TALK   24
3   INFLUENCES   35
4   COMPETITIVE NATURE   38
5   SIMON THE FISHERMAN   74
6   STRATEGY   90
7   THE VOLVO EXPERIENCE   97
8   FROM THE VOLVO 240T TO THE…..   103
9   MG METRO 6R4   115
10 BRITISH RALLY CHAMPION   140
11 PROTEST IN THE TROSSACHS   166
12 FROM THE SUBLIME TO THE ….   188
13 THE MOTLEY CREW   197
14 CONTROVERSIAL TOUR   203
15 CELEBRITY CO-DRIVERS   210
16 SOMEONE STOLE MY HELICOPTER   226
17 SCOTTISH RALLY CHAMPION   235
18 LAND ROVER: THE BEST 4X4XFAR   256
19 BREAKFAST WITH "BARBARELLA"   271
20 FLIGHT OF THE F-15   278
21 LOOKING INTO THE ABYSS   294
22 THE BIGGEST INSURANCE CLAIM …   303
23 MONTE CARLO OR BUST   311
24 CHANNEL OF DISCOVERY   326
25 M-SPORT   334
26 A DIFFERENT PERSON   341
Appendix – Main Results   354

I must admit, when I heard that the title of this book was going to called *"David Gillanders"*, I was not in the least bit surprised, but when I heard what the sub-title was, *"I do all the talking!"* I just *had* to laugh out loud, because talking is what David Gillanders *is* all about.

I knew of David in the early eighties, but it was really in 1987, when both of us were competing in our MG Metro 6R4s, that we became firm friends. After the first round of the British Rally Championship, David and I had to return home immediately the rally ended, so we both journeyed from Bournemouth to Heathrow together and of course, typical of David, he introduced me to the British Airways Executive Lounge, which I'd never been to before, and that's when our real friendship started.

David is very much an individual – there's not a single word I can use to describe him. He is certainly a larger-than-life character who is great fun to be with, and he was also very smartly dressed at my son's wedding in August, 2015 in his Carnegie tartan trews and waistcoat.

I would say that what David has achieved from a driving perspective, given his hand disability, has been remarkable. How he's done it, what he's done, and being the flamboyant character he is, it would be easy to think that he would have been the same behind the steering wheel, but in fairness he was actually a very composed, controlled and calculating driver. What I mean by that is that he had very few accidents, so if he'd started younger, he could well have gone on to greater things than what he actually achieved.

Here's David (he's the one in the tartan trews) having a laugh with two of my former WRC drivers, Henning Solberg (left) and Mikko Hirvonen, at the occasion of my son's wedding. Photograph: Gladys Gillanders.

As an orator – well, what can I say? He's really just fantastic fun to be with, particularly in male orientated company. For example, if in the middle of a shoot with a lot of guys, he'd always have these amazing tales to tell, and many of them are within the covers of this book. He also has an incredible knack of understanding people and working out just how far he can actually go. He's very brash, but on the other hand he's very clever, and he knows just what the boundaries are which is quite unique considering he's such a forceful and powerful character.

I think the big thing for him was the fun we both had before the Granite City Rally, his home event, in 1987, and during the competition as well. His words to me the night before were:

'You come up here (to Aberdeen) boy, and I'm going to whip your posterior.'

Well, perhaps not those exact words….

But, of course, I replied:

'Obviously, David, it's your home rally but there's no way, absolutely no way, that you're going to beat me.'

It was really good banter and I think in the end it was a scored draw. I led the rally until I went off the road and retired, and David subsequently won.

We started a business relationship a good number of years ago when David was working with Jaguar Land Rover (JLR) and he basically helped M-Sport get its foot in the door there. Since then we have done a few projects with the manufacturer and David has been the catalyst for those programmes.

As far as his life story is concerned, I think that it's fantastic that it has been collated. I cannot remember all of his adventures but it's brilliant that they have been put down on paper for others to read and enjoy. Some of his tales of things that he has done are truly amazing. He's fished the best fishing, he's shot the best shooting, and he's driven the best rally cars. Whatever he's done, he has done it at a very high level. His shooting is fantastic, and he is a very good driver, but this book is also about the people that he's met along the way. And because of his character he has been able to have some truly incredible discussions with people, and had many interesting and entertaining encounters with a number of high ranking individuals.

For me, reading about the people he's met on his travels, and at Skibo Castle, is what I think many people will find very interesting. Obviously, the motor sport aficionados will find the rally stories really entertaining. It's a fantastic and fascinating mix, and this makes for a highly unusual and enjoyable read.

What he did for everybody who had been involved in his success when he won the British Championship in 1987 with Ken Rees was previously unheard of. He took everybody, and that included all the mechanics and their wives, and put them up in Gleneagles Hotel for two nights as a gesture of gratitude and appreciation for the support he had been given that year. For all his outgoing personality, underneath he's basically a very generous, soft hearted man, although it doesn't always come across this way.

From my perspective, David is always generous and very appreciative of what M-Sport (previously known as Malcolm Wilson Motorsport) has done for him. This was especially true in 2013, when, amidst all the World Rally Cars and the racing Bentleys that were being prepared in my very high-tech workshop, he charged in with his somewhat low-tech *'Miss Moneypenny'*, a 17-year old Nissan Micra that he and Gordon Hutcheon had acquired to compete with on the *"Monte Carlo or Bust Banger Challenge"*.

The horn blasted loud and long, the lights flashed off and on, and the car screeched to a halt in the middle of where all the mechanics were working, and David just simply demanded attention. He jumped out, shouting:

'Get this damn car fixed for me – we're on this long event to Monte Carlo!'

He had all the mechanics running around for him, but that's just David – he can get people to do all sorts of things for him.

I am delighted to write this Foreword for him and I am really keen to see how successful his book is. I hope you enjoy reading it as much as I have enjoyed hearing his amazing tales of fun and adventure.

I have never read a life story quite like it!
'Yes, David certainly does all the talking!'

Malcolm Wilson.

PREFACE

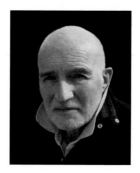

It might be difficult to believe, but I swear by the content of this book. The stories deserve to be told because I don't know how much time I have left. The threat of another heart attack is never far from my mind.

I believe that the stories inside this book are nothing short of incredible. I hope you enjoy reading about the cars that I have driven, the motor sport events I have competed in, the aircraft I have flown in, the boats I have sailed in, and the numerous and varied incidents I have been involved in over the years.

Above all, I hope you will share my enthusiasm for the many fantastic people I have had the good fortune to meet, become acquainted with, and befriend, during my lifetime of adventure.

It all happened to me, and I have done all the talking!

I hope you now enjoy all the reading!

David F.A.B. Gillanders

DEDICATIONS

To Gladys, my long suffering, caring, beautiful wife and best friend, my eternal gratitude, friendship and love.

To my daughter, Nicole, and her two children, Finlay and Amelie, my love.

To my son, David, my love.

ACKNOWLEDGEMENTS

I wish to thank the following people and/or organisations who have, either directly or indirectly, past or present, contributed in some way or other to my life, and thereby the content of this book:

Aberdeen Royal Infirmary; Keith Adams; Alan Banks; *"Autosport"*; Peter Barrett; Paul Batchelor; Willie Bauld; Robert Beck; John Bennie; Dave Bignald; Dr. Peter Bodkin; Chris Bodsworth; (The) British Army; Duncan Brown; William Brown; Scott Brownlee; Burdumy Motors; George H. W. Bush, 41st President, United States of America; Gill Buyers; Henry Cameron; Lauren Chalmers; Dick Cheney, 46th Vice President, United States of America; Alison Cheyne-Hamilton; Tom Chisholm; Dr. Francis Clark Snr; Bill Clinton, 42nd President, United States of America; (Simon Clubb Photography, *('www.simonclubb.com')*; Annie Cobb; Simon Mervyn Cobb; Tom Coffield; Roger Crathorne; Bill Cruickshank; John Davenport; Muriel Davidson; Howard Davies; Deeside Golf Club; Tommy Dreelan; Frank English; *"Evening Express"*; Bob Ewen; Paul Fairbanks; Ferret Fotographics; John Fife *('www.jaggybunnet.co.uk')*; Ross Finlay; Jane Fonda; Martin Forrest; Karen Fyvie; Gartrac Ltd; David Elder Campbell Wattie Gillanders *(my father);* David Gillanders Jnr. *(my son);* Doris Ogilvie Gillanders *(my mother);* Gladys Gillanders *(my wife);* Nicole Gillanders *(my daughter);* Martin Gillespie; Lord Glamis, (17th Earl of Strathmore); Mike Gower; Gavin Green; Mark Grierson; Nicky Grist; Ronald Herd; Martin Hirst; Gordon Hood; John Horton; Graeme Howard; Chris Huish; Gordon Hutcheon; Paul Hutcheon; Bob Irvine; Jaguar Land Rover; Peter Jeffrey; Dr. Robert (Bob) Jeffrey; Gareth Jones; Leon Joubert; Eddie Kelly Motorsport Photography; Malcolm Lamont; Bob Leckie; Nicky Lindon *('www.6r4.net')*; Mike Little; Frank Love *('www.raceandrally.co.uk')*; Brian Lyall; Kevin MacIver; Fergus McAnallen *('www.rallyretro.com')*; Ken McEwen; Colin McMaster *('www.mcklein.de')*; Colin McRae, MBE; Ian McRae; Dr. Malcolm Metcalfe; K. Michael *('www.trawler-photos.co.uk');* Charlie Bruce Miller; Jim Milne; Chris Money; The Morgan Motor Company; Richard Murtha; Graham Neish; Paramount Studios; David Pearson *('www.motoprint.co.za')*; Colonel Carl E. van Pelt, USAF; Tony Pond; Gerry Potter; *"(The) Press and Journal";* Steve Pugh; Jonathan Pulleyn; Ken Quaife; Michael Quaife; Rod Ramsay; Roger Reed; Ken Rees; Wolfgang Reitzle; Dave Richards; Brian Riddell; Geoff ('Jolly') Roberts; Jim Robson; Campbell Roy; Amelie Rutherford *(my granddaughter)*; Finlay Rutherford *(my grandson);* Timo Salonen; Peter de Savary; (The) Scottish Rally Championship; Dawn Simpson; Cecil Smith; Gary Smith; Joe Smith; Ray Smith; Steve Smith; Speedsports (Ruthin); John Steele; Sir Jackie Stewart, OBE; George Stroud; Jim Sutherland; Tommy Sutherland; Roger Swan *('www.motoprint.co.za')*; SwedeSpeed; Derry Taylor; Göran Thobiasson *(GeTe Rallyfoto)*; Tobias Tobiasson; Brian Thomson; Sandy Topp; *'Trend' ('www.trendmagazine.co.uk')*; Angela Torney; USAF Air and Ground Crews; Björn Waldegård; Gary Walker; Jerry Weintraub; Chris West *('www.chriswestphotography.net')*; Martin Whitaker; Drummond Whiteford; John Whyte; Jeremy Williams; Bob Wilson; Malcolm Wilson, OBE; Ken Wood; Graham Yule.

ALSO: SPECIAL ACKNOWLEDGEMENTS ARE DUE TO: Jack Davidson, for all his research, knowledge, typesetting and photo-journalistic efforts; and to Ross Baird, for his help and patience, without which this book would never have come to fruition.

PLUS: All of my mechanics, technicians, coachbuilders, sponsors and numerous unnamed photographers whom I could not find, or get in touch with.

Apologies are offered to anyone I may have omitted in error.

Chapter ONE

INTRODUCTION

I thought I was invincible!

I really thought I was invincible!

I never gave much thought to my health until 2006 and that was when I underwent a medical examination prior to applying for my annual competition licence. The resultant electrocardiogram on January 19, 2006, gave me a huge shock because it indicated that I needed urgent surgery and this would necessitate receiving a triple heart bypass operation. One week later, on January 26, I had that surgery.

Following the operation I was able to carry on with life much as before, but on December 21, 2014, my health began to further deteriorate to the extent that I had the first of three heart attacks. The second of which was on March 2, 2015, and the third was on November 11, 2015. I had another episode early in February 2016, and now, as a result, I realise that invincible I am not, and that my time on this planet is finite.

Accordingly, I felt that I needed to put something down in writing for myself, for my family, for my friends, and for anyone who knows me, or for anyone interested in the sport of special stage rallying or in adventure.

I have been very fortunate to have been involved in motor sport all of my adult life, especially in special stage rallying during the fabulous Group 'B' era. It was quite special, but it will never happen again. The sport will never be allowed to build and drive hugely powerful supercars like those used in the 1980s any more.

I was extremely privileged to get to drive a factory-provided MG Metro 6R4, which was the 'Pride of Britain', and there are some stories in this book that might make people think, *'W-o-w! That was rallying in the real sense!'*

The title of my book, *"DAVID GILLANDERS – I do all the talking!"* is pretty much self-explanatory, especially the talking element, because I have probably talked since the day I was born.

Although I am a bit of a comedian in many ways, I do have a wealth of knowledge on a great myriad of things. I was never the quickest in a car. In fact I was never the quickest at doing anything, really, but I have been very reliable and, yes, there is nobody quite like me, even if I say so myself!

I say this because, amazingly, I can go to hotels, or onto golf courses, or attend other functions, even today, some decades after I stopped competing, and somebody, somewhere, might make an approach and ask:

'Are you David Gillanders?'

To receive a question like that, somewhere along the line I must have made an impression (on some people, anyway) so that's the reason for the name of my book.

I was still in motor sport in 2006, but pretty much on the periphery of it all, but in order to compete, like every other driver, I had to qualify and obtain a competition licence. My previous licences were a full international 'C' racing licence and an international rally licence, both granted by The Motor Sports Association (MSA), the governing body for motor sport in the United Kingdom, and which is affiliated to the world governing body of motor sport, the Paris-based Fédération Internationale de l'Automobile (FIA).

Every driver who applies for an international motor sport competition licence has to undergo an annual medical, but when a driver reaches the age of 45, he, or she, must also obtain, and present, a written report of a stress related electrocardiogram (ECG), but as this rule only appeared in 2006, I had no previous reason to check for any heart problems.

Accordingly, I went along to the Aberdeen Royal Infirmary (ARI) to get the procedure carried out, and I failed. I failed! *I couldn't believe that I HAD FAILED!* And I certainly couldn't think why this should have happened because I didn't drink, and I didn't smoke. *(I'll talk about the drink later in the book because that's a story on its own).*

The consultant cardiologist chap in charge was a lovely man by the name of Dr Malcolm Metcalfe who would go on to become the Acute Senior Associate Medical Director in the Infirmary. Anyway, he said at the time:

'David, we need to give you an angiogram, and that means we are going to put dye into you and check your system out.'

So, fine, I went along with that and had my system checked out, but halfway through the actual procedure there was a deathly silence in the room, and I didn't know why. I was whisked back to the other room and I remember it like it was yesterday.

It was 7 o'clock in the evening when Dr. Metcalfe came walking into my room, where my lovely wife and best friend, Gladys, had already joined me. He sat on the end of the bed and said:

'David, I have something to tell you. You have what's known in the business as a widow-maker.'

I looked at him and asked:

'What's that?'

'Technically, you should be dead now, but you will be dead in maybe three months unless we give you a triple heart bypass.'

That was a bit of a shock for Gladys, and especially me, because I had just come back from Bahrain where I had been busy working on the Formula One circuit doing a lot of hard, stressful stuff out there. There was no pain, no angina, no nothing!

Nevertheless, I had to get an x-ray taken and when I went to see the heart surgeon, Dr. Robert (Bob) Jeffrey, I showed him the x-ray which prompted a jocular response to lighten the mood:

'Who belongs this x-ray?'

'I do!'

'You're joking?'

'No, I'm not joking.'

He asked if I was doing anything next week.

'Why?'

'Because you're with me next week!'

Exactly seven days later I had my triple bypass operation, but I remember distinctly saying to Dr. Jeffrey at the time that I needed to be fixed in eight weeks. (Rally drivers don't get operations, they get serviced and fixed).

'Why is that?'

'I've been invited to compete in Bahrain in a pro-celebrity race supporting the Formula One Grand Prix, and I want to go there and do it.'

'David, you won't be fit in eight weeks. You will be out for at least three, maybe four, or even five months.'

'No, no, I need to be fit in eight weeks.'

Anyway, the surgeon did a great job, and amazingly, eight weeks later I was on the circuit at Bahrain and completed the race. I did feel awful, but I *had* made it and I *had* raced.

The need for a triple bypass operation, or 'service', was the first indication that not all was well with my 'engine'. The 'filter' was getting clogged up, to use rally parlance, but you have to understand, from a rally driver's point of view, if you open something up and take out the faulty bits, you fix them and put them back in again, with new pipes. Don't you? It's sorted! You have to believe they are fixed. Of course, that is a very simplistic way of looking at things.

But it wasn't fixed. It wasn't sorted. After I had my first heart attack at the end of 2014, the cardiologist gave me what was called an angioplasty, but that didn't last, and I had to go back ten weeks later to have three stents inserted by Dr. Metcalfe and this seems to have worked.

However, from my point of view, I have a total lack of confidence in my 'engine'. My heart, or 'oil pump', as far as I know, is not damaged. It seems to be alright but I'm on a barrowload of pills just to try and keep things ticking over at 1,200 revolutions per minute, so to speak, using beta blockers and blood thinners. The list of medication goes on, but this gets me back to the start of this story.

I wanted to write this book before these pills stop working. I really, and honestly, believe that I am nearing the end of the stage although I'm still not out of the woods, so to speak. I expect to have to undergo a stress test in the not too distant future, but I feel that the next time I have a problem with my 'engine' my number might well be up. And so, true to my nature, I'll keep going flat out, in top gear, until that time comes.

And that's why I decided to write down my lifetime of adventures in this book. I hope it gives you as much pleasure as I had talking about it, as Jack Davidson did listening to it (well, that's what he said), and now you, reading it!

Chapter TWO

BORN TO TALK

I was born and given the name, David Francis Alexander Barrey Gillanders, in May, 1950, in Aberdeen, on the north east coast of Scotland, but there was a problem. I had a 'disabled' left hand. Back then it really was tough to live with such a disability, whereas today, with the advent of new technology and some incredible medical advances, there is considerably more knowledge and help available to assist similarly afflicted people.

When my mother and father took me into their lives they very quickly realised that I had an issue, so they decided to seek out a surgeon in Aberdeen for advice on what to do. This is what I was told the surgeon had said:

'We'll remove the left hand, it's the easiest option.'

That certainly would have been the easiest option (for the surgeon), but I have to stand up for my father and mother, because they declined. Instead, they said:

'We'll take David down to Harley Street in London.'

That's what they said, and that's exactly what they did; they drove me to Harley Street, in a three-wheeler Morgan sports car. Just think about the state of the roads in 1950. There were no motorways, and no service stations, but they drove the three-wheeler all the way to London (and back) and I really can't imagine how they did that.

The current distance from Aberdeen to London is 545 miles, and that can now be achieved entirely on dual carriage-way or motorway, but that certainly wasn't the case so soon after World War II. In fact, it wasn't until December 5, 1958, that the first motorway opened in the UK, and even then that was only just over eight miles of the M6 Preston bypass.

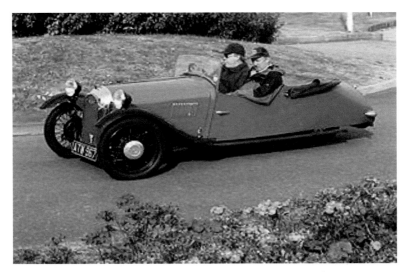

A typical 1950s 3-wheeler Morgan.
Photograph: Courtesy of the Morgan Motor Company.

Three-wheeler Morgans were in their day popular cars, but to drive all that distance with me, a baby, is just mind-blowing. I must have been on my mother's knee all the way there and back. There were no safety belts then, and certainly no carry-cots, or car seats, far less any room for one.

The Malvern Manufacturer decided to discontinue production of the three-wheeler Morgan in 1950, and my guess is that my old man probably negotiated a deal to buy a cheap one first! It's no wonder that he later became a successful car dealer. In 2011 Morgan started to produce their modern interpretation of H.F.S. Morgan's classic three-wheeler.

Anyway, my parents duly met a specialist in London, and whoever he is, or was, I wish to thank that person from the bottom of my heart, because he said:

'We can save his hand. We can do certain things to it to help him.'

They amputated one finger, but whatever else they did it's what I've got now – and that's a functioning unit. It hasn't stopped me from doing anything, so I have to take my hat off to my father and mother for having the strength of character to stand up for me and take that decision in the face of the original medical advice. My parents would have had no money in 1950 as my father worked as an engineer on the buses in Aberdeen, and my mother looked after me.

My condition was identified as 'Syndactyly', which is joined digits of, in my case, the left hand. Apparently, it is one of the most common congenital malformations of the limbs and can affect one in every 3,000 babies. It can be classified as simple or complex, the latter when it involves either the bone and, or, the nails of adjacent fingers. I suppose I must have the complex classification.

It figures.

Fingers like mine fail to separate into individual digits. This separation usually happens in the early weeks of the embryologic development, but where does the word 'syndactyly' come from? It's all Greek to me, as they say, but I am reliably informed that the name actually comes from two Greek words, namely, 'syn' (together), and 'dactyly' (fingers or digits).

I have never been very interested in my heritage, but for the interest of the reader the following will give a flavour of where I came from.

My mother's father was Major Francis Webster. He served with the Gordon Highlanders during World War I and was awarded a medal after he sabotaged some German guns. The Allies had been in danger of being overrun, but he 'spiked' them by removing the breach blocks, which he then put in a bag and ran away! He was a bit of a character, my grandfather, very colourful, and always properly dressed. He was every inch a major in the British Army.

My mother, Doris Ogilvie Gillanders (nee Webster), was a very good singer, and a very good-looker in her day. Mother and father were great ice skaters, which is where they met. I cannot imagine my mother and father skating, but they did. They probably met at the hugely popular Donald's Ice Rink in Spring Garden, Aberdeen, sometime in the 1930s. In those days ice skating was a big thing. Mother was the weaker of my two parents as my father, David Elder Campbell Wattie Gillanders, to give him his full title, was a very dominant person. He went on to found and develop one of the most successful Volvo agencies in Britain, which of course took its toll on family life. She did not have it easy.

*My mother,
Doris Ogilvie Gillanders,
and me, aged around eight.*

In the early days, we lived in Torry, a district of Aberdeen to the south of the River Dee, where there was a particular emphasis on the fishing industry. The city itself straddles two rivers – the River Don to the north and the River Dee to the south. What is not very clear is the origin of the name 'Aberdeen' although it is well recognised that 'Aber' means 'at the mouth of' but the remainder is somewhat more contentious. Some people, myself included, favour that 'deen' is an amalgam of the 'Dee' and the 'Don', but I didn't learn that at school!

Mother did a great job in bringing me up, especially with my hand disability. It *was* difficult, and I remember going to school and being bullied when I was a young boy. It's all very vague now, but I do remember certain things at school that weren't pleasant at all. I was called names and all the rest of it because of my hand. Children can be very cruel, *really* cruel, but did that make me stronger? I don't know. They say it does, but I really don't know.

School Days

My earliest memory is of going to a nursery school in Kincorth, a district adjacent to and just south west of Torry, in Aberdeen. I was howling, I remember, *really* howling because I did not want to go. I also remember falling down the stairs and landing on top of a glass bottle and almost taking the thumb off of my *right* hand which would have been a real disaster. I had been carrying a pint of milk up the stairs when I slipped, and my hand went down onto it. I am right hand dominated and any such accident would have been disastrous.

After that I went to Broomhill Primary School, on Broomhill Road. It was housed in an imposing three-storey granite building, the type of which helped give Aberdeen its 'Granite City' moniker.

After the Eleven Plus exam I went to Ruthrieston School. This was situated on a road parallel with the River Dee on Riverside Drive, but my overriding memory of school was of getting the belt. It may have been called the strap in the better schools, but it was the 'belt' I was more acquainted with. In those days the belt was part of growing up and I was belted dozens of times because I used to talk a lot. I talked a lot in class and I still talk. I think it's something I was born to do.

I *do* like to talk.

From my perspective I can't remember anything positive about Broomhill Primary School, or Ruthrieston School, but I do remember that Ruthrieston was a very uncompromising school, and the pupils there were wild and tough. Thankfully, Ruthrieston was turned into flats, but of all the schools in Aberdeen at the time, Ruthrieston had, along with Kaimhill in Garthdee (further up the bank on the River Dee) some of the hardest cases in my day.

In Ruthrieston, the first thing that happened to me was a beating when I walked through the school gates into the playground. Pupils were standing there with their schoolbags full of something heavy, and as I approached they started to attack me. That was the initiation rights for getting into Ruthrieston.

The bullies at that school were simply animals; I can't remember their names, but I can still visualise them. Even the teachers were terrified. Everybody was scared of them. The boys were tough, but some of the girls were tougher than the boys! I am pleased to say that as I grew older that particular 'system', or culture, gradually disappeared, and by the time I became a senior Ruthrieston pupil the older pupils didn't batter the younger ones as they came in through the gates for the first time. I think I actually did some good there.

I have no idea how I survived it, honest to God. I was bullied, and I was certainly belted by the teachers, but once again, that was normal for the time.

I *know* I was not a good scholar. I was pretty lazy and simply not interested in anything. I wasn't sports minded: I didn't like athletics, or football, but I *could* throw a cricket ball because my right arm was much stronger than my left. I was also a pretty pathetic swimmer because I simply did not like going in the water.

Overall, I was a bit of a dud at school. I certainly wasn't an outstanding pupil and I am probably not the type of pupil that the teachers remember, unless it was for talking. They might say:

'Oh aye, Gillanders! I remember him well. I belted him heaps of times.'

My English teacher was Mr Brown. I really did not like him. That was probably because he used to belt me a lot, and what's more, he used to put my hand over the table, so that I couldn't get my hand down to pull it out of the way. Then there was the physical education instructor – I forget *his* name – but he put my good hand over the door knob to give me the belt.

Today, this form of corporal punishment is not allowed and the perpetrators would be charged with assault, but do I regret it? No I don't. Was it a part of growing up? Yes it was, and do I think it was right? Yes, I do. If a person steps out of line, then punishment should be given, although 'getting the belt' made absolutely no difference to me; it didn't change me. I didn't become a maniac, and still I kept on talking….

I hated school, really hated it, and I couldn't wait for 4 o'clock to come and thus escape. In fact I couldn't wait for 1965 so that I could leave the school forever.

Mods and Rockers

After I left the school at 15 I became a 'Mod', yes a 'Mod'. I'd green shoes and tight pants, I know, I know. I wore white collars, and I'd hair in those days. I was *'Oh, my God!'* just the 'bee's knees' and I also wore hipsters!'

In the 1960s and 1970s the two main youth sub-cultures were the Mods and the Rockers. The latter group usually centred on their motor bikes and black leather jackets. They

29

wore biker's boots or soft shoes called 'brothel creepers'. The common rocker hairstyle was called a pompadour, and they tended to favour the 1950s music of rock and roll, played by artists like Eddie Cochran, Gene Vincent, Bo Diddley, and Elvis Presley.

The Mods centred on fashion, like me in my green shoes and tight pants, and often rode scooters, although I was more into four wheels than two. Mods tended to wear more clean-cut outfits, and enjoyed rhythm and blues, as well as beat music and numerous bands like The Who, The Small Faces and The Yardbirds.

I'd go to all of the dances at the time, and because of my left hand – back to my left hand – I found that I was still a little bit hesitant, not embarrassed, but just plain hesitant. I would ask one of the girls to dance in a place in Aberdeen called 'Madam's' (imagine calling a place 'Madam's' now-adays...) However, I should explain that 'Madam's' was named for a lady who assumed the title, 'Madam'. This was to add a bit of panache to what were essentially dancing classes for the schoolchildren. Well, 'Madam's' was part of the Cowdray Hall, an arts and entertainment venue, located on Blackfriars Street, off Schoolhill. There was a small unimposing door, and this was the entrance to 'Madam's' and inside was the dancing school where I went to be taught how to ask a girl up for a dance. The girls would be on one side and the boys on the other and the woman in the middle was called 'Madam', of course, and she would say:

'Right, boys, ask a girl to dance.'

So all the boys walked up, and some even ran, but of course all the good looking girls were immediately taken. The next problem I faced was when I put my right arm round a girl she would automatically take hold of my left hand. Invariably, her right hand would be much bigger than my left hand and I could see her thinking, *'What the hell's going on here?'* That kind of thing did make me feel self-conscious about asking girls to dance.

I'd also go to the nightclubs in the city, and of course the Beach Ballroom at the seafront was the largest of the entertainment venues. It's crazy thinking about it now, but the boys would go round the ballroom floor in an anti-clockwise direction and the girls would travel in a clockwise direction, or vice versa! There'd be a fight or two as well, usually the Mods versus the Rockers, but for variety it was sometimes the Rockers against the Mods!

There was a lot of fighting in those days. It was a big thing to have a fight, and as we used to say:

'You cannot imagine what we got up to back then!

Then I happened to meet Gladys Anne Cooper, the lovely, beautiful, Gladys, and that was me! That single encounter changed my life completely, because she then became my girlfriend.

Cars, Cars, Cars

I was once asked if I felt I had had a good education. I probably did, although I didn't pay much attention to it because the minute I was 15 I managed to get a job in a place called 'Local Wholesalers'. There, I became an auto electrician for Bosch. My job was to make batteries. I know, *make* batteries! I had to get the cases, and the electrodes, and then fill them up with acid and charge them. This is what happened in 1965. I became a battery maker although I also ended up making dynamos and distributors, both of which would be classed as alien tasks today, and I repaired them too.

Then I went to work with my father who had set up Gillanders Motors in Fraser Place, just off George Street, in Aberdeen, and it was here that I really became interested in cars. He gave me a Renault 4L Van to drive at night, and on one occasion I was chased all over Aberdeen by the police.

I actually drove it up and over the Broad Hill, all 94 feet of it. The Broad Hill is actually the highest point on the seafront, running from the north to the south. A few of my friends and I would congregate at the beach, at the east end of Aberdeen.

The Broad Hill (right) doesn't look nearly so high as it did in the late 1960s when I had my Renault 4L van.
Photograph: Jack Davidson.

I was in my 4L van, right outside the beach ballroom where there's a large roundabout. In those days I had a big klaxon horn fitted to the Renault and I also put RedEx, a petrol fuel system cleaner, into the carburettor, yes, into the carburettor, not into the tank, and this created a huge smoke-screen out of the exhaust!

I also had the wiper washers angled to the side so that I could soak people as we drove along the street, and I had a big foot press to play with.....

'Oh, ye've absolutely nae idea (what we got up to!)'

At the roundabout, I pumped in the RedEx, and then went round and round and round, about 20 times, until I couldn't see a thing – there was no wind, and the smoke obliterated everything from sight, but then the police arrived and said:

'STOP!'

'Aw, I'm nae stopping...'

I nearly ran one bobby over, then I turned left and up the Broad Hill. I just drove straight up and these two policemen were so fat they couldn't chase me. They were at the bottom screaming at me and I was at the top laughing away. It was dark, and the area was covered in smoke, of course, but eventually they went away to get some help, so I nipped back down and went home, but what I had forgotten about was that on the side of the van, emblazoned in big bold lettering were the telling words, Gillanders Motors....

The next day the police arrived at the garage to see my old man and, well, 'he wasn't happy!' He said:

'That was a good advert, son!'

He took the van away from me for a month.

Yes, I'd say that the Beach Boulevard and Union Street in Aberdeen were definitely part of my growing up.

My old friend and former co-driver, Ross Baird, actually knew my father before he knew me. He worked for him in Roy Thomson's Garage, but he got to know me a lot better when I phoned him up one day from Hazlehead Park in the west of the city. That was because I'd a problem with my van. I had taken it to the public park in the middle of winter, ostensibly to learn how to drive on snow. I soon found this huge, predominantly flat, white area, well it would be white, wouldn't it? So I started to drive on it, slide all over it, and basically learn all about car control. All went well until I decided to plough through the snow bank to get onto another nice flat expanse of ground. The problem was that this 'snow-bank' was actually a drystane dyke, (a stone wall built without mortar) and was the boundary for the second nine golf course!

Overlooking the snow-covered second nine-hole golf course at Hazlehead, and the rather solid drystane dyke. Photograph: Jack Davidson.

The van was 'marmalised' at the front end following the impact, so as well as phoning Ross, I got my other pals, Jim Robson, and Derry Taylor to also come along. Together we extricated the Renault and took it back to Fraser Place to fix it before the old man saw it.

I used to hang around with a bunch of lads of the same age group. They included the likes of Jim Robson, Bob Leckie, Jim Milne, Derry Taylor and John Whyte. We were not only car daft, but also interested in motor sport, and we discovered that the best way to compete sensibly was to join the local motor club – The Aberdeen and District Motor Club. The ADMC has probably been the biggest influence in my life because I very quickly realised that driving up and down the Boulevard *wasn't* the thing to do. By this time, I had a lovely green and white Mini Cooper S, with the registration number, 'ERG 574D'. It was my pride and joy at the age of 19.

Jim Robson also became a big influence on my life, but more about him later. Jim and I became close friends and we would build the gearbox and shave the cylinder head and then put twin choke weber carburettors onto the Mini and slowly, but surely, also add such things as performance-enhancing straight-cut close-ratio gears, straight-cut idler gears and also a limited slip differential. It became quite something to drive, although it only had around 90 brake horsepower, which today is nothing, but in the late 1960s and the early 1970s it was considered quick, and difficult to drive as well. Every time I depressed the clutch pedal to change gear, the direction of the car would veer to the left, but when I accelerated again, it would veer to the right. Hairy stuff.

Gladys travelled everywhere with me, so there was often the three of us driving around, but the minute I dropped Gladys off at her home I'd take a trip round to Jim's garage in Hammersmith Road, or he'd be at my garage down at Fraser Place. That was it, we did nothing else. It was *the* really boring thing in my life as far as Gladys was concerned.

It was cars, cars, cars, and more cars…..

Chapter THREE

INFLUENCES

My mother was a huge influence on me, especially after my father passed away. She became the matriarch, the strongest member of the family. By then, of course, I was fully functioning and I knew exactly what I was doing and where I was going, but nevertheless she was very eloquent, had a great memory, was a lovely writer and had a great voice. She also did a lot of charity work and helped out at the Gordon Highlanders' excellent Museum on Viewfield Road, Aberdeen, in no small way because of her father, Major Francis Webster.

She loved helping out at the institution which actively preserves and shares the legacy of the famous Gordon Highlanders Regiment and she was really proud that her father served with them.

Father was a very driven man, and we didn't really know each other too well. He was often in his own world, and I mean that in the nicest possible sense. In other words, he simply did his own thing. When he left his work on the buses, he rose to become the sales manager for prominent city garage owner, Roy Thomson, selling Rootes Group cars, but he was always interested in (and also thought about) selling continental cars.

As I mentioned earlier, Ross Baird had previously worked for my father when Roy had both the Singer and Simca agencies in Guardian Motors. Ross said that they weren't allowed to have Singers in the same showroom as the other Rootes Group cars, but when that changed, Roy decided to move the agencies to a showroom on Great Western Road in Aberdeen. Father remained very interested in continental cars in general, but Volvo in particular; in fact, he used to sell the

Swedish marque when he wasn't on official duty, and it was always Ross who went to Buchanan's, the main distributor in Glasgow to collect the new Volvos and take them north for specific customers.

After father left Roy Thomson's business, the family took on the Renault agency in Fraser Place, Aberdeen. We set up Gillanders Motors and started selling both Renault and Volvo products for a number of years. After this, we moved to purpose-built premises to solely concentrate on Volvo, and we also created a Gillanders Motors business in Peterhead too, because at the time, the fishing industry was big in the 'Blue Toon'. We thought it would be good to have an outlet in the far north-east and our Austin Rover Dealership there fitted in with our overall plan. My MG Metro 6R4 actually came through Gillanders Motors in Peterhead.

Originally, I drove the 62 mile round trip every day to run it and, in the showroom, I met a lot of fishermen over the years. Not only that, I also went to sea! Yes, I actually went to sea in a seine net fishing boat – with Simon the Fisherman!

Simon Cobb, although most folk know him as Mervyn, or Merv, is a good friend of mine. He was the engineer on the vessel, but that's a story for later where I will also explain his two names. The trip to sea was very interesting, but never, ever, to be repeated although there were other things that were repeatedly repeated….

My Wife – Gladys Anne Gillanders

The lovely Gladys. This is a great story, a lovely story in fact. Gladys Anne Cooper and I met on Friday, April 7, 1967, and it's amazing that I remember it so clearly. She was 15 at the time, and I was 17.

I had gone to a youth club which posed as a nightclub. It was called 'The Place' and it was situated in Skene Street, opposite the Aberdeen Grammar School. The building was originally a church, before being converted into flats, but back in 1967 it was called 'The Place' and if you were a member, you were called a 'Place Face'.

They had a little coffee bar there, and as well as a disco-thèque and live music. One night I was standing there playing one of those table-top slot football games when my attention wandered. I was distracted by a girl who had just walked in. She was wearing a green coat with tan shoes, but the thing that got me was her hair! It was a beautiful bright colour – she was most definitely a redhead – and *really stunning*. I looked over, but as she was standing with her back to me all I could actually see was her *l-o-v-e-l-y* head of hair. I thought to myself, *'I've got to speak to her. I really have to.'*

Gladys tells me that I was out on a date with another girl at the time, but I really don't remember that. I was a bit embarrassed to go and speak to her and so I asked a friend:

'Go and ask that girl if she'd like to speak with me.'

That's what we did in those days. We were just kids. Anyway, my friend went over and asked her, and she said she'd speak to me, so it all started from there. She always blames her hair for ending up with me.

Gladys has been, is, and remains, a remarkable wife and friend – she's still my best friend today.

Chapter FOUR

COMPETITIVE NATURE

The Fintray Hill Climbs of the early 1970s were huge events and they were always held on Sundays when there were no other sporting attractions to compete against. Football matches were held on Saturdays, but there was little, if anything, to entertain the public on Sundays. At its peak the hill climb attracted well over 5,000 spectators at the biggest British Championship events where drivers would take their saloon cars, sports cars, sports racing cars, single seat racing cars, and rally cars, up the 725 yard, 12 foot wide, asphalt course. It doesn't sound much, does, it? It's very short and narrow, but speed hill climb events are very much a precise and specialised form of motor sport.

I remember my first visit to the hill climb: I took the bus to the Parkhill Bridge on the outskirts of Dyce, to the north west of Aberdeen, and then walked three miles to the venue. Gladys would have been with me at the time because I dragged her along to everything.

I also remember standing watching the single seaters and various weird looking 'specials' that folk had built themselves, and I recall the smell of a racing oil by the name of Castrol 'R', made at the time by the Scottish Burmah-Castrol Oil company, and I thought, *'W-o-w! I want some of this!'*

The drivers were all very flamboyant and Health and Safety Risk Assessment wasn't around in those days. The competitors were characters, and I could get up close and talk to them, mix with them, and hey, who was I? I was a 'nobody', but there I was, rubbing shoulders with these very famous hill climb drivers.

I believe the speed hill climb at Fintray would have been one of my first competitive motor sport events, because it was 'softer' on the car than the 'Granite' was. I had to think long and hard about competing on the Granite City Rally special stage event because I'd have to fit a sump guard and the like to protect the underside of the car, whereas with the hill climb, an ordinary road going car was sufficient.

I was attracted to motor sport because of the element of competition. I liked beating the others and I definitely wanted to win. I wanted to be better than anybody else, whether it was in Autotests (known as Driving Tests in the 1960s and early 1970s), or on night (road) rallies, in autocross meetings (racing against other drivers round a grass or stubble field), or on the speed hill climb at Fintray House, alongside the River Don.

Driving Tests, I have to say though, were the bane of my life insomuch that I couldn't remember where to go. I could easily do handbrake turns, having had plenty experience of them in Union Street and on the Beach Boulevard in Aberdeen, and I also managed the reverse flicks (going quickly in reverse and then spinning the car whilst at the same time slipping it into first gear and continuing in one, hopefully smooth, uninterrupted motion). I could also manage to park between the marker cones, but the more complicated the tests became, the less my brain could take in, so invariably, I'd get three quarters of the way round and stop and think, *'Oh bother!'* (or perhaps some other words along those lines), *'Is it left, or right here, or even reverse?'*

I resorted to putting bits of paper on the steering wheel to try and remember, but I couldn't, I just couldn't. I enjoyed them, funnily enough, but my brain just could not comprehend the complexity of some of the tests. If I'd had a navigator with me I'd have done much better.

It was during this time that I met and became best friends with Graham Neish. We used to compete on all the driving tests together. In fact, folk like Jim Robson, Bob Leckie, Derry Taylor, John Whyte, Jim Milne, and Simon Cobb all competed in these events. The best of the tests were the ones held inside Pitcaple Quarry, almost in the shadow of Bennachie, (the highest point in the north east of Scotland). Pitcaple Quarry was owned by the council and had an absolutely flat, smooth and loose surface, whereas the venue at Blairydrine Quarry was pretty much the opposite. I managed to get second place overall in my Renault 4L at Blairydrine, near Durris Forest, but I went one step better at Pitcaple in July, 1973, when I achieved 'FTD', the Fastest Time of the Day – my first!

It was great fun, and with Graham Neish, especially, it was a hoot. Neish played a big part of my life. We had great times together along with Jim Robson, and I recall another of the Blairydrine meetings where Robson and I shared a Mini Traveller together, along with Jim's pet Alsation, *'Rastas'*, who sat in the back of the car, completely unperturbed by it all, although I have to say the marshals did appear to be a bit uncomfortable....

In these events, I could beat the opposition in my particular class, and this was important to me coming from a childhood in which I had been mercilessly bullied because of my hand. I think my situation was similar to Sir Jackie Stewart's early life, about which he describes so well in his excellent book, *"Winning is not enough"*. Therein, he stated that he continually strived to have the best greasing bay in the country in his father's garage in Dumbuck, Dumbarton. He too, was bullied at school, labelled dumb by the teachers and others, until he was diagnosed dyslexic (word blindness) in 1980, long after he'd retired from Formula One, but by then he'd still managed to win three World Championship titles.

I liked beating the other drivers, but Jim Robson was a really good driver, and I thought to myself, *'I want to beat Jim'*. If you thought Colin McRae was quick, then my chum, Jim, was equally as good. He was the guy that everybody wanted to beat.

Jim Robson, but without 'Rastas' in his Mini, at Fintray in 1968.

Photograph: Jack Davidson.

Attacking Ruin Corner in my Mini Cooper S and only around 20 seconds or so later, some tyre-bending round the Hairpin at the Fintray Hill Climb.   Photographs: Ken McEwen.

I didn't take the hill climbs at Fintray all that seriously; it was just something I never got enthused about, although I did once compete in the Rally Car class of the Scottish Hill Climb Championship. I did

quite well, but to me, hill climbs became something to do when I wasn't rallying. It was purely a fun day out.

My cars were never set up for asphalt and I never had an out-and-out hill climb car although it was always a great day's entertainment. But did it teach me anything? No, I don't think so. I used to compete there, but I used it more as a *'fun'* event. Others, like John Whyte, who went on to win an incredible eight Scottish Hill Climb Championship titles, took it much more seriously.

Road Rallies

The first time I got Ross Baird to navigate me was in my Mini Cooper S, and we were somewhere along the B9077 South Deeside Road to the west of Aberdeen, with Gladys sitting in the back. This was his trial for being a co-driver, but I'll let Ross pick up the story:

'The information was handed in through the window because it was a 'plot and bash' style of event, where the idea was to 'plot' the reference of the next control and 'bash' on. Well, amazingly, I managed to plot the map reference of the first control, and 'Whoosh...' we went off like a rocket and arrived at the control and I thought, "Gee whiz, that's amazing!"

'It certainly was amazing as I was never renowned for being the best navigator in the world, and David, by this time, was extremely excited by this success, and said to everybody:

'Oh, I've got the perfect co-driver now, because this is just fantastic!'

'I didn't find another control all night! So why David kept me on I have no idea. The thing is, neither did he! Mind you, I did pay half of the fuel costs....'

Like Jim Robson, I competed in the inaugural Esso Caledonia Road Rally Championship in 1972, and this took me as far north as Inverness and as far south as Dumfries. However, it was Jim Robson who won the series in his sister's 850cc Mini, but even with Peter Grant as his navigator, he still had to pedal the wee car along pretty quickly.

I'd a proper navigator in the left hand seat by this time in Malcolm Lamont. He had the uncanny knack of being able to read the Ordnance Survey maps, *and* simultaneously interpret the organisers' often complex route instructions. In those days, of course, it was all about the navigator, not really the driver. When I had a good navigator my role as the driver became pretty incidental. In a road rally, the navigator would simply state:

'Ok, sit here for 10 seconds to allow me to plot a map reference'.

Then he'd command:

'OK, now we go.'

The organisers seemed to have a knack of teasing out the weirdest and most complicated sets of instructions to hand to the crews at each time control. It was usually obscure enough to test the best of them. Navigators like Malcolm Lamont, Roger Reed and Peter Grant had their work cut out in spite of the route being timed at a 30mph average. It could be a struggle for the drivers to get to the next control in a timely manner, but of course, I did try my very best…

Most of the time it was good fun, but very dangerous. The amount of times I nearly had a huge accident in the middle of the night was incredible. Such events started at exactly one minute after 11 o'clock on a Saturday night and the half-night road rallies went on until around 3 o'clock in the morning, but the all-night events went on until breakfast at 6 o'clock the next morning. I even took Gladys with me sometimes; she'd sit in the back, but never complained once, and was never car sick either.

The First Stage

One day, in the early 1970s (I think it was possibly 1971) I rather naively entered the biggest motor sport event held in the north east of Scotland, the ADMC's Granite City Rally. The rally had turned from being a night time navigational road event in 1967 to a daytime special stage rally in 1968.

It was my first special stage rally, but what a baptism! The only problem was that having a taste of it merely whetted my appetite for even more. Many of the top foreign drivers used to visit the Granite City Rally, and I used to think, *'Wow, look at their cars!'*

I remember that day in April when the rally started from the Skean Dhu Hotel in Dyce, the one at the eastern edge of the airport. I had plenty time to view the top drivers off at the start. The number '1' car was sitting outside, and that was the gleaming Ford Escort RS1600 of Roger Clark, *The* Maestro, and a legend in his own lifetime.

I'm not 100% certain as to which year I first entered the event. Despite searching high and low I failed to find an entry list, but if it was in 1971, then Roger's co-driver that day was none other than Stonehaven's Hamish Cardno, the then deputy editor of *"Motor"* magazine and he and Clark went on to win it. Hamish almost made a career of co-driving with legends: he co-drove Finnish Superstar, Hannu Mikkola, to win the 1972 Scottish Rally in an Escort; and he also co-drove for Scotland's top rally driver of the time, Duns farmer, Andrew Cowan.

Meanwhile, I was there, sat outside the Skean Dhu, totally transfixed by it all; I stared wide eyed at the stationary Escort and whispered to myself, *'Look at this!'*

Then, out from the front door of the hotel, came the man himself, Roger Albert Clark, the man with the same initials as the RAC Rally (which he would go on to win twice). He had his racing suit on whereas most of us in the lower ranks didn't wear flameproof racing overalls in those days. We just had jumpers and jeans.

I said again, *'W-o-w, look at that!'*

I was only 50 feet away from him when his co-driver handed him his driving gloves, and I thought, *'That guy's cracked it!'*

He jumped into the car and switched on the ignition: the engine bellhousing made a lovely tinkle, tinkle, tinkle sound, then 'crack', the engine fired up. Then he drove away and I whispered again, *'My God!'*

My start number, however, I do remember – it was 120, and there were 120 entrants! I finished 110th, so I beat ten people. Well, that was it! I said to myself,

'This is what I want to do with my life!'

I wanted to be a rally driver. This was what I really wanted to do! I bought some Webster Hyperion Remould tyres for the rally but that day they all fell to bits on the gravel; I remember too that I didn't want to bash my car because it was my road transport as well and I was really annoyed that it had been chipped by the flying stones thrown up by the front driving wheels. Actually, I was quite furious, and I even slowed down on the straights because I didn't want to wreck the underside either.

Overall, though, I remember coming out of the first forest stage thinking to myself, *'Whoah! Yes! This is maybe something I **can** do!'* Maybe David Gillanders the rally driver was 'born' that day, driving a Mini Cooper S through the forests of Aberdeenshire.

That was really the start of it all, my love affair with cars and competition. I think I was born to be a driver, I really think I was; I passed my driving test first time without any problems whatsoever, and then matched that on my motor bike test.

Roger Clark and Jim Porter in typical
"Sideways to Victory" pose on the Granite City Rally.
Photograph: Ken McEwen.

However, I now regret my snow driving escapades in Hazlehead, and my Union Street Racer days where I used to speed away from the traffic lights and go west to Rose Street and then east to the Castlegate, sometimes even venturing down to the beach promenade, and also round (and round, and round) the 'RedEx' Roundabout, but that was all part of my growing up. I, and the other boy racers, *had* to do handbrake turns in Union Street, and we *had* to do handbrake turns on the Boulevard, and we *had* to be chased up the Broad Hill...

Fun Days

I enjoyed the co-driving company of both Ross Baird and Graham Neish, and in fact they shared the 'Hot Seat' for a number of years. Graham and I started doing special stage rallies and we really had a great time together. I remember one event with him in my Mini Cooper S: we were on a forest stage by the Holy Loch, close to Dunoon on the Cowal Peninsula, near to Faslane, the naval base on the River Clyde. We had been motoring along quite quickly when all of a sudden, Neish shouted loudly:

'STOP the car! STOP! STOP! STOP!'

So I did, and asked:

'What's the matter? What is it?'

'There's an effing submarine, there. Look!'

A submarine had literally popped out of the depths of the Holy Loch and was about to berth. This was the first submarine Graham had seen, and he wanted a better look.

'Graham, we're in the middle of a stage!'

'But I've never seen an effing submarine before....'

That might provide a flavour of the fun times we had in my early days of motor sport, but there was another incident that will further illustrate this and that was when I competed on the Granite City Rally in the same car. The Start Marshal of one particular stage was none other than Aberdeen's George Stroud, a very quick driver in his day, particularly in his Saab. I think he had a 96V4 model, with his distinctive registration number, '9 EEV'.

46

Well, George had a bit of the devil in him really, but nevertheless I had a lot of respect for him, both as an individual and as a driver. Anyway, he asked:

'How are you doing, David?'

'Oh, I'm ok, but I'm not doing very well.'

'Well, you've got forty five seconds to go....'

(before my due start time) –

'.... and if you'd like to go now, just go....'

Well, I just took off and I think we were about the third quickest overall on that stage! It was a short stage to get a 45 second flyer. I was truly saddened to learn that George had passed away in August, 2011.

George Stroud in his Saab on the 1970 Scottish Rally.

Another quick driver from Aberdeen in the 1970s was music shop owner, Charlie Bruce Miller, in his Mini Cooper S. Always the gentleman, Charlie was the first to congratulate me after I won the Granite City Rally, and on being the first Aberdonian to do so. I really appreciated that.

Charlie Bruce Miller in his Mini Cooper S, here co-driven by Peter Jeffrey.

Photographs: Jack Davidson.

'PRG 1M' on the 1974 RAC Rally

In 1974, I got my hands on a Volvo 142S, with the registration number, 'PRG 1M', and I had decided that with Ross Baird we'd do a season in this, on the big stage so to speak, and there was none bigger at the time than the RAC Rally of Great Britain!

I managed to secure some sponsorship from Barratt Industrial Buildings, the construction company with the oak tree logo, although Ross felt that this was tempting fate somewhat, given that we were going to be thrashing through the woods. Nevertheless, the Snowman Rally was the first event with it, and Jimmy McRae won in a standard road-going red coloured Ford Escort RS1600 that he'd borrowed from another driver.

I'll let Ross take up the story:

'I remember I was asked at the halfway halt about what position we were lying in? I looked at David, and David looked at me and said:

'I don't know. Who cares? Does it matter?'

'Och, I'll have a look at the results then.'

'I then returned to David:

'Hey min, do you know we're lying 8th overall?'

'What? Naw, dinnae be silly.'

'And then I said:

'Do you see that standard looking red Ford Escort over there? Well, that's the guy who's leading. And he's leading by miles...'

'Oh, really?'

'I would say that there was definitely a lack of professionalism but we did 'up our game'. We kind of had to, as we had a responsibility to our team and sponsors.'

Ross continued:

'Because of the sponsorship I was always interested in 'PRG 1M' from the promotions angle. I organised the livery and put it on the car to make sure it was correct. I also kept on thinking that, as a co-driver, we were about to take this car out on not just any old rally, but the RAC Rally of Great Britain! And we're going to be doing this in a spanking new

Volvo, a thing of abject beauty. It really was a beautiful car and our start number was 150.

'I thought, "Hell, I had better do this properly," so I went out and bought the full set of one inch to the mile Ordnance Survey maps to cover the entire route which went from England to Wales and looped into and around Scotland before returning south of the border again. Or it might have, if we had reached that far... I even got a box specially made and the maps were meticulously filed for use. My intention was to prove how professional we could be and I spent the best part of a week plotting the entire route onto maps, and had them folded up in order. I knew exactly what I was doing, and then we pitched up at 'Scrutineering', where the event officials checked the car for eligibility and safety.

'David and I were right behind the world-famous co-driver, Brian Coyle, so I decided to go forward and ask him how he managed his maps:

'How to you work your maps in the car, Brian?'

'Oh, I don't use maps.'

'What! What do you use then?'

'An Esso Roadmap.'

'And that, allegedly, is what he used all the time he co-drove for Andrew Cowan. He never bought an OS map in his life, not for rallying anyway... and I had spent not only one week of my life plotting the route, I had spent £140 in buying the maps in the first place! That hurt. Not only that, we went off in the wilds of Wales somewhere, with very little usage of the maps. We ended up in a ditch but the Volvo was just so heavy, we couldn't get it out without a recovery vehicle.

'The RAC Rally was peculiar in that it had to have marshals at every corner, and they were not allowed to move from their positions. We had actually gone off within sight of two marshals' posts, but neither group could come and assist, and so that was more or less the end of the campaign with 'PRG 1M' on the RAC.

'One of the high spots we did have, though, was at a Vauxhall Plant, near Ellesmere Port. It sported various types of roads, surfaces and cambers, and was used as a special stage. They also had a roundabout there which was surround-

ded by a natural amphitheatre where hundreds and hundreds of spectators gathered to watch the action.

'We were told afterwards that David had taken this roundabout in a most spectacular manner, beating even the Works Volvo driver, Per-Inge Walfridsson, for style and content. He had just been through about three cars earlier than us, but the spectators said that he was not nearly as quick through there as we were... but perhaps they really meant not so spectacular!

'There was another incident on the event – there were usually several when David was on a rally – but this one happened when we actually arrived at some sort of farm area going far, far, far too fast, and we were suddenly faced with a huge problem – to head towards a huge tank which sported a warning sign that said "Acid!", or head into a sewage area. I don't recall why I didn't call this out in advance, but David had been driving by following other drivers' tyre marks through this stage, and he thought, rather speedily:

'I'm not going into the acid tank.'

'The only other choice was to aim for the sewage pit, so he threw the big Volvo sideways and we went right into the pit and out the other side and into a massive rose bush, so from ending up falling into a manure pit we actually came out smelling of roses!

'We could have done well on that RAC if we hadn't got stuck in the ditch that I mentioned earlier, but as I'd followed Brian Coyle's example, I hadn't been using my maps, and by the time we got out of the culvert I hadn't a clue where we were. When I looked at the route map I saw that the route went all the way round in a huge loop, so I thought we would take a short cut through the forest. There were no control boards, no officials, and by this time, no marshals either, so our service crew followed us through.

'We got out of the forest, but then realised that we only had a few minutes to get to the nearby stage, near the market town of Machynlleth, in Powys, Wales. David had to drive like a lunatic to get there on time, as that was our only chance of remaining in the Rally, but I also remember we entered the outskirts of the village, and hit a humpback bridge at a fair *old rate of knots and went flying, literally flying, and flying so high that I ended up looking down on the 30 mph sign instead of looking up at it!*

'But then I looked forward to see a police car….

'The policeman was good, to be fair to him, but what a bollocking he gave David:

'What a bloody speed you were driving at - that was absolutely ridiculous! Now, how long have you got to go into the control?'

'One minute.'

'Well, you are waiting here for two.'

'And that was the end of our rally. He could have had David's licence for ever for that display of aerobatics.

My Volvo 142S on the Welsh International Rally in 1975. Photograph: Fergus McAnallen (www.rallyretro.com).

*'Once out of the rally I planned to have a good long sleep. In fact, on more than one occasion on previous rallies I have nodded off on some special stages. And, as David has said, his driving was never about being the fastest of the fastest (which is probably why I fell asleep). Remember, it was a big Volvo, with comfy seats, and the heater was on (it **was** November, after all), and it was very easy to nod off. Half the time the radio was on too. It was pure fun. The rally was almost an afterthought.'*

"I know where I'm going…"

I remember competing on the 1975 Granite City Rally in that Volvo. The ADMC had it planned that one of the special stages would be the Fintray Hill Climb, but in the reverse direction – downhill! I cannot remember who was actually in the 'Hot Seat', but it couldn't have been Ross or Graham as they both knew Fintray as well as I did. Anyway, I said:

'Well, there's one thing for sure, we're going to be quick in here because I know where we're going…'

Aye, right! The route entered the forested area of Fintray from the north and quite soon after getting the hang of driving on the loose surface the next instruction from my co-driver was:

'Hairpin Right, onto tarmac!'

This was where the finish line of the hill climb course was, and 200 yards later it was:

'Hairpin Left!'

Normally, I would be taking this corner as a 'Hairpin Right' on an actual Hill Climb, but I had no problem with it whatsoever. I accelerated down the straight and over a slight brow to what is called 'Combine Corner', but on this event it was a sharp right hander (going downhill, remember) and with an adverse camber. Then I thought, *'Oh no, it's downhill this time. Wait a minute, this is all wrong, and – BANG – backwards off the road I went.'*

I eventually got out with the help of the spectators.

Opposite Lock during an ADMC Autocross meeting.

An advert in "The Press & Journal".

The Droopsnoot

Ford Escort RS2000s were produced as Group '1' cars in the mid seventies, but a tuned version of the road car, which had a pinto engine with carburettors, an atlas axle and a rocket gearbox, along with all of the latest improvements available at the time. These were incorporated into the rally cars by a company called F. English of Bournemouth, a Ford Rallye Sport (RS) Dealership in the south of England and a sister company of Maranello Concessionaires. The rally department was run by Chris Bodsworth.

Bodsworth approached me because he thought that such a liaison would give his business publicity north of the border. Personally, I thought this was strange, as they were in Bournemouth, right on the southern coast of England, and I was in Aberdeen in the far north eastern area of Scotland, a distance apart of some 600 miles in those days.

Powering the Ford Escort RS2000 out of the hairpin in Durris forest (my favourite stage) on the 1978 Granite City Rally. Photograph: Frank Love (www.raceandrally.co.uk).

Well, English of Bournemouth gave me the parts for nothing, because I bought the RS2000 from them. It was the

53

model with a 'droopsnoot' front end which made it quite distinctive. They provided the kit of parts which would have normally have cost around £2,000 or £3,000 (a lot of money back then) and I, in return, agreed to emblazon 'F. English of Bournemouth' on the side of the car and later, with a sunstrip over the top of my windscreen!

Ross Baird remained as my co-driver and we ran the car on several events. It really was a 'hoot' because we'd no service crew, two spare wheels in the boot, and we drove it to the events, competed in it, and then drove it back home. We did this for an entire season of the Scottish Rally Championship. I don't have the results, but we did alright in it, most of the time.

There was one event, though, that I didn't do too well on. That was on the Hackle Rally, when I rolled the car. All of the panels were bent, the roof was kinked, and the screen was cracked, but we were in a hurry to get home because the car was still in a driveable condition.

I had just left Stonehaven and was heading north on the old A92 (this was before the authorities reclassified it and turned it into a one-way southbound route off the now renamed A90) and I got the car very sideways just under the railway bridge, by the entrance to the local golf club. But in true rally style, I just 'kept the boot in', and held a power slide through the corner with the inside front wheel dangling away in mid-air because of the stiff suspension. But there, in front of me, was a Police Ford Granada coming in the opposite direction.

I straightened the car up, but as I did so, I saw the blue lights come on. The policeman turned round and chased us all the way to the Bridge of Muchalls, but he only managed to catch me because I had slowed down to 70 miles per hour. The policeman did eventually manage to actually stop me, and when he got out of his car and ran up to my window. He was panting and peching (breathing hard, and with some difficulty), and then blurted out:

'What the... '

He was bawling and shouting:

'I've been trying to keep up with you two bastards for the last eight miles!'

He'd really lost it, the policeman. Then he looked in the window and pointed to Ross, and asked:

'Is this guy dead?'

'Well he could be.'

Ross was sound asleep but he woke him up by banging on the passenger window.

'How the hell can you sleep with all that noise and sideways driving going on?'

And from his slumbers, Ross replied:

"Nae problem for me, pal. I've slept on some of the forest stages, never mind the public roads."

Then he turned his attention back towards me:

'Right, I'm booking you. Your rear light bulb's gone.'

Meanwhile, the car would not have looked out of place in the wrecker's yard, but all he did was book me for having an inoperative rear light, although the exhaust was blown too. It was obvious that we'd need to get some more parts from our sponsor. I'll let Ross explain our sponsorship deal:

'F. English had done their homework well and the English of Bournemouth campaign was really a very clever piece of marketing. They'd recognised David as having a lot of talent and with the way that mail order was going at the time, they felt they could steal a march on all the Scottish garages by marketing much earlier, and with a wider range of products.

'It had become as easy to get parts from the south of England as it was from the local dealers in Scotland. And it was successful too.

'We carried no spares, had only two extra wheels, and, as I mentioned earlier, we used to drive to, compete on, and drive back from the events in this car. The only time this strategy nearly failed was on the Hackle Rally, (the journey home from which David has previously described) where we rolled the Escort and I do remember saying to David:

'There's a great big rock there, so don't hit it.'

'BANG!'

Above: One careful owner....   *Photograph: Ross Baird.*

Below: It needed a lot of new parts!

The 1977 Welsh International Rally

In 1977 we decided that we would compete on the Welsh International Rally and soon afterwards we found ourselves in Llandudno, the seaside resort in Conwy County Borough, which was hosting the event, and I remember we had some great fun the evening before the actual start. Chris Bodsworth accompanied me and the rest of the team to a rather classy restaurant for a meal. Gladys was there too, but I'll let Ross take up the story:

'Well, this Norwegian appeared on the floor and it trans-pired that he owned the restaurant. Nothing unusual about that, you might think, but he had a guitar strung around his neck. Now, picture the scene in a nice, quiet, and smart restaurant in the heart of the Welsh town. Then this big Viking appeared with his instrument... That, in itself, might have been quite pleasant, but then he started to sing in his high-pitched voice with a strong Norwegian accent, parading around the tables in full serenade mode...

'I'm a Rhinestone Cowboy....'

'What a laugh! I thought I'd wet myself. It was some night and very, very entertaining.

'The next morning, we were outside and David asked:

'Where are we going?'

'Up there, to the Great Orme, and this is right up your alley, pal; it's like the Fintray Hill Climb – but on steroids!'

The Great Orme.

Ross continued:

'The Great Orme is a prominent limestone headland on the north coast of Wales and overlooks the Irish Sea. The road around it hugs the vertical cliff on the inside and that in turn sits atop a vertical drop into the briny below. It soon became our turn and when we got the instruction 'GO!' we took off up the tarmac special stage like a bat out of hell. We were certainly in the top three or four fastest round there.

'Fast, straight out of the box – that's David's secret. He could turn the speed on immediately from the start and was as quick on the first stage as on the last. We got to the end of Great Orme special stage and thought, 'Ooyah boy, let's have more of that!'

'In addition to that fantastic special stage, there was a network of dual carriageways in the north of Wales, and it said on the road book, in huge letters, "WHEN YOU REACH THE ROUNDABOUT DO NOT UNDER ANY CIRCUM-STANCES WHATSOEVER, GO LEFT".

'The reason: it would entail a journey of 26 miles before we would be able to return to the rally route. I must have said that to David at least five times, five times, five times, five times, five times, yes as much as five times, as we approached the junction. So what did the boyo do? Yes, he turned left....

'For heaven's sake, David, what did I say to you before we reached the roundabout?' (It is just possible that I might have expressed a different version of some choice words that loosely resembled the same meaning).

'We were on the motorway, so what did the boyo do? He simply turned right over the central reservation as there weren't so many armco barriers around in those days. At least he indicated that he was going to turn right! So over we went, clatter, bang, thump, and down with a bump on the other side, and we shot up the slip road and joined the cars on the correct route. We didn't even lose a space in the queue for the next stage!

'But the car in front of us was holding us up – and behind the wheel was a doddering old driver who was driving very slowly – so we pulled out and 'whoosh' we went by. We were going like stink down the outside, and then David shouted:

'I've no brakes! I've no brakes!'

'He eventually managed to bring the car to a halt. We stopped behind a lorry, but it was too close for comfort as the tailboard of the HGV ended up only inches away from our front windscreen! Apparently, David had ripped off the brake pipes going over the central reservation after we (or rather, he) had erroneously driven onto the motorway.

'That RS2000 though, was great fun. It was Group '1' and a true laugh-a-minute car. It was also standard, but at one point in its life we got a fancy one-off camshaft for the Pinto engine. At around 30,000 miles, the Ford Capri used to suffer from what was called 'camshaft knock' and this was a special one designed to stop that. For some reason we got a hold of it for the Escort and it allowed the engine to rev like it had never done before.

'There was another incident on the Welsh Rally when we descended a very slippery snow-covered, open forest track on one of the special stages. We were whistling down the hill like there was no tomorrow in front of what looked like thousands of spectators, and David, for some unfathomably stupid reason, thought he saw something and braked. This simply caused the car to spin and we ended up facing the wrong way, and in a ditch.

'Remember, the car was emblazoned with 'F. English of Bournemouth' on the side, and we were in Wales. We were almost up on two wheels with David's side of the car down in the ditch, and my side nearest the road, with all of those people watching. There were thousands of spectators on the Welsh, just like the RAC and Scottish Rallies in their halcyon days, but none of the spectators moved an inch to assist us, until I finally managed to get my door open. I stood on the centre console and shouted:

'Come on you Welsh bastards, give us a push!'

'And all I heard was a lone voice which said:

'Oh, they're not English at all, mun, they're actually Scottish!'

'And with that the car was manhandled out of the ditch, and we got on our way with a toot of the horn in gratitude.

'That RS was the best fun. It was one car, two people, two spare wheels (which was actually too much weight in the boot), and oodles of laughter.

'Then there was the time on the Granite City Rally where there was a half-way halt somewhere, at Alford, I think, and everybody else had their service vans, lots of mechanics, and plenty spares to service the cars. The teams all queued up at *the burger vans for their lunch, but we had Gladys who appeared with Prawn Cocktails for us:*

'Would you care for a Prawn Cocktail?'

'Merv (known as Simon to David) had literally been out spectating, as he only had to wash the little beauty. That was our car serviced while we ate the prawns in front of Simon the fisherman! Then we went on our way.

'We designed the car so that we wouldn't have to really service anything. We simply tightened everything up prior to the events and rarely had to do anything during the actual rallies.'

All-Purpose Motor Car

As well as competing on stage rallies, I also did some Driving Tests, as well as Autocross events and some Fintray Hill Climbs in the car. In fact I did absolutely everything with it because it was totally reliable and a 'fun' thing to drive. Gladys and I actually went shopping in it at the weekends, because it really was an all-purpose motor car. I thoroughly enjoyed it and although it wasn't fast, it was good fun to drive.

Fun at Fintray: Sideways round Ruin Corner in 'RFX 300R'.
Photograph: Ken McEwen.

During the entire year we competed in the 'English of Bournemouth' car we never had one mechanical failure; the car never missed a beat on any of the Scottish Rally Championship events.

I believe that the Scottish series is one of the best around, but it's miniscule in comparison to what it used to be. I remember individual entry lists of up to 200 crews back in the old 'Burmah Rally' days in the west of Scotland in 1976. What an entry!

That particular year the Burmah Rally was won by Finnish Legend, Ari Vatanen, a hero of mine, in his Ford Escort RS, and it wasn't a surprise to me when he won the World Rally Championship in 1981. The special stage mileage of such events, including the Granite City Rally, used to be close to 100 miles in total, but nowadays, all of the events are pale shadows of their former selves in length, partly due to costs, but also due to the time and manpower needed to run them.

In its heyday, the Scottish International Rally was a grueling six day event, whereas now it's over a weekend.

Going well on the Burmah International Rally in my Droopsnoot Ford Escort RS2000, in 1978. (Photograph: Tom Coffield & Chris Money).

Spectators and Enthusiasts

Motor sport would be very much the poorer without spectators and enthusiasts. In fact we could not have special stage rallying without such people because they are the life and soul of the sport. I have no doubts about that because spectators have helped push me back onto the road many, many times. I've have been off, off, off, and right off, and I simply would not have regained the track without their help, their efforts, and of course their enthusiasm.

I remember once competing on a hill climb at Kinkell Braes, on the outskirts of St. Andrews, high above the cliffs overlooking the North Sea. It was sometime early in the 1970s, and the local club used this caravan park out of season for their hill climbs. It was always windy and 'baltic' there during the break in the camping season, from October to March, so guess when they held their events? Yes, in March, and in October....

Anyway, the St. Andrews and District Motor Club had arranged for the winner of a local radio station competition to become a co-driver for a day, and, as it happened, the unfortunate motor sport enthusiast winner got me as his driver. I got the unsuspecting chap strapped into my Ford Escort and I duly sped up the hill and stopped at the top when he said, rather shakily:

'I can't go back down, I can't go! I can't...'
'What do you mean?'
'I can't go. I can't handle it.'
'What do you mean?'
'I think I have a problem!'
'Ach, you'll be fine.'

We were the last to go on the next run as well, and I whizzed through the flying finish (where the car had to break a light beam to stop the clock), but when I stopped, the enthusiastic radio station interviewer approached me with the microphone and asked:

'Well, what do you think of it so far?'
'I thought it was really good fun.'
'But can I interview your passenger?'

'Oh yes, my passenger.....'

But my passenger had started to walk away from the car, rather ungainly I have to say, towards one of several public toilets on the site, and he was just about to enter the facility when the interviewer caught up with him and said, live on radio, remember,

'Tell me, what was it like?'

'I'm sorry, I've just shit myself!'

I used to help out at the Aberdeen and District Motor Club Press Days prior to the Granite City Rally and quite often they would have a reporter from one or both of the city's two main newspapers, *"The Press and Journal"* and it's more local sister paper, the *"Evening Express"* in attendance.

One year, I happened to chauffeur a columnist from the evening paper. He wanted to experience and write about the sport and my role was to provide him with an express ride in a rally car. Although my passenger was a slight man, he was a former sporting champion in his own right, and he was also a presenter with the then *"Grampian Television."*

I got him into the sculpted bucket seat, and tightened the full harness belts, then slapped a crash helmet onto his head, but soon afterwards he said he'd never go in a car with me again! I think it had a lot to do with the fact that although the ADMC had acquired all of the required permissions from the Forestry Commission, and shut the stage, it appeared that the local forester didn't seem to know about the press day, and had trundled somewhat unsuspectingly onto the forest track, towards my full-flowing, opposite-lock, sideways-motoring flat in fourth gear, Ford Escort RS2000.....

W-E-L-L, I had been driving round this particular curve doing something in the region of 90 mph when I suddenly came upon this van. The forester didn't see us, or perhaps he couldn't quite take in just what he was seeing in front of him, and to this day I don't know how I missed him. My passenger turned fifty shades of white.

It was pure luck, not skill that saved us. I was in the ditch, but didn't hit the brakes or anything like that, and thankfully, I managed to steer round the forester.

The Group 4 Ford Escort RS1800

I then got my hands on a Ford Escort RS1800, with the registration number LBO 2P, and although it did not have all the 'right' bits on it, we finished third on the snow-covered Snowman Rally on rather skinny Nokian Hakkapeliitta tyres, more commonly known as 'Hakkas'. These Finnish tyres were designed for exactly the kind of conditions that the Snowman Rally often had.

The Torlundy Stage of the Snowman Rally.
Photograph: Frank Love (www.raceandrally.co.uk).

I was pretty good in the snow, especially over golf courses, but when the going got slippery I seemed to excel. I was never the quickest under normal conditions, but was always very competitive in inclement weather, particularly when it was slippery underfoot. And if the conditions were tight and twisty, I could still be fast.

Top speed, though, was always scary to me: anything over 100mph and I'd think, *'Hell, I can die at this speed.'* If the stage had a flowing nature to it and was quite technical, then I could drive that extremely well. I remember the Bennachie Stage on the Granite City Rally – that's a 'Yahoo!' stage, if ever there was one. The road sweeps left, then it sweeps right, then it sweeps left again, and right once more down to the finish. It's a fantastic stage and I have always been competitive there.

Ross also reminded me about an incident we had whilst going up a hill in Craigvinean Forest, about one mile west of Dunkeld, just off the A9, so I'll let him take up the story:

'I remember that hill in Craigvinean. We were on the Scottish Rally, and I said to David:

'Now look, David, we're in the top ten here, so just screw the nut.'

'But the further we got up the hill the more the tail end of the car went out, ever more sideways, and even further sideways, so I said to him:

'David, nobody is watching, nobody's interested and nobody's catching us either. But did he listen? No! The back end of the car hit a bloody great tree and spun the front round and down we went into a ditch. We were on our side and there was absolutely no way that the car was going to get out without mechanical intervention, and that wasn't likely to happen immediately.

'I opened the door, stood on the transmission tunnel (a bit of déjà vu here, I thought to myself), and said:

'Are you alright, David?'

'Aye, I'm ok,'

'Then he let out an almighty scream.

'Oh, my God! He's hurt himself.'

'Apparently, the hot oil from the gearbox had oozed its way through and out of the gear lever's rubber gaiter, and drips had landed on his side and started to seep through his overalls. It was boiling hot too! Anyway, we both got out.

'I then wandered down the stage towards the start, and by this time, all of the later and less experienced crews had passed. I tried to stop them to get assistance, but I wasn't very successful, and, as I was really fed up by this time, I thought I'd walk further down the track towards the start to speak to the marshals and try and get some help. I kept in the middle of the stage and hardly moved off to the side for the slower cars

that appeared at roughly one minute intervals, until I heard something really quite incredible approaching…

'*I was unaware that Stig Blomqvist (who would go on to capture the World Rally Championship in 1984) had been running late in his Works Saab 99EMS. Well, he came hurtling round the corner like a bat out of hell, and I could see his eyes – they were on stalks – and he must have thought:*

'*Va i helvete…. Flytta dig jävla idiot?'*

Or, in plain English:

'*What the hell… Move you bloody idiot!'*

'*The Group 4 Ford Escort RS1800 that David then owned looked almost identical to that of the Scottish Champion, Donald Heggie. Both cars had a blue and red colour scheme, with white diagonal stripes. It was brilliant, but on one particular rally, on which we had been going well, we suddenly slowed down on one specific stage, and noticeably so, so I asked David:*

'*Why are you slowing down?'*

'*I've just had a premonition.'*

'*A premonition, aye.'*

'*A premonition of what?'*

'*I just got a flash of my car upside down in the ditch.'*

'*That was Heggie, you twat. We just passed him!'*

'*I've had a premonition… Aye, right!'*

The Archerfield Rally-Sprint in 1979 was held in the grounds of the 17th century Archerfield House and comprised both gravel and tarmac surfaces.

Photo: Frank Love (www.raceandrally.co.uk).

Frank Love, the motor sport photographer, confirmed that the drivers each had a journalist in the 'hot seat' for their runs and such runs were held over both directions. Being a knock-out type of event, the elapsed time determined whether the driver would go through or not. There were something like 20 competitors there, including Jimmy McRae, Drew Gallacher, Donald Heggie, Willie Rutherford, Allan Arneil, Ken Wood, Bill Taylor and even circuit racer, Bill Dryden. I had a lot of competition and I can't remember my own result, although I believe Heggie beat Gallacher to win the event.

On the 1979 Granite City Rally with Ross Baird.
Photograph: Sandy Topp.

Ross Baird had taken a break from his co-driver duties, but returned a short time later, and I think he is best placed to describe what happened after this little interlude:

'I do remember it was much more fun in the early days, but after I had a break from co-driving, I found that David had somehow stepped up a gear.

'I recollect, on one occasion, when we were in the queue to start a particular forest stage we were behind Russell Brookes, one of the UK's top drivers. David had been gradually creeping up the seeding ladder and had been running in the top five or six in the RS1800 by this time. I

wasn't surprised at that, but whilst waiting in the queue, I was very surprised at David when he went up to Brookes and was downright abusive to the Englishman when he said:

'I'm telling you now, if you hear two 'toot toots', it'll be me right up your backside, so move over.'

'I was really shocked and I remember thinking at the time:

'David, you do realise that was Russell Brookes?'

'Brookes was actually the British Champion-elect in an Escort RS1800 in 1977, and David had just told him to move over in no uncertain terms! But we actually did catch him so he was vindicated in his action, although Brookes didn't move over.

'David had become more of a 'known' figure and I must admit we had people who championed our cause. One such individual was Ross Finlay, a superb journalist, and a lovely man too. He was very helpful to us, surprisingly so, as David could be rude and quite abrasive at times. But Ross, being the gentleman that he was, could see through the facade to take notice of his undoubted driving ability, and therefore he tended to be very kind to us in his media reports.'

With Ross Baird on the Bank of Scotland Rally in 1979. Photograph: Frank Love (www.raceandrally.co.uk).

I have a myriad of stories about motor sport and of special stage rallying in particular and one such story involved tyres. As you can imagine, tyres were critical, and still are, so thank you, Robert William Thomson, for inventing the pneumatic tyre in 1846, but rally tyres – that was something else. In a rear wheel drive car, on a forest rally, I could rip off the edges, the rubber blocks which provide lateral grip, in around twelve miles, but I later got some experimental 'knobblies' from Dunlop.

Ditch hooking could often result in a puncture. Photograph: Jim Sutherland.

These knobblies came with extremely hard sidewalls, in order to avoid puncturing. Dunlop, though, had gone the opposite way from the likes of Goodyear, Michelin and Pirelli, who had instead concentrated on a programme of developing tread patterns and compounds.

With Ross Baird on the 1980 Snowman Rally.

Photograph: Jack Davidson.

A puncture usually didn't stop us; it would merely delay us a little! We'd only stop to change a wheel if a flat tyre happened near the start, or midway through a special stage, but if it happened near the end we'd simply carry on to the finish.   Photographs: Jack Davidson.

The problem was that the Dunlop tyres had absolutely no 'give' in the sidewalls and as soon as I dropped the clutch, the rear wheels spun round, and then ripped out of the tyres. In an instant I had two punctures! This happened on around three or four stages on the trot, so I handed them back to Dunlop.

It was never really tyre issues that put me off the road; it was usually driver issues! Yes, I'd go off the road but I never seriously damaged the car. I think I was always unlucky inso-much that I usually got embedded in a ditch or something, and not be able to get the car out, rather than suffer from any serious accidents.

Lifting a wheel round Ruin Corner at the Fintray meeting on June 17, 1979. *Photograph: Jack Davidson.*

Sideways all the way, and on June 5, 2015, BBC Scotland's "Landward" programme televised this still photograph of my effort. Photograph: Jack Davidson.

My first NCR (New Class Record) was at Fintray in my Ford Escort RS1800. I made the ascent in 34.44 seconds, but I can't imagine how I ever set any records because I never went out there to try to break them. I just wanted to see if I could go round the bottom bend sideways from start to finish.

And I did, and I managed to stay on the track. The front half of the car may have been on the grass, but the important bit, the rear end, remained on the tarmac, and that generated all the power I needed to slide round the corner.

Sideways again, this time on the Renagour Stage, Trossachs Rally.

Photograph: Jim Sutherland.

I mentioned much earlier that Fintray was a serious hill climb, but a fun event for me. For John Whyte, though, it *was* serious stuff, so Jim Robson, Bob Leckie and I got together and treated ourselves to even more fun by moving John's braking point forward about 50 feet closer to the corner!

John was very much a meticulous, scientific kind of driver, and he'd carefully worked out that he needed to brake at this specific point before the first corner, and to give himself a visual aid he placed a syrup tin at the trackside at exactly the location he'd need to apply the brakes, and that duly became his braking point, until we climbed over the fence and moved the tin a bit closer to the bend...

The fastest special saloon cars reach around 80 mph on the approach to Ruin Corner, the first bend, but when John arrived at competition speed in his Mini Cooper S and put his foot on the brake pedal he suddenly realised that his braking point was not exactly much of a help to him.... To this day, John still denies this ever happened, but it is a good story!

Chapter FIVE

SIMON THE FISHERMAN

The MFV "Mary Croan".
Photograph: Courtesy Annie Cobb.

Simon Mervyn Cobb has always been known to me as Simon, although most people know him as Mervyn, or Merv. Anyway, he had a 998cc Mini at the same time as I had my Mini Cooper S, and we used to work on our cars in either his garage or mine, and through this mutual interest we became very close friends. We have remained so ever since. Many years later he came to work with me at Skibo Castle.

He was already an Approved Driving Instructor with his own "Liberty Driving School", so named after his last vessel.

Simon, you see, was indeed a fisherman.

Because my family had the Austin Rover dealership in Peterhead, I felt that I needed to understand fishing; I needed to understand the people who came into the showroom to buy cars, and therefore I needed to go to sea. My father goaded me into volunteering as he thought I wouldn't be able to stand it.

So I said to Simon, who was at the time, the engineer of the deep sea seine net trawler Motor Fishing Vessel (MFV) *"Mary Croan"*:

'Listen, if you have need of a crewman, I'll join.'

I forgot all about it, but one day he phoned me:

'David, one of my guys has come in sick, so could you report to the harbour in Peterhead on Monday? You can join the boat for a sail, and go out fishing!'

'No problem.'

The day before I was due to go out I had been talking with one of the guys, who said:

'Oh, listen, the sea sickness…,'

But before he had stopped talking I had jumped in somewhat confidently:

'That won't be a problem to me, I'm tough!'

*'No, no! Sea sickness **is** a big problem. What you should do is this: you should eat bread, or rolls, or buns, dry, without margarine or butter, and keep your stomach full. You need to do this because the problem is when you are sick and empty the contents, but continue to be sick, you retch all the time. It sounds bad, but be full of food.'*

I remember going to a local baker in Peterhead where I bought a dozen rowies (a rowie is a bit like a flattened French croissant, the North-East's take on a breakfast roll).

Well, I sat on the dockside, and stuffed myself with these dry rowies, buns and bread – I ate a ton of them – and Simon came along and said:

'Are you ready?'

'Ready? I was born to do this. It's not a problem!'

But Simon had a wry smile on his face, as though he knew something was heading my way, and I didn't…. He got me a sou'wester, the traditional, collapsible oilskin hat that is longer at the back than at the front to protect the neck, plus boots, oilskins, and all of the necessary kit, because I was to become an actual member of the crew.

I was no sooner onboard than we had to cast off and sail round the pier to get 'iced up'. This meant taking the boat to an ice trader who filled the hold with ice. This was to keep the fish fresh once caught, and I thought to myself, this is dead easy. It was flat calm, a beautiful sunny day, and I was sitting there enjoying myself. Once filled, the boat turned round and finally left the Harbour of Refuge.

The North Sea can be dangerous, and many years ago it was decided to build a new harbour of refuge. There was a lot of discussion as to where it would be located. Would they select *"The Birthplace of Scotland"*, the ancient town of Arbroath, where the Declaration of Independence was made on April 6, 1320 and where they still produce speciality smoked haddock by the name of Arbroath Smokies? Or would it be the Granite City of Aberdeen, or even the ports of Stonehaven, or Peterhead? All were considered, but the South Bay of Peterhead was selected as the best possible option, and it thus became the Harbour of Refuge.

The skipper of the MFV *"Mary Croan"* was Tommy Sutherland, and his vessel was a 'white fish' seine net steel trawler of some 75 feet in length. It was built in Campbeltown, but registered in Inverness, and sailed out of the fishing village of Hopeman on the Moray coast.

I thought that the guys sailing onboard were all 'nutters', and by that I mean that they would sail when nobody else would because the price of fish would be much higher during inclement weather. Peterhead was considered to be the biggest white fish port in the UK.

Anyway, if there was a 70 mph wind blowing a 'hoolie', to me it would appear like it was a hurricane, but that rarely stopped these guys. They would still go out because if they brought home a catch that nobody else had managed to get, they would reap the benefit. These guys would sail, irrespective of weather, and I kid you not, *irrespective of weather*.

We left the harbour walls behind, and I when I looked back I thought to myself, *'What a bloody idiot!'*

I couldn't swim, well not very well, and certainly not all the way back to the beach. Mind you they did tell me that if I fell into the North Sea I'd be dead within minutes so it would make no damn difference anyway. This was all so I that I could stand and talk to fishermen about selling cars to them. As I said:

'What a bloody idiot!'

I watched the harbour of refuge disappear very slowly, and I mean v-e-r-y slowly, and, honest to God, we must have been doing all of seven miles per hour. I don't know the actual speed, but it was helluva slow.

Slowly but surely the harbour disappeared from view, but here's the funny thing. The same guys I had been talking to onshore had been speaking normally to me (well as normal as Doric can be) but at sea the guys started to speak what sounded like a 'foreign' language; they all sprang funny accents, they all whistled, and they all squeaked…. it was like they were Martians (not that I've ever met a Martian, you understand) but I figured that this must be the way they get into their sailing mindset. It turned out that what they had been speaking was a very broad Hopeman version of Doric, the dialect of the north east of Scotland!

The drill was that we would paint the boat on the way to the fishing grounds, and touch up all the white bits. I don't think I painted it much, but I sat around and watched what was going on, and it wasn't that rough.

It seemed alright, and I thought, *'well, we're only going to go out for about 100 miles, do a bit of fishing and then come home, weren't we? Can't be that bad, can it? Huh! My memory tells me otherwise.'*

We sailed all day, and as sure as day turned to night, I asked:

'Where do I sleep?'

I was motioned to go below.

'Down below' consisted of holes in the wall, looking for all the world like holes a worm had cut out. They were tubes in effect, and the crew had to slide into these apertures, pull down the netting and that was it but to me it was more like a worm being buried alive. In any case, I had to sleep on the floor because all of the tubes had been taken!

I didn't even get forty winks that night, what with the boat heaving, the stink of diesel, and the constant noise of the engine. But I have to say that the food was good, apart from the fact that condensed milk was used in everything, absolutely everything.

The toilet on board was no bigger than a regular broom cupboard. The pan was open to the sea, and what the skipper usually did when somebody was on the throne was to keep the boat on an even keel, but when I first went onto the throne, I felt the boat tipping... This in itself was fine, but then the skipper turned it sideways, and *'boof, slap, whap'*, I got an injection of millions of gallons of water, right up the backside! It blew me off the seat! It was like a sea water enema straight up the arse! The bastards keeled over the boat just at the tip of a big wave, and, and of course the guys were all standing outside waiting, indeed *wanting* it to happen.

Simon said there was a design fault in the plumbing, and when the boat rolled all the water disappeared and left only the water in the 'U' bend of the toilet, but when the boat rolled back the compressed air forced the water in the toilet to shoot back up the seat. This was the incentive to not stay too long on the throne. I thought it was an induction for the new members of the crew....

The other thing that used to drive me nuts was that the crew of eight slept in the same cabin, but they kept the light on. I kept getting up to switch it off, but the next watchman came down and switched it back on.

It took forever to get anywhere, because this was most definitely not a speedboat. Not only that, the sea got rougher with a swell of maybe, 15 to 20 feet. To Simon and his crew this was flat calm, but to me, it was bloody rough! In a trough, all I could see was a mountain of water in front of me, and a mountain of water behind, and then the boat would shoot up over the top and I could see for miles.

The skipper turned to me and said:

'As the new boy, you're on duty tonight.'

'What does that mean?'

'Well, you've got the midnight watch.'

Apparently, they always gave the 'duff' guys the midnight watch.

'That's no problem to me.'

I went upstairs into the wheelhouse at half past eleven at night to relieve the current watch, but he was fast asleep! There was a bell that was supposed to ring every 30 minutes to waken any watchman should he nod off, but this guy had stuffed a jacket in the bell so that he didn't get wakened up. We'd been steaming for three or four hours, with no bells, no lights, no radar, no nothing, including no watchman!

This was in the seventies, the halcyon days of the North Sea Oil and Gas Industry, and there were drilling ships, rigs, and platforms all over the northern sector, and us, a wee dot on the ocean, but one which had me onboard!

We'd been sailing blind through the night, so when I took over my shift, I made sure the bell would ring. I was alert. In fact I was totally alert. I had the searchlights on and I was peering into the darkness to make sure the boat didn't ram another boat, or worse, an oil rig.

After what seemed an interminable length of time, we arrived at the fishing grounds, and that, I have to say, was truly spectacular. We shot the net, which was huge: it was around 200 feet in width and was all lead-lined to sink to the bottom. Then big trawl boards were dropped over each side of the boat to spread the net at the blunt end, the stern. Then the skipper spun the boat round in a wide arc and as the net started to get pulled in it got buoyant with fish and up it came, popping out of the water, a bit like a minuteman missile. It just exploded from the surface. Then they took off the ties. It was spectacular to watch as the cod dropped into the hold.

I was wondering exactly how many cars I would subsequently sell to the fishing fraternity as each catch of between 25 to 50 tons in weight would have been worth anything up to £25,000 to the skipper and his crew. I thought, at this rate, we'd be filled up in minutes and I'd be home by teatime.

'Aye, right!'

We cast the net again. Out it went, and disappeared under the surface, but then there was an eerie silence. The hydraulic winch motor had packed up, and the crew couldn't pull in the net. I asked Simon:

'What happens now?'

'We've to hand-line it in, haul it onboard, hand-over-fist.'

The crew all got together and gradually pulled the net in. Not only that they managed to open it to allow the fish to escape, otherwise they would have been unable to lift the full catch onboard. These nets cost a fortune, so there was every incentive to save it. I said to Simon:

'I guess we're going home now?'

'No, we're off to Lerwick in the Shetland Isles.'

'Sorry? Lerwick? I need to go home.'

'No, David, you're out here for a fortnight!'

'Simon, for heaven's sake, I said I'd be out for a few days. I said I would do it, and I've now done it. I have experienced it, so I now need to go home.'

We were well on the way to Lerwick when a Royal Navy Fisheries Protection Vessel approached us. I was reminded of the so-called *"Cod Wars"*, a series of three confrontations between the United Kingdom and Iceland over territorial waters and fishing rights in the North Atlantic. The third cod war actually ended in 1976 but as this was only three years later, there could well have been a number of remaining tensions. We were duly hailed:

'Ahoy, "Mary Croan", this is the Royal Navy Scottish Fisheries Protection vessel, "Westra" and we intend to board you for inspection.'

I say it was the *"Westra"* but it was a long time ago, and it could easily have been the *"Orkney"* or one of several Fisheries Protection vessels.

Of course the "Mary Croan" skipper agreed to allow the Royal Navy to check the logbook, the catch, and the mesh sizes of the nets. So, over came this inflatable dinghy and the sailors, all dressed in smart uniforms, jumped onboard. They then checked everything that they needed to and found that all was in order. When the checks were completed the skipper presented a package of fish to the Navy Captain and his crew, as a matter of courtesy, you understand.

The FPV "Westra".
Photograph: K. Michael, (www.trawlerphotos.co.uk)

My mind, however, was in full overtime mode and I quickly came up with a plan. I asked one of the navy sailors:

'Where are you heading to next?'

'Lerwick.'

'Listen, can you give me a lift?

'What do you mean?'

'I need a lift? I can't be on this boat any longer.'

I explained who I was, and why I needed off. So he got onto the R/T (Radio Telephone) to his Captain:

'Sir, we've got a guy here, who says he needs to get back to the beach.'

'Permission granted.'

'Perfect!'

Simon mentioned later, before he could wink, that I had stated 'goodbye' by saying:

'That's it. Sod this, I'm off.'

I literally stepped off the *"Mary Croan"* onto the Royal Navy dinghy.

'Guys, I'm going. I'm away!'

The swell was such that I just had to time my jump with the nearest wave to the height of the trawler and then step over. We sailed over to the Navy vessel, with Simon and the rest of the boys all watching my progress.

I got to the bigger vessel, and looked up. The side of the ship must have been about 30 feet high; it was like the north face of the Eiger! With the *"Mary Croan"*, I just stepped off, but this was different and I thought to myself,

'How the hell do I get up there?'

There was a rope ladder that the rest of the navy crew just shimmied up, but the guy in the dinghy turned round to me and asked:

'You don't look too happy?'

'Well, left hand, you know....'

'Don't worry, we'll throw a rope down for you.'

They threw a rope down and tied it round me, then the guy said:

'Now what to do is this. When the dinghy rises and falls with each wave just wait until the biggest one arrives and step

onto the ladder at the top. Take the biggest wave you can get because then you just have to step onboard.'

Well, the waves kept coming, and they got bigger and bigger and then I spotted one.

'Oh, this is a BIG one.'

So I stepped onto the ladder at that point, but then, the next wave along was even bigger. It was at least ten feet higher and it just took me clean off the rope ladder and all of a sudden I was left hanging by this rope.

All the guys onboard the *"Mary Croan"* knew this would happen, and I could hear them hooting with laughter. I could hear them clearly, but the Navy guys soon pulled me up backwards and got me on the deck and dumped me like a wet fish. The crew then took me to meet the Captain, who said:

'Welcome aboard, Sir. Would you like to have your clothes cleaned?'

They washed, dried and ironed my clothes and then I sat down with the Captain and his senior officers in a white table-clothed mess – this was the Royal Navy, where things were done properly. I had a lovely breakfast and was shown to a nice cabin, not a hole in the wall.

I can't remember when the Captain said we'd reach the port of Lerwick, but this thing was going at 100 miles per hour compared to the *"Mary Croan"*. We approached another trawler which the Navy boarded, but soon after that we came across an Icelandic Gun Boat. We almost collided with it and subsequently had a bit of an argument. It was very much reminiscent of the cod war incidents in the fifties, sixties and the mid-seventies.

So there was me, far out in the middle of the North Sea. I had survived the fishing onboard the *"Mary Croan"*; I had survived being washed from the rope ladder during my transfer to the *"Westra"*, but the question in my mind was this: would my luck hold as we came perilously close to colliding with the Icelanders?

When two vessels sail parallel, in close proximity, it stirs up a turbulence of water between the two ships and the vortex can effectively suck each vessel in closer and thus create a very dangerous situation. It could have easily ended up being a ramming issue and yet another international incident. It might even have started a fourth cod war!

The two captains, one British and the other Icelandic, were at least talking to each other, trying to push each other. I just sat in the Bridge, and said:

'This is great. This is fantastic!'

They had guns at the front (the bow), so I asked:

'Can ye nae just take that big thing in the front and go BANG?'

We eventually arrived in Lerwick harbour and I said my thanks and goodbyes to the Royal Navy crew. I made my way up to the main hotel on the island. Remember, this was in the middle of the busiest days of the oil and gas industry. It was frantic, frenetic even, with Lerwick a huge cog in the wheel of the industry. Vessels used the port until bursting point, and helicopters used the island as a stop-off point en route from the oilrigs to Aberdeen, the self-proclaimed Oil Capital of Europe.

I arrived at the hotel which was owned by Luigi Stucci. It was either called the Shetland Hotel in Lerwick or the Lerwick Hotel in Shetland (there were two such hotels) but I cannot remember which one it was. I knew Luigi from his days in Aberdeen, so I went in and I asked, the receptionist:

'Can I get a room for the night please?'

'Which planet have you come from?'

'What do you mean?'

'They're sleeping ten to a room just now!'

'Well, I'm not sleeping ten to a room. Can I get an executive suite?'

'Ha! You are a comedian.'

'Well, I would really like to get to Aberdeen tonight.'

'Have you booked? Have you booked an aeroplane?'

'Booked an aeroplane? No!'

'You have come off a foreign planet!'

'I'll easy get on a plane.'

It's all of 25 miles from Shetland's capital to Sumburgh Airport, right on the most southerly tip of the island, so I took a taxi and on arrival I went straight to the British Airways ticket desk and asked:

'Single to Aberdeen, please?'

'Sorry, where have you come from?'

It must have been extremely obvious that I'd come from the same planet I'd been on earlier...

'I've just come off a Royal Navy ship, actually,'

I was trying hard to impress.

'The next flight will be in two weeks.'

Obviously she *wasn't* impressed.

'You are joking?'

'You do realise that this is the busiest time the North Sea has ever experienced? I'm sorry, there's no chance.'

I went outside and got a payphone (there were no mobiles in those days) and I phoned Gladys:

'You're not going to believe where I am.'

'Where are you?'

'Shetland. I was hoping to get home because "Top of the Pops" is on tonight and I want to see it.'

How sad was that?

'It looks as though I'm going to be here for a couple of weeks.'

'What do you mean?'

I told her the whole story, and she was resigned to me being away a little bit longer than planned.

'Look, I'll just be on 'stand-by' as somebody surely, will fail to turn up.'

I hung up then started to walk out when suddenly an offshore oil worker ran in, shouting loudly, and looking for the Shell charter flight to the Granite City:

'Shell for Aberdeen, Shell for Aberdeen!'

A woman standing over by a gate said to him:

'Hurry, the flight's about to leave.'

I thought to myself,

'Nothing ventured, nothing gained.'

And so I continued to go outside, but then I turned and quickly ran back into the terminal, shouting:

'Shell for Aberdeen, Shell for Aberdeen!'

A woman standing over by a gate said:

'Hurry, the flight's about to leave. Follow your mate over there, and do hurry! There's not much time.'

So I ran like hell down the tunnel and out and onto the Shell chartered plane. The turbo props were spinning and the door was about to close, but this guy, and me, got onboard. We got the last two seats at the rear of the aircraft and the flight attendant then asked:

'Where's your pass?'

'My pass, oh my pass, yes, my pass....'

Well, I patted my shirt, patted my jacket, and patted my trousers, but of course I couldn't find my pass…

'Oh never mind, we've no time, just let's go.'

The cabin crew shut the door and I kept praying, *'Oh, please God, take off. PLEASE take off. If I get arrested in Aberdeen I'll be ok with that, but PLEASE take off.'*

We taxied along the perimeter and got as far as the island would take us, to the North Sea side in fact. We turned into the wind, a westerly as it often is in Shetland, and built up speed, and 'whoosh', we took off just as the Atlantic Ocean lapped the shores of the west coast of the island. To let you understand, the runway runs the entire width of Shetland at its most southerly point, and there's no room for error. I stifled a shout, *'Oh, you beauty!'*

I had sat down next to the guy I had followed from the terminal, and he asked:

'What rig are you off?'

I mentioned some rig or other that I'd heard of, but I cannot remember exactly which one it was, and he said:

'Oh! That one; I was on there two - three months ago. How's it going?'

'Fine, we're going great!'

'Are you pumping sand?'

It sounded like he said 'sand', but I really wasn't very sure, obviously.

'Oh yes, pumping. Oh, yes, barrowloads.'

'Really?'

'Oh, we've been pumping that for weeks.'

Everything I said seemed to make sense to this guy which in itself was quite remarkable.

'That's really unbelievable. You must be producing?'

'Oh, producing, yes, we're producing…'

But then I stopped him and said:

'I tell you what, I am really tired. I've just come off a continuous night and day shift and I'm absolutely whacked. I'd like to get some sleep.'

'Understand, I understand.'

'Phew!'

It was pouring with rain when we landed at Dyce, and all the passengers were pushing to get into the terminal and under cover, but the doors were closed while the security personnel checked us in. The guy with the clipboard was checking in everybody, and I thought to myself, *'Well, I'm going to get arrested now, but it doesn't matter, I'm home in Aberdeen.'*

But, the way people were backed up, the check-in guy hadn't a hope of catching everybody. The doors suddenly opened, and I managed, somehow, to sneak round and past the security guard without being stopped. I got a taxi home and stepped in through the front door, when Gladys said:

'I don't believe it…'

I got to see *"Top of the Pops"* after all!

At the time I was very friendly with a man called Norbert van Beelen. He happened to be the general manager for Shell International's Wells, and he'd bought a lot of Volvos from me over the years, so I phoned him up the next day and said:

'Norbert, listen, I have something to tell you. I bagged a seat on a Shell chartered flight from Shetland to Aberdeen yesterday. I beat your security out, and I beat your security in after I landed at Dyce.'

'David, all you needed to do was call me and I would have arranged it for you, but now you have told me about security, I will be taking some action to tighten up our procedures.'

So that was my trip with Simon, the Fisherman. I'll never go again, not least because the *"Mary Croan"* sank off the Inner Hebrides by the Ascrib Islands near Loch Snizort, to the north west of the Isle of Skye, only about 12 months later. Apparently, there had been a fault with the radar (and had I known that during my trip, my eyes would have been on stalks during my watch). Where it showed land as being two miles away, the vessel was actually right on top of it, and in the dark it hit some rocks.

Simon was asleep at the time, but he woke up when he felt the judder, and when he reached the wheelhouse he could see that the vessel was rising and falling in the swell between two towering cliffs.

As he was the engineer, he had to go below to the engine room where he found that the boat was quickly taking on water. The pumps failed to halt the flooding, so the crew got out the life rafts and launched them whilst a *"Mayday"* signal was transmitted.

Unfortunately, one life raft inflated upside down, but the other inflated correctly, with its beacon intact. The eight crew members abandoned the vessel with seconds to spare before it capsized and sank. One crew member managed to get onboard the properly inflated life raft but the wind took it away from the other raft.

Simon said that it was extremely fortunate that there had been a chemical trawler nearby and that it had picked up the *"Mayday"* call. It had subsequently shadowed the *"Mary Croan"* and when the crew of the tanker spotted the life raft beacon they chased after it and picked up the sole occupant. Luckily, the fisherman managed to tell them that the other seven members of the crew were still clinging to the other, upturned, life raft.

Normally, the crew members would have righted the raft but that would have taken a lot of energy to do so, and given that they expected to be rescued in a few minutes, they did not do this. Instead, it took between 20 to 30 minutes for the tanker to search and find them in their searchlights.

By this time, all seven trawlermen, including Simon, had become exhausted, hypothermic, and curled up into a foetal position, each with their arms wrapped round the ropes at the side of the life raft. Another few minutes and I'd have lost a good friend, and six other fine men would have been lost too.

Simon did go back to sea (I would have become a land-locked landlubber had that happened to me) but he continued and skippered his own boat which he named, MFV *"Liberty"*. It was a multi-purpose boat for single trawl, pair trawl, or seine net fishing until all of the bureaucracy, black fishing, legal quotas and such like started to bite. He gave up his precarious life at sea when he gratefully accepted the Government's Decommissioning Scheme.

Simon is as good a driver as he was a fisherman, and so he brought *"Liberty"* back to life, reincarnated as a Learner Driving School in Aberdeen. He also took up karting at the age of 46 and raced a 125 gearbox kart for 14 years, won the club championship three times, and became the Scottish Champion at the ripe old age of 60 with a class four gearbox kart and Energy chassis. He also turned to motor cycles for leisure and toured Europe with his wife, Annie, on a Ducatti.

One thing is for certain, I will never, ever, go to sea again. I'll stick to fishing on the lochs and rivers from now on!

I prefer the more traditional method!

Chapter SIX

STRATEGY

Much of my competition driving was done *prior* to the innovation of power steering, and because of this, my preferred technique for steering was actually my right foot! I could steer my car round a bend in the forest track through the application of more power when driving a rear wheel drive car, and I only had to steer into the skid. The photograph, below, illustrates my point: although not on a forest track, the technique employed is much the same. More power to the rear wheels would increase the angle of attack whereas less power would pull it back into line.

Steering with my right foot whilst cornering....

Photograph: Jack Davidson.

However, I was always conscious of hairpin bends, especially in a left hand drive car, but I was definitely 'ambid-extrous' because I could drive from either side of the vehicle although I actually preferred left hand drive. But if I came to a hairpin in a left hooker and wanted to change up soon after the bend, I'd come in relatively straight, apply the hydraulic handbrake and induce a slide. This would allow me to position the car perfectly for a fast exit with a touch of opposite lock as necessary and then push the pedal to the metal for full power. Simultaneously, I'd change from first to second gear with my right hand and hold the steering wheel with my left.

The biggest problem for me in that sort of situation would have been a bump in the road, so I was always conscious of reading the surface 100 yards or so in front to check for any depression that could maybe cause a deflection of the steering wheel. That never actually happened, but I was always very much aware of such a possibility.

My right foot was always flat to the floor, either on the brake or on the 'loud' pedal, but mainly the latter! It was either 'on' or 'off', 'up or down'. There was no half-way house for me.

When I was rallying, my driving strategy was to try and go as quickly as was humanly possible in the first two or three special stages. This was to try and get a wee bit of a lead, and accordingly I'd go into the first stage and try very hard and take a few more risks until such time as I built up that lead. That particular strategy could easily backfire, especially if I happened to cut any bends, pick up a puncture or two, or knock off a corner of the car, such as a wheel and suspension unit. I did do that a couple of times.

However, if I managed to get through the first few stages unblemished, I would have, when I was at my peak anyway, a lead of five or six seconds. And from that I would build up a further cushion. When my opponents saw that I was beating them – and they, presumably, would have been trying just as hard as me, it would have demoralised them to an extent, so I suppose psychology actually did play its part in the early days of my motor sport career. If I managed to get a lead of 30 seconds or so I was happy, and no way would I let such a lead slip, barring mechanical disaster, a puncture, or a visit to the vegetation.

*On the Granite City Rally, 1979, with Ross Baird in my
Ford Escort RS1800. The rally was won by Malcolm Wilson
and Terry Harryman in their similar car.
Photograph: Frank Love (www.raceandrally.co.uk).*

I did some left foot braking in the early days with my Mini and other front wheel drive cars, and even with my rear wheel drive 240T. This was especially true when I had to 'spool up the turbocharger' in the Volvo. I *had* to keep my right foot on the throttle to keep the revs and turbo up, *and* brake with my left foot, but this generated so much heat that the standard brakes just couldn't cope. *(There's a lot more of my Volvo exploits in Chapter 8).*

With various four-wheel drive cars, I *had* to employ a left foot braking technique and although I could do it, I was not an expert in the art.

*The 1981
Granite City Rally.*

*Photograph: Frank Love
(www.raceandrally.co.uk).*

Gartrac

When the Ford Motor Company introduced only it's second front wheel drive car, the Escort Mk III, in 1980, the rallying fraternity were somewhat disheartened given the huge sporting successes achieved by its rear wheel drive predecessors. I began to think that I'd have to change my strategy, perhaps even my driving style, so I began to look at my connections to see what my options were because my Mk II, 'LBO 2P', had been replaced by another Mk II, 'OSO 151W', although it too had become a bit dated. Mind you, if I'd kept one of them, I could have done well in the historic category that has burgeoned over the intervening years. In case any non-motor sport reader is confused about this, the historic category refers to the age of the *car*, not the *driver!*

Wheel waving to the crowds round Ruin Corner, Fintray.
Photograph: Jack Davidson.

I had, by this time, developed an extensive list of contacts and one such connection just happened to be with a fellow competitor, the double Scottish Rally Champion, Donald Heggie, from Cupar in Fife. Late in 1983, I made contact with Donald to see if he'd sell me 'KSR 896X'. This was a Gartrac G3, essentially a Mk 3 Ford Escort but with the complete running gear of a rear wheel drive Mk II. I wanted to get something different and I considered it sufficiently unusual at the time.

Donald's car looked (outwardly) similar to any road-going Mk III Ford Escort, and as such anyone could have been forgiven for thinking it had front wheel drive, but Gartrac, who were a small sheet metal fabrication company at the time I was first introduced to them, had converted it from front to rear wheel drive and given it a G3 suffix. Allegedly, the G3 was reputedly faster than Ford's front wheel drive RS1700 Turbo!

Donald had used the car with varying success levels in 1982 and 1983 but the best he could achieve was 3rd place on the Granite City Rally on what could well have been its first outing. He took my Mk II, 'OSO 151W', in part exchange and so I began my association with Gartrac.

Originally based in Farnham, Gartrac moved to near Guildford, Surrey, in the south of England. The business had been formed in 1970 by Dave Bignald and Bill Payne who originally worked for the Alan Mann Racing Team in 1968. Through this they built close ties with the Ford Motor Company and provided the Works team with suspension parts and running gear for the ubiquitous Ford Escort Mk I Rally Cars. Dave and Bill were involved in the development of Ford's GT70 sports car as well, although Ford later decided to concentrate on Escorts instead.

The speciality that the Gartrac outfit provided was in the supply of either new or re-worked atlas axles. They became renowned as the finest fabricators and builders of these for competition cars. They were also the original Works Fabricators who provided fabulous 'big-winged' flared wheel arches on the Mk I Escorts, and later, they created slightly subdued wheel arch extensions for the Mk IIs. My association with Dave Bignald and Gartrac would reap huge benefits over the following years and many of the incidents we had together appear in some of the later chapters....

To be honest, though, I didn't think that the G3 was anything special; I didn't much like it, even though it had Macpherson strut rear suspension rather than springs. Mind you, it was obvious that Gartrac had done a lot of work on it and I have to say, it looked good, but, as they say, *"looks aren't everything"* and that was borne out over the fact I didn't really get any good results with it.

I persevered with it for a while before I hired it out to Chris Bellamy, a friend of mine. He ran it for a year or so before I sold it to Aberdeen-based Dutch oilman, Klaas Zwart, who, before he left the city, subsequently 'totalled it' on an event somewhere. Klaas left the north east of Scotland to live in the south of Spain, where, near the town of Ronda, he built his own racing circuit and also funded the stunning Ascari KZ1 sports cars.

My Ford Escort G3 on the Loch Carron stage of the John Wilson's Bedroom Stages Rally in 1984. Photograph: Frank Love (www.raceandrally.co.uk).

And below, reminiscent of an earlier image ....
...Déjà vu, perhaps? Steering my G3 with my right foot.

Photograph: Jack Davidson.

It was part of my maturing I suppose, given the fact that the G3 doesn't stick in my mind as being anything other than a fun car to drive, but it was a good, well-built car. More importantly, however, was the fact that it was through my association with Gartrac that I started to deal directly with the boss, Dave Bignald, and this, ultimately, helped me to get my hands on an MG Metro 6R4.

Oops! Maybe this is why I didn't achieve any decent results with the Escort G3 as this overshoot at the famous Blairadam Gates on the John Wilson's Bedroom Stages Rally illustrate – pass the duvet, please!   *Photograph: Jack Davidson.*

Chapter SEVEN

THE VOLVO EXPERIENCE

Gillanders Motors was a very successful Volvo Dealership from the mid-1970s through to the mid-1990s and, for our size, my father and I had the most successful Volvo outlet in Europe. Volvo had what they called the 'Top Car Salesman's Club', and the top 250 Volvo salesmen and women were taken on trips round the world as a reward. We were the top dealers in Britain every time, and father thought it good for me to go on these trips.

I have been many places and had some incredible experiences with the Swedish Car Manufacturer, but the following encounter is definitely one I will never forget. This particular trip began in Gothenburg on the western side of Sweden for an overnight stay first, and in the evening, I and quite a few of the other Volvo sales personnel entered a discothèque.

Unfortunately, a fight broke out in the disco and I just happened to get involved in the fracas. I got hit over the head with a bottle, but I managed to hit the guy back with the boom of a microphone. I knocked his teeth out, apparently.

We were all arrested and incarcerated in the local police station and of course, the boss of Volvo had to come and get us out, but because Volvo was HUGE in Sweden at the time, this gentleman had a lot of clout and as a result, we all received a dressing down for our misdemeanours. Nevertheless, the next morning we boarded a specially chartered aircraft at Landvetter, the second largest airport in Sweden, and headed north to a town in the Municipality of Finnmark, in Norway, high up and well inside the Arctic Circle, where they say it is night all day and day all night, depending upon the time of year.

Our destination was a place called Alta on the Altafjord near the two islands of Stjernøya and Seiland, close to where the World War II German navel base was located, near the Kåfjorden fjord. I understand that this is where the German battleship, *"Tirpitz"*, was sunk.

Anyway, we were all onboard this private jet late in 1984. We thought nothing more about it, as we were all pretty drunk at the time and I also had a big bruise on my face from the fighting. Most of us were half asleep too. The flight was well underway when the aircraft suddenly dropped like a stone. It yawed this way and then that way and everybody became very concerned and really quite uncomfortable. Then, almost as suddenly as it dived, the aircraft levelled out, and the pilot announced over the intercom:

'Ladies and gentlemen, we are really sorry about the turbulence, but we've just flown over the magnetic north pole (or something like that) *and it momentarily knocked off our automatic pilot mode but we have regained control and everything's fine.'*

None of us knew any better about the accuracy or otherwise of such a statement like that, but it certainly shook us up. We had just begun to settle down again – about an hour later – when the pilot made a further statement:

'Ladies and gentlemen, we have a major problem.'

When you are flying, you really do not like to hear an announcement like:

'We have a major problem'.

The pilot continued:

'If you look outside the aircraft to our right hand side you will see a Russian Air Force MiG.'

And there it was, a fighter aircraft sitting about 500 yards off our starboard wingtip, with the pilot pointing for us to land. That was bad enough, but the pilot then made a further announcement:

'Ladies and Gentlemen, if you care to look outside the aircraft again, this time to the left hand side, you will see another MiG, on our port wingtip, and that pilot is also pointing for us to land.'

Then suddenly, one of the MiGs opened fire, with what I presumed to be machine guns or cannon:

'Brrrrrrr, rat tat tat....'

All I could see was a huge trail of tracers shooting off into the distance. I thought: *'Bloody hell, this is exciting!'*

Then the pilot came over the intercom again:

'Ladies and gentlemen, perhaps you don't know this, but quite a few months ago the Russians shot down a commercial jet after it allegedly and unwittingly strayed into what was restricted Russian airspace.'

Our incident en route to Alta happened during the daylight hours, but the Korean Air Flight 007, a Boeing 747-230B, had strayed into Russian airspace following a breakdown of its navigation system. It had been flying at night, and was therefore less visible as to its identity.

The captain of the Volvo flight continued his address:

'They can see we are commercial; we have identified ourselves through our automatic identification indicator, but the Russian pilots are having none of it. They want us to land and so, ladies and gentlemen, we have to land immediately. We are to land in Russia.'

The IFF system (Identification, Friend or Foe) is an identification system designed to enable military and/or civilian radar systems to identify any aircraft and to thus determine if they are friend or foe, although IFF could only positively identify friends, for obvious reasons.

Well these Russian pilots would have none of it, and the guy sitting next to me, a Belgian, started to panic:

'It's a disaster, it's a disaster.'

'Why?'

'Oh, they'll shoot us.'

'Don't be daft'

'Oh, they'll shoot us. They'll certainly shoot me. I'm a Belgian, and they hate the Belgians. They'll shoot me. Could we swap passports?'

*'No, why would I give you **my** passport?'*

'Well, I'm telling you, they'll shoot me.

'Don't be daft, nobody will get shot.'

Anyway, we made a very steep descent, and by now everybody was strapped in tightly. I was trying to hide my passport inside my pants, and all the rest of it. It's strange the things that go on in your head in situations like this. We landed and taxied to the far end of the airport, and when we came to a halt the doors were flung open and Russian troops stormed onto the plane with their Kalashnikovs, or some other semi-automatic rifles. They poked people in the ribs, and manhandled the passengers a bit before being forced to march off the aircraft and onto waiting trucks. I even tried to get my case, but was rather unceremoniously pushed away from it. They ordered us:

'Leave everything!'

We had to climb aboard canvas covered wagons and when the soldiers tightly tied the flap down off we went. It was pitch black inside, and everybody was jabbering away rather excitedly, and nervously, especially the Belgian who kept on saying:

'We're stuffed. We're stuffed.'

(Or some other flaming Flemish words).

I said to myself, *'I'm British, nobody's going to shoot me. In fact, I'm Scottish, for Christ's sake. I'll talk my way out of this.'*

The Belgian was far from happy. He kept on saying:

'David, we're screwed.'

At the time, the Russians were considered the enemy. They had been 'taking no prisoners' and the idea of 200 plus political captives would be a great coup for them, I thought. The boss of Volvo was there, along with some other top management from the car manufacturer.

We were driven around for about 20 or 25 minutes, before we stopped and reversed down a steep slope and came to a halt at the bottom. The canvas was thrown open, and the way it was, this Belgian and me were the first off. We all got pushed around a bit too.

It was a very compact location, and dark. We were forced to go towards a huge hangar-like door, but much, much bigger. Well, you can imagine: the little Belgian's imagination had begun to run riot. He said:

'That's it. When that door opens, there'll be machine-gunners and they'll mow us all down.'

'For God's sake!'

I had challenged that, but, by this time, I had started to almost believe him. I was actually thinking, *'Hell. This **is** a **bad** situation I'm getting into. When the door opens, I am going to run in screaming. If there's a gun in there, I'll go sideways, which means that everybody else will get shot, and I'll disappear into the hanger and run away – just like my Grandfather Major Francis Webster....'*

The door started to slowly crank open. It was red in colour, and about 25 feet in height. It creaked open, very, very slowly, and when it got to about the width of a human being, I just took off! I started screaming and yelling and ran inside the hanger. I ran to the left-hand side as I went in and was ducking and weaving just waiting for the machine guns to go off when suddenly my feet gave way and I fell down what felt like a chute. This, I found out later, was a form of industrial tubing, just like the kind the builders use when demolishing a site and one which gravity takes the rubbish down and into the skip. I went whizzing round and round in the pitch black, totally disorientated, and at the end I came out of it and, *'whoosh'*, I landed – not in a skip, thank goodness – but onto a cushioned mat on the floor. I was immediately enveloped in a world of strobe lights, loud noise, and a discothèque in full swing.

All of a sudden, the whole place erupted. I picked myself up and everybody started cheering! Dozens of people were there, clapping hands at the success of this elaborate ruse. We *had* landed in Alta, but the Swedes, with their sense of humour, had planned the whole thing. The MiG jets, the captain and crew of the chartered jet *and* the 'Russian' troops were all part of it!

'*Välkommen till Alta!*' they shouted:

'Welcome to Alta!'

'*W-o-w!*'

I was asked if I enjoyed the trip.

I didn't reply directly, but said:

'Well, the Belgian didn't enjoy it… so when he comes in you'll have a lot of explaining to do!'

The Belgian actually wrote a letter of complaint to Volvo Sweden soon afterwards because he panicked. By God, did he panic! He thought his time had come. He actually got me starting to think my time was up too but nevertheless, I stored this experience for the future…..

'Tack så mycket, Volvo.'

Thank you very much, Volvo.

Chapter EIGHT

FROM THE VOLVO 240T TO THE METRO 6R4

With Graham Neish on the '85 Kayel Graphics. Photograph: Steve Pugh.

Left: On the limit in Craigvinean Forest. Photograph: John Fife.

Setting the car up for a left hand corner on the Hackle Rally.

Photograph: Willie Bauld.

If my earlier Volvo experience was something special to remember, then I have to say that my Volvo 240 Turbo experience was even more memorable. It was certainly more remarkable and infinitely more rewarding.

As the owner of a Volvo dealership I had excellent links with the factory, so I decided to try my luck and approach Volvo Sweden to see if they would give me a car to compete with. The Swedes' reaction was positive, and so I flew to Karlstad, the capital city of Värmland, on the northern shore of Lake Vanern where they had their factory. It was there that they presented me with a 1983 Volvo 242 Turbo Group 'A' Racing Car, with the chassis number 242 083003.

The nomenclature used by Volvo for the '200' series of cars was such that the '2' indicated the series type, and the two subsequent numbers identified the number of cylinders and doors. Although my car was technically a 242T, in other words, a '200' series, four-cylinder, two-door saloon, it was more commonly known as a 240T.

With Graham Neish on the Snowman Rally.
Photograph: Jack Davidson.

I acquired this particular one through Volvo Motorsport, although it was actually me and my mechanics at Gillanders Motors who converted it from left to right hand drive. It was a huge job, and our biggest problem was the exhaust manifold which was at the *'wrong'* side. This resulted in the soles of my shoes melting because my feet were immediately next to the turbo pipe on the other side of the bulkhead. The down pipe used to get white hot on the long stages, I kid you not, and I often went through a pair of shoes per event!

I really loved the car though: it had over 300 brake horse-power from the 2.1-litre turbocharged engine, but its Achilles' heel was the rear axle and my Volvo, as well as the factory cars, suffered from axle failures. Because of this I commiss-ioned Dave Bignald's Gartrac company to manufacture and modify a rear axle based on an atlas axle from a Ford Capri 3-litre, incorporating a ZF limited slip differential, fully floating drive-shafts as well as AP Racing disc brakes. Two units were made for me, and one for Volvo Motorsport.

Gartrac and I took this axle to Sweden to show Volvo and they bought half a dozen units to put into their Group 'A' racing cars. The units were unbreakable, but they weren't homologated (sanctioned) in Group 'A' for use in 1985. But because I had used the axle 'in period' it is now deemed acceptable and has since been homologated. I believe that my old car is registered in Sweden with FIA papers along with the homologation documents which make it eligible for a number of historic events.

Corgi Toys made a model of a Volvo 760 (not a 240) in my very own livery.

After the Volvo secured its reliability it became a 'hoot' to drive. Yes, it had 300 horsepower, but it had 300 hp either *'on'* or *'off'* because of the turbo lag (this *was* in the early

days of turbocharging); the time delay was between one
second and one and a half seconds, and to put this in context I
had to put the right foot down on the accelerator at least 50
yards *before* the bend for the thing to wind up, to spool itself
up in effect, and when it really 'lit up', I mean, *'Christ!*
Everything went!'

*Above: I'm tugging on the 'Emergency Exit' lever after failing
to stop the beast at the end of the Railway Line in Cymer, on
the 1985 Kayel Graphics/Peter Russek Rally (or whatever it
was called that year)... Below: On the Port Talbot Rally at
Cregan in 1985.* *Photographs: Steve Pugh.*

The Volvo really had no brakes to speak of and it had rubbish suspension because all of the bushes were standard, and therefore it was very soft in the ride, but, God, it could go! I often saw 100 mph and more on the speedometer going down a forest stage, but all the time I was thinking to myself,

'It'll never stop!'

In Cardrona Forest on the 1988 Scottish Rally.
Photograph: Tom Chisholm.

This is the best bit about the story, though, because ultimately it was my Volvo that provided the opportunity to get into an MG Metro 6R4, and this little piece goes back to one of the first rallies that the 6R4 competed on, and I'll let John Davenport, who was in charge of the Austin Rover Group (ARG) motor sports programme at the time, explain:

'The first appearance of the 6R4 on an event was on the York National Rally on March 31, 1984, about a month after ARG had launched it at the Excelsior Hotel in West London, on February 24 that year. Tony Pond set fastest times on each of the first eight stages and then a cam lobe broke up on the V62V engine (this power unit had just one camshaft and pushrods because it was a 'shrunk' Rover V8 power unit).

'The Mewla Stages in late August was the first time that ARG ran the car – in public – with wings.'

There's more from John in the next chapter, but my introduction to the Metro 6R4 was on the Autofit Stages in July, 1985, an event I had entered in my 240T. The organisers of the event had devised a 45 mile route through the Cowal Peninsula of Argyll and Bute and this comprised eight forest stages plus a downhill thrash on the Rest and Be Thankful, an old military road and a former hill climb when used in an uphill direction! I was seeded at number 6 in my Volvo with Graham Neish, and we were waiting in the queue at the start when suddenly, this *'thing'* appeared.

All of the top drivers in the event were looking at this *'thing'*, and of course, it was like something from outer space with, fins sticking up, and wings above that, like it was on steroids. It was four-wheel drive, mid-engined, and blue and white, but when Tony started the V6 engine, the noise was so incredible, I just had to say:

'I want one of those…'

Of course, never in my wildest dreams did I think that I'd get one… Tony, who later became a good friend of mine, said that ARG had planned to run through the stages as a test exercise in preparation for the RAC Rally that year and this was confirmed by Ian McRae, the Clerk of the Course of the Autofit Stages, who said:

'Tony Pond was a bona fide entry and as such ran as car number '1'. ARG chose the Lanarkshire Car Club's rally because it was one of the nearest events date-wise following the official launch of the car, and they needed a quick win, and a quick win was exactly what they got!

'The only downside was felt by George Marshall who finished 2nd, and that was because Austin Rover's win cost him £1,000 in prize money from General Motors – that's what he would have pocketed had his Vauxhall Chevette HSR been placed in first position.'

But back to the first stage: Tony and his co-driver, Rob Arthur, waited in line at the start, with this *'thing'* at the control. As I was car 6, I had a five minute wait before it was my turn in the Volvo, so I ran to the top of the hill to watch this *'thing'* take off.

I couldn't believe it…. I simply could not believe it!

When Tony dropped the clutch the *'thing'* just simply disappeared: it went from 0-60 miles per hour in just over three seconds on the loose surface and after that it kept on accelerating! I could hear it howling away into the forest. The rest of us there were totally gobsmacked, and these were competitive drivers of the calibre of Jimmy Fleming, who won the Scottish Rally Championship in 1983, the aforementioned George Marshall, who would go on to win it that year (1985), Murray Grierson, who would go on to win two championships, in 1987 and 1993, and Jimmy Girvan who would win the title in 1990 and also in 2008.

In a rather less than polite exclamation, we all asked:
'Is this the future of rallying?'

I spoke with Tony at the end of the event and he said he was up to 20 seconds per mile quicker than any of the other drivers, that's 20 seconds *each and every mile*, not *two* seconds, but *20* on some of the stages. However, on two of the stages he'd some problems with a puncture and a bent steering rack, so that reduced his winning margin to an average of only (only) five seconds per mile. He and Rob won the event outright by three minutes and 35 seconds!

Obviously the 6R4 was quick, and I never felt I'd get one, but if you don't ask, you don't get, so I phoned up a man called Rod Ramsay, the then Managing Director of Austin Rover Scotland, and he said:

'David, I'll get you an interview, so why don't you go down and have a go?'

The last word on the 1985 Autofit Stages goes to Ian McRae who, as Clerk of the Course, quite proudly stated that interestingly, the co-driver of car 32 was none other than Colin McRae at the age of 16, with John Gray behind the wheel.

By the end of the season I had realised that I had moved on from preparing my cars privately. I realised, that if I was going to progress from being the talented amateur that I was (well I *had* won a few things by this time) I *had* to go for a Works (factory) team; and I *had* to have a professional car preparation contractor because up to that time everything had been done brilliantly in-house at Gillanders Motors, by Joe and Steve Smith, a father and son team, and also Gary Smith and Martin Gillespie. Joe, Steve and Martin built the cars, and they came with me to all of the events. They were really immense. They were my 'rocks' and they gave up their time at the weekends to become rally mechanics and support me in my efforts, and I am eternally grateful to them. They were brilliant, absolutely brilliant. So too were John Steele and Geoff ("Jolly") Roberts, two highly capable mechanics from the then fledgling Malcolm Wilson Motorsport team whom I contracted with.

I also have to thank Graham Neish a lot for his friendship, encouragement and motivation, especially on rallies, so I think I'll let him explain our relationship:

'I think David is getting worse the older he gets; his memory is ten times worse than mine, and mine's bad.... He doesn't remember the detail and he always likes to be the hero but he's still the same old David though – you either like him or you don't like him. I happen to like him a lot; he's great fun to be with but you just have to take David the way he is, and if he starts speaking a load of rubbish, just tell him so!

'David needs people to speak to him, but when I was first introduced to him through a mutual friend called Ally Freeland, my first impression was that he was a bit obnoxious and didn't speak to me at all, and yet he was only the fastest delivery driver of motor spares in the world at the time – in his Renault 4L van!

'However, after a few meetings, the subject became motor sport orientated, and so we began to converse. I had by then joined the Garioch Motor Club in the town of Oldmeldrum in Aberdeenshire, whilst David had been cajoled into joining the Aberdeen and District Motor Club.

'David and I used to compete against each other in the autocross events that were held at Udny Green and Pitcaple, but when we got to know each other really well we did a fair bit of spectating together. We also went north to Inverness to watch the Snowman Rally, and see (in particular) the fantastic Alpine Renaults, and after that we watched the action

on the Scottish Rally. It didn't take us long before we started to think about competing, albeit in separate cars.

'We each competed on the Granite City Rally in the early seventies: he was in his Mini Cooper S and I was in my smaller engined Mini, but after a time we joined forces and David and I did the rally he described earlier, the one that overlooked the Faslane Submarine Base. I felt we were going so slow that I could actually look out and enjoy the scenery! Seriously, though, David was not the fastest driver, and he'll admit that; that honour fell to Jim Robson who was easily the quickest of the crop of drivers in the north east of Scotland at the time, but David, in my opinion, was ultra safe. I'd even go as far and say that he was one of the safest drivers around.

'I always felt comfortable with David at the wheel, even as he gradually increased his speed, and this is where I think I came back into the equation after his droopsnoot days with Ross Baird in the Ford Escort RS2000. He'd had the Volvo 142S as well with Ross, but it wasn't until I sat alongside him again, on the Granite City Rally in his Group 4 Ford Escort RS1800, that I got a real eye-opener. I was gobsmacked by his new turn of speed at the wheel of 'OSO 151W', but after a few of the forest stages I was up at the top of the screen just trying to keep him going – I kept shouting at him:

'Keep it going, keep it going!'

'If I shouted it once, I shouted it hundreds of times, and as a result we got a fine result on the event. He was a good, safe driver, but he didn't have the speed initially – that came with sheer hard work whereas I would go out to the pub at nights. David, though, would instead go out and practice in the snow (on the Hazlehead Golf Course, for example...) but I like to think that I just made him believe in himself. I pushed and pushed and pushed, so we had a sort of marriage, although it wasn't a marriage made in heaven as we used to argue a lot. There was a lot more speed to come out of him.

'David was friendly with Donald Milne and one day, Donald phoned to say that he planned to do a recce of the stages on the Snowman Rally:

'How?'

'By helicopter, my helicopter.'

'Donald volunteered to take the two of us, so David and I drove west to meet up with him at his house near the old Kincardineshire town of Banchory, fairly close to where the famous salmon leap is on the Water of Feugh. The three of us managed to squeeze into Donald's helicopter with Donald himself on the left, me in the middle with the maps, and David in the right hand seat. We took off and flew north to look over the stages, but all we could see was snow.... so we turned round to head back home. We had decided to follow the Cabrach, the A941 road from Rhynie to Dufftown, but when I spotted the Grouse Inn I said:

'God Almichty! There's the Grouse Inn doon there.'

'Donald asked:

'What's the Grouse Inn?'

'It's a wee pubbie. Maybe we should just drop down and have our lunch?'

'So that's what we did. Donald popped the helicopter down onto the car park and the landlord, his wife, and wee daughter came out to see us. They hadn't seen anybody for three days as the roads had been totally blocked with snow-drifts. We asked if they were open and they invited us in to get a plate of soup. 'I had a pint and David had a soft drink, but Donald, well he was 'driving', so he'd a bowl of soup before we relaxed with a game of pool. Eventually, we returned to the helicopter, took off and flew direct to Kintore, where I stayed at the time. Donald dropped me off (not literally) by the field by my house, and he and David headed back to Banchory.

Sideways in the dust. Photograph: Mike Gower.

112

Sideways on the slippery stuff.

Photograph: Jim Sutherland.

'We didn't win that Snowman Rally, be we did win the Autumn Stages in the Volvo from Gordon Smith who had initially been announced as the victor. It was a big shame for him, but when the organisers checked all of the time penalties they spotted an error in the calculations and we were subsequently promoted to the win.

At the start of the Border Rally. Photo: Kevin MacIver.

'Drivers and co-drivers have a special relationship, they have to have, and the element of trust comes into it. David depended on me to give him the right instructions at the right time, and I depended on David to get me home safely, which he always did.

'That special relationship extended to our respective spouses, Gladys and Edith. The four of us went on David's and Gladys' honeymoon to the Norfolk Broads! Edith and I thought that we'd travel in style in a Volvo but we ended up going in a Renault 11. We spent a week on a cabin cruiser and were wakened early each morning by David who had actually got up at the crack of dawn to fish from the boat – on his honeymoon!

Postscript:

Strangely enough, my Volvo actually came up for auction at Bonhams, the privately owned auction house in the UK, in 2015. I was seriously tempted to buy it back as it was still resplendent in its Gillanders Motors decals! They sought bids in the region of £55,000-£70,000, but what would I do with it nowadays? I think it would just sit and gather dust and that would be a shame.

Photograph: Courtesy of Burdumy Volvo, Sweden.

Chapter NINE

THE MG METRO 6R4

Trying very hard! With Ken Rees in the MG Metro 6R4.
Photograph: Sandy Topp.

Where do I start with the MG Metro 6R4?

Well, I can start by stating that at the time the car was announced I had an Austin Rover dealership in Peterhead and that certainly helped me a lot in terms of getting my hands on one.

In October, 1986, I witnessed Ken Wood secure his third Scottish Rally Championship title. He was driving an MG Metro 6R4, but I had been impressed with his abilities behind the wheel before: in 1984 he had won the championship driving a Rover Vitesse SD1, but before that, in 1982, he took the title in his ex-works Triumph TR7 V8, and each time he was partnered by co-driver, Peter Brown. That *has* to be a unique record, securing three titles with three different models, from the same manufacturer, every second year, and all with the same co-driver! I'd go so far as to say that that's a motor sport trivial pursuit question in the making, wouldn't you? Ken's exploits in the Metro certainly encouraged me.

Full opposite lock on the Penmachno North special stage of the Skip Brown Rally. Photograph: Steve Pugh.

When I had my big blue Volvo bus that we used to tow the rally car all over the country, it was all about having fun, especially with Graham Neish in the ranks. Everything was a hoot, whether it was drinking and rallying, or rallying and drinking, (before and after the events) but if we broke down on a rally, we'd head off to the nearest pub for more drinking. If we finished the rally, we considered that a bonus and, yes, another reason for more drinking.

It was a huge laugh from start to finish. There was nothing serious about it, but when the 6R4 era started I thought about it long and hard and had to 'fire' all of my mechanics. This, as you can imagine, didn't go down too well as they were no longer involved in the preparation of my car in-house. I *had* to become more professional and so I went to an external car preparation company to carry out that work. It was tough, really tough, and Graham was eventually replaced. However, I must stress that this was *not* of my doing. That was not my choice; it was Dave Bignald of Gartrac who actually made that decision. He said that I needed to get someone more professional because they were a professional outfit, and that they needed to maintain a professional image.

Prior to the co-driver decision, Austin Rover Group's Rod Ramsay kept his word and I was duly invited to meet the ARG motor sport supremo, John Davenport. I said to Dave Bignald that if I was going to go in and see John Davenport then I'd need to go in mob-handed; I couldn't go in myself. I needed somebody with me, and he agreed to come along. This was for an interview to potentially become a driver for ARG the following year, and if successful, I would also get some funds from the midlands manufacturer to run the car.

Anyway, we both arrived in Longbridge, an area of Birmingham, to meet 'the Boss'. We entered a large room in the complex and found that the number of drivers there was incredible. They were *all* there, wanting to get their hands on a Metro, just as I was. I recognised first rate drivers like the amiable Finn and eventual Lombard RAC Rally winner, Pentti Airikkala, waiting along with a number of Americans, Germans and Russians. All were superstars in their own right. Also there was Jimmy McRae, the five times British Rally Champion from Lanark, and me! We were all queued up at Davenport's Door, waiting for our interview!

I said to Bignald:

'We've no chance. Look at the quality (of drivers).'

Jimmy McRae was a legend in Scotland at the time, and much, much better than me. There just seemed no way I would get one; no way would I get past these guys. Anyway, my appointment was timed for 2 o'clock and Dave and I were beckoned to go in, and the first thing Davenport said was:

'I remember you! A Volvo wasn't it?'

John Davenport was *the* motor sport man in Austin Rover – he was 'the Boss'. You are talking about *'God'* in his day (purely from a motor sport perspective of course, although Stuart Turner was also *'God'*, when he was with the Ford

Motor Company, although he mainly recruited the top Scandinavian drivers).

"The Boss", aka John Davenport.
He complained that I had cropped this
picture of him so much that he'd lost
all his hair!

Photograph reproduced by kind
permission of John Davenport.

I remember the interview very well – and John and I have since become good friends. He was there, wearing a pink shirt and sitting behind his desk when he said:

'Ah! Gillanders, I have to tell you something which you won't remember, but I have to tell you anyway. I did this rally some time ago and had not long finished the event. We were all going home, when one of my engineers said:

'Listen, you need to see this guy in the Volvo.'

So I asked him:

'Why? What do you mean?'

'You've got to see him.'

The engineer insisted:

'He's a flaming lunatic, but you just have to see him. It's a laugh. You simply have to watch the guy!'

Davenport continued:

'We hung around at the last stage and heard a funny noise coming from the forest,' (this would have been because the Volvo had a turbocharged engine – it didn't have a roar like a conventional car. Instead, it emitted a sort of 'flat' exhaust note):

'And this thing burst over the top of the hill and into view, completely sideways, so sideways you would not believe it, and we were all just looking at it thinking 'the guy's run out of brakes. He's got no brakes!'

The Austin Rover boss said I flashed past him and his crew and then he started enthusiastically again:

'You were on opposite lock to here, opposite lock to there, and on opposite lock to here again, and it stuck in my mind, so I'm glad to meet up with you.'

That's the reason I got to see John Davenport. It was mainly because of the Volvo, and that's why that car became so special to me. I had decided that I would go in with a completely different attitude altogether because I suspected that the others would be pretty much on their knees praying and pleading to get their hands on a 6R4.

John Davenport said:

'What can I do for you?'

I responded with:

*'No, it's what **I** can do for **you**! I'm an Austin Rover dealer, and you want to give me a car **because** I'm an Austin Rover dealer.'*

Whether I could drive the car or not made no damned difference, but Davenport finished off by saying:

'Well, that was a very good interview, thank you very much. Just go outside and wait, please.'

So Dave and I went outside, where he said:

'We've no chance.'

I agreed:

'Not a ghoster, but we'll have to wait.'

We waited an hour and the door opened and 'God' beckoned us in. Honestly, he picked up a set of car keys, threw them into my hands and said:

'If you can find the car that those keys belong to, you can have it!'

There were something like 200 MG Metro 6R4s out the back, all in white, and we'd one set of car keys....

Wall-to-wall Metro 6R4s and all white.....

Photograph: Keith Adams.

Can you just imagine it? These cars did not have remote locking and unlocking on the key fob, so we ended up having to try each and every Metro door lock. Neither were they stacked in chassis number sequence. We started with one, then two, then three, then four.., then five.., to 54, 75, 111, 151, 164, 177, 182, 195..., until we eventually found 'our' MG Metro 6R4, *our* Supercar, *our* chassis 082, with the registration number, 'C670 JSU'. I can just about remember saying (almost whispering) to Dave:

'Can you believe this?'
'David, it's incredible.'
'But we've got a 6R4.'
'I know...'

Well, the Metro wouldn't start, obviously, because along with all of the other pre-homologation 6R4s, it had been stuffed into this car park and left for some time.

However, as I flew home via the proverbial cloud nine, Bignald made arrangements to return with a trailer and collect the car along with a large pile of parts. Unfortunately, the pile of parts we were given were not the 'right' parts initially: all of the Works cars had 4:1 differentials and also the very best equipment including special gearboxes, and in addition, the engines had also been taken to the Nth degree of tuning. Eventually, though, I did get all the 'right' bits, but, early on, I was a 'nobody' compared to the other 6R4 drivers.

Being a 'nobody' meant that my car had the lesser 'Clubman' specification but if I had been a 'somebody' I would have been given the 'International' version. Mine would only go from a standing start to 60 mph in four and a half seconds, or from nought to 100 mph in 12.8 seconds, but the 'International' specification engine and ancillary parts, which I ultimately graduated to, would do the same measures in three point two and ten seconds respectively.

John Davenport has a few memories to tell, so I'll let him take over here:

'In this modern age, memory is something you buy to stick in your computer, but for us older guys, we have to rely on good old biological neurotransmitters somewhere in our

hippocampus. Thus it is that I cannot say with certainty as to when I first met David Gillanders.

'I did compete on the Granite City Rally a few times in the early 1970s with such luminaries as Chris Sclater and Billy Coleman, so it is possible that David and I first met in some Aberdeen drinking den in the aftermath of one of those rallies.

'Certainly, David did compete on the 1974 RAC Rally in a Volvo 142S when Hannu Mikkola and I retired in North Wales with broken wheel studs. He probably drove past us without passing the time of day, but one thing I do know for sure is that we met at the Autofit Stages Rally in Argyll on May 18, 1985.

'I can be certain of that date because this event was held only two days after Austin Rover Group launched the definitive version of the MG Metro 6R4 to the media at the spectacular Knebworth House, near London.

'After this we scuttled up the A74 towards the Cowal Penisula in Argyll and Bute, where the car was going to have its first try at a real rally.

'I recall a ferry trip from Gourock over the River Clyde to Dunoon and then a day spent dodging the Great Highland Midge (Culicoides impunctatus), an infuriating little insect that is more commonly known as the Midgie, around Loch Eck, and praying that Tony Pond and the 6R4 would do their stuff. They did. But while we were watching some of the stage action, I couldn't help but notice a Volvo 240 Turbo that was chasing the Vauxhall Chevette HSRs, Opel Ascona 400s and Ford Escort RSs in the most spectacular fashion.

'Of course the driver was David, and later, while we searched Dunoon for food and drink, we had a chat during the course of which he enquired about the possibility of acquiring a 6R4. Well, very shortly I would have 199 of the things to dispose of, so I told him that his prospects were excellent.

'However, it wasn't until late in 1985 that we finally got ourselves together to sort out a deal. Accompanying David at that meeting was David Bignald of Gartrac. He had been preparing other rally cars for the Aberdonian, including that Volvo 240T. With a little help from his friends in British Car

Rentals, and the slush fund that we called "Private Owner Support", David got his 6R4 and with it a deal to run it in the British National and Scottish Rally Championships.

'During 1986, David started racking up the results, particularly in Scotland, but the 6R4 was still a bit new, and when the ARG Works cars of David Llewellin and Malcolm Wilson retired from the Scottish Rally with worn engine valve seats, it was David that came through and saved our face by finishing 4th overall.

'Then of course, Group 'B' got banned and the ARG rally programme died on its feet, although 6R4s were still allowed to compete in the National Championships where, I am glad to say, David won three events outright in 1987 and stacked up enough points to win the title.'

Thanks to John Davenport, my very first event with *my* supercar was on the Snowman Rally based in Inverness, a most beautiful part of Scotland. This was in mid-February, and located high in the Highlands, and as such it meant that it was usually the nearest thing the UK had to a snow rally.

At the time I still had Graham Neish as my co-driver, but I'd not driven the car before I was flagged off from the start. I drove it along the main road to the first special stage, and soon realised that the noise was incredible. We didn't have ear defenders, and we'd no intercom. In fact we'd nothing like that in the early days of the MG Metro 6R4. We couldn't hear a thing, other than the V6 engine, and I certainly couldn't hear a word Neish said to me.

You have no idea just *how* noisy these cars were.

Anyway, I had to try out the acceleration on the road section to the first special stage and I ended up saying:

'Bloody hell, this is something else!'

And I had the 'slow', Clubman version....

I'll never forget it.

We sat at the stage start and Neish said to me:

'Are you ready for this?'

'Let's give this thing a bit of laldy.'

Translated, that meant to do it with gusto.

'Jesus Christ!'

I dropped the clutch – and remember, this was a *small* engined 6R4 – the *big* engined version did not come until later. It went off like a scalded cat. I mean, *really* like a scalded cat, and howled to match! I crashed it at the first corner! I had gone in far too fast and just couldn't slow it down on the snow. I thought to myself, *'W-o-w!'* (If you believe that's what I actually uttered, then you'll probably believe anything!)

I shouldn't really have been surprised, as the Formula One Williams Racing Team had been involved in the 6R4's early development. Anyway, we did get back on the road at that first corner by using the car's superior traction to its full potential, although I had knocked off the spoiler and a few other bits as well.

As I said, my car was the 'Clubman' specification version. It had a 3-litre 90-degree, 24-valve, V6 engine which developed some 250 brake horsepower through a five speed gearbox to all four wheels. The power to weight ratio was fantastic, but even more powerful was the 'International' specification version which came with 410 brake horsepower. Originally, ARG used the Rover V8 engine and chopped off a couple of cylinders at the end, but then made new cylinder heads and blocks to create a new engine. The intention was that Austin Rover would compete against the other Group 'B' supercars like the Audi Quattro Sport, the Peugeot 205 T16, the Lancia Delta S4 and the Ford RS200.

This four wheel drive, short wheelbase, purpose-built rally engine had enormous power driving all four corners, and that was totally alien to me. Did we finish? Yes, even with that earlier 'off'. Graham and I finished 2nd overall to Donald Heggie and Iain Mungall in their Audi Quattro by just over a minute, but we, in turn, were over a minute ahead of Ken Wood and Peter Brown in their 6R4, and they'd been driving theirs for a longer period of time. I did win the Snowman Rally a couple of years later.

Ken Wood was always my nemesis because he had his MG Metro 6R4 as well. His car was marketed as *"Britain's Noisiest Crisp"*, because it was sponsored by the Golden Wonder potato crisp manufacturer, although I think Ken was a wee bit envious because I, technically, had the 'Works' car, compared to his private one. He could certainly drive.

Air Traffic Controller, Ken Wood, in full flight. Right: Me at the start of the Granite City Rally in 1986. Photographs: Jack Davidson.

Gradually, I got better and better results with the 6R4 and I managed to finish 4th overall on the 1986 Scottish Rally – my best ever international result. Finnish driver, Mikael Sundström, actually won the event in the Works Peugeot 205 T16, and Englishman, Mark Lovell, was 2nd in the Factory Ford RS200. And 3rd, only (only) five minutes faster than me in my MG Metro, was Swedish driver, Björn Waldegård.

Summertime in Scotland can often be wet and cold; summertime in Scotland can sometimes be hot and dry! Stand long enough in the one place and you might get all four seasons in one day, but on this particular event, in June, the dust was a huge problem. All the official Works 6R4s broke down through the ingestion of such particles; they had sucked in the dust and blown their valves, but my Gartrac engine had been fitted with an old-fashioned oil-filled air filter which worked well enough, although my engine was pretty much knackered by the end.

We had been lying in 4th position overall just before the final day's action when we went to start the engine in Parc Fermé.

Night-Time Service for the 6R4 on the 1986 Lloyds Bowmaker RSAC International Scottish Rally. Photograph: Derry Taylor

This was the area where the competition cars were kept overnight and security marshals were stationed to ensure that no additional and/or illegal servicing could be carried out. When I got access to my car and tried to start it, there was no compression when I turned over the engine. I prayed:

'Come on, baby, catch, catch, catch!'

I cried out time and time again and eventually, one cylinder fired up, then two, then three, then four, then five, and then six, the last one. We breathed a sigh of relief, but Neish said to me:

'You know, we're never going to finish.'

'We'll keep going and see what happens.'

Super-Swede Waldegård, in his Works Toyota Celica Twin Cam Turbo, was just in front and I said to myself:

'I want to beat him and be 3rd on the Scottish Rally.'

I got to the start of the next stage and said to Graham:

'We're going to give this thing laldy.'

I did beat the Swede on the stage and I thought to myself,

'Yes, I can beat this guy. Who the hell's Björn Waldegård anyway? I'll blow him clean off. 'I am going to beat him!'

125

Aye, right!

Björn Waldegård wasn't the inaugural World Rally Champion in 1979 for nothing, was he?

Flying high with Ken Rees on the '87 Granite City Rally.
Photograph: Courtesy of Scott Brownlee.

I got to the start of the next stage, and was sitting waiting in the queue, ready to go when the door opened, and in leaned the tall Swede. He said to me, somewhat incredulously:

'What the hell do you think you're doing? Do you realise you are the only 6R4 left in this rally, and suddenly, you're trying to beat me? I'm crawling through these stages. You will be 4th and you will take it. You will not go any faster because you won't catch me, but you will break your car trying.'

And I then thought to myself, *'You know something, I believe you, because you're Björn Waldegård!'*

That's true. He told me to slow down. I would never have caught him, and I *would* have broken the car trying to catch him. Anyway, we made it, and it was one of the first international finishes for the MG Metro 6R4. The official Works team had gone home earlier, and that included John Davenport himself and all of the Works mechanics.

They all pissed off and left us on our own! We were furious because they could have, and should have, stayed on and supported us. We were not best pleased because, normally, in such a situation, when a Works team retires all of its cars on an event, the factory mechanics and team personnel usually rally round any of the semi-works teams, or privateers even, to ensure that their marque gets to the finish.

I could hardly believe it; I had the only 6R4 running at the end of the Scottish International Rally, and Graham and I had just finished in 4th position overall. Much of the credit for that had to go to the Swedish Superstar, and I was really saddened to learn that Björn had passed away on August 29, 2014.

Right: An actual photograph of Björn Waldegård 'peeping' out of his 'peep' hole window of his car on that Scottish Rally. Photograph: Göran Thobiasson.

Landing after a jump on the Autofit Stages, one of the last events I did with Graham Neish.

Graham Neish (right) and I had a fantastic partnership in the rally car – it really was a laugh-a-minute, enjoyable time. Photograph: Courtesy of the Scottish Rally Championship.

I progressed with the Metro but had to lose Graham Neish. I missed his sense of humour and his fun, because he was a bit like me, a comedian. The more professional members of Bignald's outfit considered Graham to be too much of an amateur at this particular stage of development of the Gartrac Motor Sport Team. The car itself was certainly professionally prepared and maintained, with the support of the factory, and I had responded and upped my level of skill in driving this very demanding car. Gartrac said I *had* to get a more pro-fessional co-driver, and for the first time, the name of Ken Rees was mentioned.

Graham, you see, wasn't really interested in doing the notes beforehand, or even the service schedules, because he was more interested in competing on the actual events. The problem for the Gartrac team was that they would arrive in the morning and expect to have all the times and locations sorted out for them, but all Graham would say was:

'Here's a map; you'll find all the references on the Rally HQ Notice Board where you can plot them.'

To be fair to Graham, though, in the early days of stage rallying, the service arrangements could generally be rather vague, with something along the lines of:

'We'll see you at the first layby on the A-class road by such-and-such village.'

I did understand Graham's point of view.

Devilla Forest, a classic. Photograph: Jim Sutherland.

I have to emphasise that I didn't know a thing about any of the kind of stuff that had been going on. Bignald, apparently, wanted his mechanics to get from Graham, *exactly* where the service points were to be positioned. He wanted to know that they were going to be, *'here, here, here and there'*, so to speak, but Graham was always somewhat vague about the actual locations.

I never actually fired any of my co-drivers: Graham Neish stopped because of time constraints originally, and Ross Baird had to stop through work commitments. My second stint with Graham, though, was brought to an end when Bignald said:

'Look, we must get you a professional co-driver.'

He demanded that I should have a professional in the co-driver's seat, and give 100% of his time. I must say, though, that the times I had with Graham, in particular, were the greatest I had in terms of fun and enjoyment.

Anyway, that's when Ken Rees came into the frame. I certainly did not fire Graham. He was at the time, and I am pleased to say, still is, my best friend (other than Gladys). The decision to free Graham was down to Dave Bignald and Gartrac. Nevertheless, Graham has some views on this, so I think I should I let him explain his thoughts of our time with Gartrac and the Metro:

'The pinnacle of my career, and probably David's (in respect of a single event), has to be the aforementioned 4ᵗʰ overall finish we had on the Scottish International Rally, although David and I nearly fell out on the last night of the event because he thought he was going to go on and win it in his MG Metro 6R4....

'He rightly felt annoyed that Austin Rover did not leave their service crews behind to look after him after the Works Metros had retired and their service teams had departed before we had actually finished the rally.

'Nevertheless, David was undoubtedly the 'Star' by taking the only remaining 6R4 through to the finish!

'He also put his trust in me when we finished the competitive sections of the event outside Glasgow. The organisers had a large car park and the first three cars got a police escort to take them to the Holiday Inn in the city, but the car in 4ᵗʰ place (us), well, we had to lead the remaining cars to the finish and he didn't think I'd find the hotel. Well, I did, and we secured one of the best ever international results for the MG Metro 6R4.

'After the Scottish Rally, our paths became separated. My services were no longer required, primarily because Dave Bignald had made the move to replace me. I have to say, though, that it was the right decision for David because he would go early to his bed at night, whereas the service crew and I would go and have a night out on the town. On some of the events the following day, I'd have a pretty sore head, but with some coca-cola and a mars bar I soon returned to some semblance of normality. However, from my perspective, it was not at all professional, although I have to say it was a very enjoyable time in my life.

'David, though, had reached another level. He had proven his speed, and his reliability was there with that Scottish Rally finish. It was a fantastic result for him, and his performance on that event, coupled to the fact that he had won the Group 'A' category in the Scottish Championship with the Volvo 240T the previous year, cemented his growing reputation and helped him to get the uprated 6R4.

It really was an excellent opportunity. He was the right driver and bloody safe too. The car usually went to an Austin Rover showroom for publicity prior to an event and it could easily have been returned there after the rally, still in pristine condition. He never really damaged the car, and it never blew up when I was his co-driver.

'David always did what the sponsors required, and that helped enormously. As far as his motor sport was concerned, I think he had too much confidence in himself not to be successful.'

I have to say that it was a huge wrench to part with Graham as my co-driver, and learn to work with someone I had never heard of before, a fellow by the name of Ken Rees. The new pairing teamed up in time for the 1986 RAC Rally, so I'll let Ken pick up the story at this point:

Ken Rees –
'I got a phone call from Dave Bignald of Gartrac to see if I would be interested in co-driving for David Gillanders on the RAC Rally.'

'As there was no internet at the time, I did not have any immediate information on just how good, how safe, or how quick David actually was, so Gartrac arranged a test day at Gaydon, in Warwickshire, where ARG had a vehicle proving ground. I made my way there and that's where and when I first met him.

'Being the big businessman that he was, he happened to announce his arrival by flying in with his helicopter. I found out that this turned out to be David's normal, bombastic, important style and I thought to myself, "I don't know if I can put up with ten days of this...."

'But anyway, we had our test run, and although David appeared to be a little distant, I still said 'yes' and Dave Bignald subsequently organised our entry on the RAC Rally.'

The 1986 Lombard RAC Rally

I had a prior shooting engagement at Glamis Castle, near Forfar, the county town of Angus, in Scotland. This was held about the same time that the scrutineering of the rally cars began and it was obvious that I would be late, but I didn't have to worry too much about this because the organisers actually delayed the scheduled time for my car to be checked over.

This was, allegedly, because of Lord Glamis, the 17th Earl of Strathmore and Kinghorne, a first cousin, once removed, of HM Queen Elizabeth. I think he might have been the boss of the RAC at the time, and as a result pulled a few strings on my behalf, but all my efforts to substantiate this have failed.

Anyway, when I arrived for the rally I was still in my shooting togs because I had just come off the plane, but nevertheless there, waiting patiently for me, was Ken Rees. This was the very first time I'd have a professional co-driver on an event, and we headed towards Bath in Somerset, England, for the start. It was a World Championship round but it was also the swansong European event for the Group 'B' Supercars. I happen to think that this event was probably the high spot of my driving career. I still have the metal competition number identification plate at home.

We got through Scrutineering and the car was, by this time, a fully fledged MG Metro 6R4; it was almost where it should have been in terms of all the proper equipment and it had the performance to match. It even had the right dashboard built in. In fact it had everything. It was a spectacular car, and at that point Ken Rees turned round to me and said:

'Are we setting the lights up?'

'What for?'

'Well, the night stages.'

'No, what do you mean?'

Anyway, I said to him:

'Stand over there.'

I pointed to an area 20 yards away.

'I'll now shine the lights on your penis because that's the correct height!'

So he walked 20 yards until I shouted on him to stop.

'Perfect, 20 yards away on your penis; the height is absolutely perfect!'

He couldn't believe this, but nevertheless we started the event and just before the start of the first special stage I asked him:

'What's your navigation like?'

'Oh, I'm a proper co-driver. In fact I used to co-drive for Dennis Moody.'

'So what was the last car you were in?'

'A Gartrac Ford Sierra XR6.'

'Have you rallied a four wheel drive car before?'

'No.'

'Well, they're slightly quicker.'

'Oh, we'll be fine.'

'Oh, you think so?'

There were no co-driving aids such as pacenotes or safety notes in those days, but all the same there was an incredible array of talent entered in the event, and the starting order could easily have been described as a 'Who's Who?' of rallying. The quality of drivers in those first thirty odd places was incredible, and for the motor sport aficionados, there is a complete list of the top 37 competitors at the end of this chapter.

'Why only the top 37?'

Well, that happened to be my competition number…

The first stage was held in a public park, and when I saw the cameras for the BBC's, 'live stage' programme, I thought to myself, *'You beauty, we're either going to go off or we're going to be on television!'*

Well, I got as far up the leader board as 8th overall, and this amongst the World Rallying elite. I was on that famous 'cloud nine', and nobody could touch me because I had a minute's lead over the car behind.

On the Lombard RAC Rally in 1986.

Photograph: Courtesy of Scott Brownlee.

There were world champions and numerous national champions ahead of me, and I was down at car number '37', where the road conditions were considerably rougher in the forests. Despite this, I would say that it was my best ever performance; I traded times with Markku Alén in his Martini-liveried Works Lancia Delta HF Integrale in front of thousands upon thousands of spectators who lined the parks and forests of the event. It was spectacular stuff and almost unbelievable!

There was one particular incident that stuck in my mind, and that involved Russell Brookes who was in his Opel Manta 400 at number '16'. I was many places behind in my 6R4, but anyway, Ken Rees said to me on a stage:

'That's Russell Brookes ahead of us.'

I felt we were just cruising through the field because I was into the top ten on this World Championship event when Ken added:

'And you're going to catch him, David.'

'What do you mean?'

'You're going to catch him.'

'It's Russell Brookes! I'll never catch him.'

*'I don't care a damn who he is, but based on your stage times so far, you **are** going to catch him!'*

'I'll worry about that later...'

I started the next stage. It was a long one of around 35 miles, and I was about half way in when I sniffed the rubber off the hot tyres, and I thought to myself:

*'I **am** catching Russell Brookes!'*

Eventually, I caught sight of flashes of brake lights in the distance and slowly, but surely, over the long and winding road, the red mist descended, and:

'Oh, yeah! I've caught him!'

Then *'Whoosh!'* the metaphorical 'horns' came out, but of course the 6R4, had its front end full of radiators and other vulnerable equipment, so I couldn't afford to get up too close and personal to Brookes' rear wheel drive car, with all the muck and gravel being catapulted out the back. I waited until we entered a downhill section where he started to drift left in true rear-wheel drive sideways style and I simply cut the corner on the inside and overtook him.

I got to the start of the next stage before him, but he suddenly pulled in right in front of me and parked up. I thought, *'The cheeky bastard!'*

So I got out of my car and went up to his door – his Perspex window had little 'peep' holes cut into it to avoid steaming up, so I knocked on his window, which he pulled back, and I said:

'Mr. Brookes, I think I passed you on that last stage.'

'Oh, that was you, was it?'

'Yes. Did you have a problem there?'

'No.'

'Ok, so why have you pulled in front of me?'

'Well, my co-driver has said we should be starting in front of you.'

'Oh, you think so?'

Anyway, I caught him again on the next stage, but at the time control he said:

'Yes, you are right, you deserve to be in front of me.'

Then he bought me an ice cream (in the middle of November) by way of an apology.

William Woollard, a BBC Presenter, picked us up on the rally, and asked me:

'David, 'I'd like to do a spot on the programme about you. You started car '37' and you're in the top ten. What a story!'

But, it wasn't a story with a fairytale ending because on the third day, the effing cambelt went and the engine blew up. Hero to zero. Finished.

Overleaf is a picture of Ken Rees and me with tears streaming down our faces on some motorway or other because the engine was well and truly broken. I probably used another word (or several) instead of 'broken', as 'broken' simply did not convey our actual feelings or thoughts at the time.

Woollard still wanted to stand and have his interview with us but I have to admit I was rather ungracious and responded somewhat impolitely….

Distraught. Disconsolate. Dejected.

Not the best of photographs, but then again, neither Ken Rees nor I were in the best of moods either after our retirement on the 1986 Lombard RAC Rally.

I flew home that night and was ill for about a month. I couldn't speak to anybody for four weeks because I saw myself as a proper Works driver on that event. I had finally cracked it: the MG Metro 6R4 and I had become synonymous and I was on my way to my biggest 'high' in the sport, but with the engine failure the event also became my biggest 'low'. I'll let Ken expand on that:

'To get into the top 20 in a World Championship event in the Group 'B' era was pretty successful, but to get into the top ten was really special, and to get up to 8th position amidst some incredible names in the sport was absolutely awesome. Unfortunately, we broke the gearbox in Grizedale Forest, right in the heart of the Lake District of England, so we changed that at the side of the road. We lost a lot of time and had to hastily head south towards Wales.

'I was really looking forward to going to my home country, so we sent a car ahead to look out for any police, traffic jams and the like. We drove as fast as we could, as

safely as possible, but in the end we 'popped' the engine. I was bitterly disappointed that we didn't get there because it would have been the last leg of the event. We got rescued and headed off in different directions; I went to Wales, and David went to Scotland.'

Photograph: Chris Huish.

The Entry List for the 1986 Lombard RAC Rally.
(For the motor sport aficionados)

1. **Timo Salonen** (Finland - *World Champion '85*)
    (Peugeot 205T16 E2)
2. **Stig Blomqvist** (Sweden - *World Champion '84*)
    (Ford RS200)
3. **Markku Alén** (Finland - *FIA Champion '78 – forerunner to WRC*)
    (Lancia Delta S4)
4. **Tony Pond** (England)
    (The first person to set an average speed of over 100mph around the Isle of Man TT Motor Bike Circuit in June, '90, driving a production Rover 827 Vitesse)
    (MG Metro 6R4)
5. **Juha Kankkunen** (Finland - *World Champion '86, '87, '91, '93*)
    (Peugeot 205T16 E2)
6. **Karl-Erik (Kalle) Grundel** (Sweden)
    (Ford RS200)
7. **Ingvar Carlsson** (Sweden)
    (Mazda 323 4x4)
8. Non Starter
9. **Mikael Ericsson** (Sweden)
    (Lancia Delta S4)
10. **Malcolm Wilson** (England - *British Champion '78, '79*)
    (MG Metro 6R4)
11. **Mikael Sundström** (Finland)
    (Peugeot 205 Turbo 16)
12. **Mark Lovell** (England - *British Champion '86, Irish Tarmac Champion '87*)
    (Ford RS200)

13. Non Starter
14. **David Llewellin** (Wales - *British Champion '89, '90)*
    (MG Metro 6R4)
15. **Jimmy McRae** (Scotland - *British Champion '81, '82, '84, '87, '88)*
    (MG Metro 6R4)
16. **Russell Brookes** (England - *British Champion '77)*
    (Opel Manta 400)
17. **Per Eklund** (Sweden – *Swedish Champion '78)*
    (MG Metro 6R4)
18. **Stig Andervang** (Sweden)
    (Ford RS200)
19. **Marc Duez** (Belgium - *Belgian Champion '89)*
    (MG Metro 6R4)
20. **Harri Toivonen** (Finland)
    (MG Metro 6R4)
21. **Harald Demuth** (Germany - *German Champion '82, '84)*
    (Audi Quattro Sport)
22. Non Starter
23. **Tony Teesdale** (New Zealand - *New Zealand Champion '82, '84, '87)*
    (MG Metro 6R4)
24. **John Haugland** (Norway)
    (Skoda 130LR)
25. **Ladislav Křeček** (Czechoslovakia - *Czech Champion '96, '98, '99)*
    (Skoda 130LR)
26. Non Starter
27. **Kenneth Eriksson** (Sweden)
    (Volkswagen Golf GTi)
28. **Lassi Lampi** (Finland - *Finnish Champion '91)*
    (Audi Coupe)
29. **Pentti Airikkala** (Finland - *British Champion, '79)*
    (Vauxhall Astra GT/E)
30. **Andrew Wood** (Scotland - *Scottish Champion '89, '00)*
    (Vauxhall Astra GT/E)
31. Non Starter
32. **Louise Aitken-Walker** (Scotland - *Ladies World Champion '90)*
    (Nissan 240RS)
33. Non Starter
34. **Alistair Sutherland** (England - *British Champion '86)*
    (MG Metro 6R4)
35. **Willie Rutherford** (England)
    (MG Metro 6R4)
36. **Ken Wood** (Scotland - *Scottish Champion '82, '84, '86)*
    (MG Metro 6R4)
37. **David Gillanders** (Scotland - *British Champion '87, Scottish Champion '95)*
    (MG Metro 6R4)

Obviously, some of these entrants became champions after 1986, me included, but I include their eventual successes here to illustrate the quality of drivers I was up against........ all the way down to number 165 – a huge entry.

What a memory to have......

Chapter TEN

BRITISH RALLY CHAMPION

After the RAC Rally I phoned up Ken Rees and said:

'I think we need to compete in the Marlboro/Autosport British National Rally Championship in 1987.'

'We've no chance doing that.'

'What do you mean? I think we should definitely do it, and in fact we'll also enter the Scottish Championship.'

'Never.'

'Yes, we'll do them both!'

I had made up my mind.

I cannot remember exactly which event of the 1987 Marlboro/Autosport National Rally Series it was and nor do I recall which hotel I was staying in (I did say that my memory was failing) but I do remember the feeling that it had finally become 'My Turn'. Yes, it was 'My Turn' to come walking out of the hotel, wearing my fireproof racing suit, with my white MG Metro 6R4 gleaming at the front door, with the number '1' on the competition panels. And when I walked down the steps I thought to myself:

'I wonder if Ken Rees will hand me my gloves?'

And he did.

'He did!'

When he handed me my gloves, I thought to myself:

'Roger Clark, pay attention pal!'

Be scared of what you dream for, because sometimes it can happen. Who would have thought that I, a bullied child and lowly guy from Aberdeen, with a bad left hand, would actually be the number '1' and driving the car that people would look at, and stare at me? It was just like the time I stared at Roger *('The Maestro')* Clark, and his gleaming white

Ford Escort RS1600 all those years ago, and thinking, *'That boy's damn well cracked it!'*

On the Granite City Rally in the early seventies, I'd see all the English drivers entered and I'd think, *'Phew, look at these drivers.'*

Back then the English crews' support vans were quite a bit better than the Scottish teams; their car preparation appeared to be generally superior, and it also looked as though they had an unlimited number of tyres. I only had about six tyres available to me in my early stage rallying days: I'd four on the car, and two spares and I had to alternate them and put the fronts onto the backs, the backs onto the spares, and the spares onto the front, but if I picked up a puncture I was basically knackered. I would have had to ask someone else for the loan of a tyre or two because the camaraderie was good back then, and this system worked well both ways. These were tough times, financially.

The first round of the British series in 1987 was the Citroën Winter Rally which was based in Bournemouth. I finished in 4th place behind the Metro 6R4s of Malcolm Wilson/Nigel Harris, John Brown/John Daniels and Ken Wood/Peter Brown. I'd never seen the rally before, far less the stages, but I found the roads to be as smooth as silk. I also thought that there was no skill required for them although they were very, very fast.

In Scotland, the forest tracks I had grown accustomed to were, I felt, a bit slower because they followed the contours of the hillsides, had a wide variety of gradients, and could quite often be a mixture of fast and flowing sweeping bends, or slow and twisty corners. There could be a lot of crests where the road might suddenly veer off to the right or to the left, and I used to compete on such tracks long before the use of pace-notes, or safety notes. Basically I had learned to drive purely on sight, with considerably more variety to contend with in Scotland. But, in some areas of England it was more like:

'200 yards, 90 left ... 500 yards, 90 right.'

Well, I thought to myself, *'This is pretty easy, why should I worry about the English?'*

I remember someone once saying to me:

'Hey, you Scottish guys can drive.'

And of course, I just had to reply:

'There's nothing to this; wait until you come to Scotland!'

Round 2, the Skip Brown Rally, used the north Welsh resort of Llandudno as its base and with it the traditional dash around the Great Orme special stage that I'd first encountered with my Ford Escort RS2000 in the 1970s. Again, Malcolm Wilson and Nigel Harris won, but I took the runner-up position to be in a very handy position in the championship which had started in England and had gone into the principality of Wales. It was now to Round 3, and Scotland's counter, the Granite City Rally, which was sponsored for the first time by NorthSound Radio.

I felt that the British Championship was a tougher series to do because it was much, much faster, and the cars looked more professional. The entry lists were also bigger down south, but that was maybe because the bulk of the crews didn't have so far to travel. I enjoyed the championships on either side of Hadrian's Wall, but most of all I enjoyed beating the English!

And I did beat the English!

That was very satisfying.

The Granite City Rally

Generally, I thought the cars of the 70s and 80s were very fragile. The events were rough and tough all the way and on this Granite City Rally, Malcolm Wilson's 6R4 suffered differential failure three stages from the end and he rolled it off the track, well into the undergrowth.

Even although I'd been the next car along, I never actually saw Malcolm off the road, and I certainly didn't see the efforts of the spectators trying to right his car. Apparently, he had disappeared over a bank and I missed it all when I passed by. I exited the forest and headed off to the next stage where I waited until it was my due time of arrival and it was whilst I was waiting there the Start Marshal asked me:

'What's it like to be leading the Granite, David?'

'I don't think I am, because Malcolm is lying about 25 seconds ahead of me and I can't catch him.'

'Oh, you think so? Well he hasn't clocked in here.' (at the time control).

'Really?'

I said, somewhat incredulously to Ken Rees, almost in a whisper:

'Wilson hasn't clocked in!'

Ken whispered back:

'Let's hang around then to see if he does. We'll wait until the last minute, or until he incurs delay penalties'.

This is how Ken Rees and I won the Granite City Rally in 1987 – it was because of Malcolm Wilson's agricultural 6R4 (above). Photograph: Ferret Fotographics (with due acknowledgement to Nicky Lindon of www.6r4.net for his assistance in obtaining the image).

We held back until the last possible time before we too would start to incur time penalties. There was a line of cars behind and still no sign of Malcolm in his car, so for the last three stages I kept on saying to myself:

'I don't believe it....! I do not believe it....!

I could still scarcely believe it even when I crossed the finish line to become the first home-grown Aberdeen driver to win the Granite City Rally since it became a special stage event in 1968.

'*W-o-w!*

I'll let Ken continue:

'*We did particularly well on the Granite City Rally. It was an important event to David, just as much as the rally in Port Talbot was to me. He was so pleased at the effort we had all put into him winning the 'Granite' that he turned round to me on the podium and said as he shook my hand:*

"*Hey wee man, that was very good. Now I'll take you to Wales and I'll win one in Wales for you.*"

'*I always remember it. It was one of those really nice phrases to hear. And he meant it.*'

Ken didn't get paid for acting as my co-driver, but I did take care of all of his expenses and I gave him a car to travel up and down from Wales to Scotland because there was a lot of mileage covered through doing both championships that same year.

Winning the Granite City Rally was very special to me and I think Ken enjoyed it too!

It was sad to learn that Malcolm's regular co-driver, Nigel Harris, had died a few months after that Granite City Rally. He was involved in an air crash in September during the Bandama Rally when a Toyota Management Cessna crashed into dense tropical forest about a minute after take off from Yamoussoukro Airport in the Côte d'Ivoire (Ivory Coast). The cause was never established but the accident resulted in the loss of four lives, the two pilots, motor sport legend Henry Liddon (who used to co-drive for the original *'Flying Finn'*, Timo Mäkinen, in a Works Mini Cooper S), and sadly, Nigel Harris too. I knew Nigel. He was a lovely man.

Ken Rees continued:

'David and I had some good successes, but he wasn't really a tarmac specialist. He didn't like pacenotes either although we took a lot of time creating them on the Manx Rally. Altogether, we spent five days making the notes, even with Malcolm's input. Then we got to the start and accelerated hard off the line. David went up four gears very quickly and when he changed into fifth 'BANG!' went the engine. That was five days' effort wrecked in about five seconds at an important time in the series.'

After the Isle of Man, Ken and I decided to compete on the International Scottish Rally to maintain our levels of performance, but rather than risk the Metro, I decided to hire a Subaru RX Turbo from Subaru Motor Sport. Because the Manx Rally was in May, and the Kayel Graphics in July, I felt that a ten-week holiday break was rather a long time to sit and do nothing.

What goes up......

My Japanese registered Subaru Motor Sport RX Turbo out for an airing on the International Scottish Rally in 1987 with Ken Rees. Photograph: Jim Sutherland.

……must come down!

Photograph: Fergus McAnallen (www.rallyretro.com).

When the championship returned to Wales, it was to the south, to Port Talbot in fact, for the Kayel Graphics Rally. Ken and I won it by 2:10 minutes from Roger Clark and his co-driver, John Robinson, in their Metro. Malcolm Wilson, however, had withdrawn his car from the series.

The photographers got their moneysworth with the 6R4.
Photograph: Steve Pugh.

After this we headed to Carlisle for the Shell Oils Cumbria Rally which was won by London based Scot, Steve Whiteford, and his co-driver, Dave Adams, in yet another 6R4, but the best I could manage was a lowly 8th overall. The fight for the title was not going to be easy, that was fairly obvious.

And so to the penultimate event of the year, the Quip Forest Rally in Yorkshire. Here, it was Ken Wood's turn to take the top spot in his 6R4. I took it a bit easy to ensure a finish, but it nearly cost me dear. It meant that the final event, the Audi Sport Rally based in Telford in Shropshire would be the decider, and I had an uphill struggle on my hands. The title race looked as though it was going down to the wire, as they say, between me in my 6R4, Trevor Smith in his Ford Sierra RS Cosworth and Russell Brookes in his Vauxhall Astra GSi.

On the Margam Special Stage en route to winning the Kayel Graphics Rally in 1987.   *Photograph: Steve Pugh.*

Although Malcolm Wilson was there as well, he had actually switched his allegiance from Austin Rover Group to Vauxhall, but their big hope for the title lay with Russell Brookes. Pat Doran, who later went on to become a four-time British Rallycross Champion, was there as well. It was tough

147

opposition, and Malcolm recognised that, so on the Friday evening before the rally, he made a suggestion to me:

'Look, David, as this will be the decider for the title, let's walk through the last special stage.'

'Malcolm, for Christ's sake....'

'David, let's walk the last stage.'

He was pretty insistent. Although the Special Stage was in Telford it felt as though I was walking through my local Duthie Park in Aberdeen. It was a flat, public park, and we walked round it and just chatted away, but did I look at the course? No, not really, because I just thought to myself, *'Somebody will have won the event before it comes to here. There's no way it's going to come down to the very last stage.'*

But why was Malcolm so insistent?

The record book shows that the 1986 British National Championship also went down to the wire, and on the very last event, Alistair Sutherland clinched the title by a mere ten seconds from Melrose driver, Andrew Wood. Everyone thought that would have been the closest finish ever to this championship, but they didn't reckon on me, did they?

Timo Salonen, the 1985 World Rally Champion, was there in his Mazda Rally Team Europe 323 4WD. He was in full practice mode for the RAC Rally which was to be held on these very stages a few weeks later.

Anyway, Flying Finn, Salonen, and co-driver, Seppo Harjanne, started at number one and Mark Lovell was at number two with one-time co-driver, the *"Daily Mail's"* Jerry Williams in a Ford Sierra RS Cosworth. I was at number three with Ken Rees and we were followed by a multitude of Metros.

The following record of the stage results are probably more of interest to the aficionados, but they do show how intense the competition was. The first Special Stage, SS1, was Dyfnant 1. It was 11 miles long and Steve Whiteford sped through in 13:02 minutes. Ken Wood was seven seconds behind, then Pat Doran a further 10 seconds slower. I was 4th, a couple of seconds down from that.

SS2 covered the four-mile Tri-Arglwyd stage where Ken Wood and I were equal first with a time of 4:17 minutes. Bill Barton was 3rd, and in equal 4th place were Timo Salonen in his Mazda, and David Williams in his Metro 6R4. Pat Doran was 6th. SS3 was the well known stage of Gartheiniog 1, and this encompassed eight miles of testing conditions, yet three of us exited the forest with exactly the same time of 8:46 minutes. One of my biggest rivals, Steve Whiteford, though, went off the track and into immediate retirement, so that was him out of the running. Crucially, in respect of the overall standings, it was Ken Wood who was in front.

SS4 was Llwydiarth and over the six mile course, Pat Doran was five seconds faster than the WRC driver, but Salonen's results would not count as he wasn't registered for the championship that the rest of us were chasing. I was 3rd, seven seconds behind the Finn.

Salonen was starting to get into his stride by SS5, the 555 CWM Celli stage, and he set the fastest time of 3:41 minutes over the three miles. Doran was next up, down only three seconds and I was only two seconds behind, equal with Ken Wood, who still led the rally at the halfway halt in the town of Machynlleth, He was two seconds in front of Doran, and I was in 3rd place, but I *had* to win the event outright to secure the title. I could not relax as the two leading Group 'A' drivers, Trevor Smith and Russell Brookes could also win the title because the winner of that category got the same number of points as the Group 'B' drivers. I was certainly under intense pressure.

SS6, Pantherthog, was about eight miles long and I recorded the same time as Salonen, covering it in 9.04 minutes, but more importantly, Doran was four seconds slower, and Wood a further three behind. Doran had, however, snatched the lead by one second from Wood and I was in 3rd place overall, only five seconds behind the man at the front.

Timo Salonen came up to me at the start of one of the special stages (it might well have been SS6, Pantherthog) and he asked me a question:

'Tell me, how is the championship going?'

'Well, it's very simple really, because whoever wins this event will be the British Champion.'

'How are you doing?'

'I'm there or thereabouts, lying in 3rd or 4th place.'

'Could I help you?'

'How could you help me?'

'Well, you're in next after me, so follow my lines.'

'Really?'

'Yes, you follow my lines.'

Well, I followed his lines as he suggested.

'Jesus Christ!'

His lines through the forest tracks were unbelievable, but I had to believe in them. Rees would back me up on this, so Ken and I went into the stage and I said:

'Where's his brake marks?'

I hadn't seen any evidence of him braking!

Anyway, we came to these long lefthanders over a crest where normally I'd see some tyre marks beforehand where the earlier drivers would have locked up briefly before taking a brow. But there were no tell-tale signs on the road; in fact, there were no marks whatsoever, so I thought to myself:

'Well, if he's nae braking, I'm nae braking!'

So, Ken and I went flying through this stage, and I mean *flying* through it. There were long lefts and long rights and when Salonen braked, he *really* braked. I could see the rubber-leaving evidence! That was some ride, but when we got to the end of the following stage I found that I had actually beaten him by three seconds!

In SS7, Pen-Lan. I snatched three seconds back from Doran when I won that seven mile test in 9:23 minutes. Bill Barton then won SS8, Bwlch, and Ken Wood was second, three seconds down. I managed to take another second off Barton who was in 4th place, but overall, Ken Wood was still in front, by two seconds over Barton, whom I had drawn level with, and we three were well ahead of everybody else.

A second visit to the eight miles of Gartheiniog, masquerading as SS9, saw Doran take five seconds off me in second place, which was disappointing, but Barton and Wood were behind me which was a bit of a relief. The final forest stage of the rally was SS10, Dyfnant 2. It was our second visit to the stage and Timo Salonen, by now, had the bit between his teeth and took the stage win along with me and Pat Doran! The overall position with two asphalt special stages to go, looked like this:

1st   Pat Doran   1:20:17 hours
2nd   David Gillanders   1:20:22 hours
3rd   Ken Wood   1:20:28 hours

My tyre tracks tell only some of the story. I was well crossed up here and that merely shows just how hard we were trying on this, the final event of the season. Photograph: Martin Hirst.

In the Group 'A' category, I had heard that Trevor Smith was two seconds ahead of Russell Brookes and so it was all to play for with only the two Telford Town special stages to go when Malcolm Wilson said to me:

'Well, are you glad you walked the last stage?'

'I can't remember it.....'

'Well, you do this stage twice and this is it. This is it! The whole championship comes down to this, the very last two stages!'

Dave Bignald of Gartrac was in the Service Park and he asked, in quick succession:

'What are we going to do? What are we going to do?'

'What do you mean?'

'What do we do? What do we do?

'What's wrong with you?'

He was having a bit of a 'turn'. He had completely 'lost it' and his equilibrium had totally disappeared.

'Bignald, you need to sit down.'

'What do you mean? What do you mean?'

'You need to sit down, Dave. Get some fresh air, and take some deep breaths. You've lost it.'

'What do we do? What do we do?'

It took a while for the team boss to settle down.

I did have the opportunity to change to tarmac tyres, but I thought that I'd just leave on the forest tyres, the round and black and knobbly things, because I had been driving with them all day long. Some of the other drivers, Pat Doran included, had changed to racing tyres, the smooth, almost bald slicks used for asphalt surfaces, but I thought that if I suddenly changed onto a different set of tyres at this point it would perhaps give me a false sense of security on specific corners.

Because the two final stages were to be on tarmac, I believed that the other drivers (me included) would cut through the corners and drag mud onto the road on the first run through, so I thought to myself, *'No, I'll stick with my forest tyres.'*

SS11, Town Park 1, was a mere 1.3 miles long, and I cleared the course in 1:44 minutes. Bill Barton was two seconds behind, but interestingly, Pat Doran was down in equal 7th place with Roger Clark.

The penultimate stage of the 1987 Audi Sport Rally, Town Park 1, in Telford, where my tyre choice was duly vindicated. Photograph: Paul Fairbanks.

I had managed to take seven seconds off Doran to lead the rally by two seconds with only the final stage of the event, in fact the final stage of the entire championship to go, and it was a rerun of this stage. I guess my tyre choice was the right one! I was also correct in my considerations that all of the drivers would cut the corners, as indeed they had. They had dragged a fair amount of mud onto the tarmac.

The atmosphere was absolutely electric; I could feel the current emanating from thousands of spectators lining the course in readiness for the conclusion of the event, and of the championship, and so we headed towards the start of SS12, Town Park 2.

I was, by now, in the Champion-elect position, when Ken said to me:

'David, I can't see the maps!'

'What do you mean?'

He panicked.

'I can't focus!'

The pressure had got to him. He, like Bignald earlier, had also 'lost it'.

'Look, it's alright. I know where we're going, and we are just going to do it again.'

And we did! I won the stage with a time of 1:43 minutes. I'd actually reduced my earlier timed run by a second and crucially, Doran was two seconds behind me. I finished the stage, and sat there, on the finish line, trying to catch my breath, and of course, I asked:

'Who's won it? Have we won?'

We both looked around searching for the times of the other drivers and then I looked down the road. I could see Malcolm Wilson in his Vauxhall Astra GTE. I saw him literally jump out of his car and he jumped up in the air, and he was excitedly going:

'Y-E-S!'

I thought that this meant that his team mate, Russell Brookes had just won, and I must admit, I thought some pretty unthinkable thoughts…. before I said to Ken:

'I think we've lost.'

'What do you mean?'

'Look at Wilson over there. He's ecstatic. That means that Brookes has won.'

Brookes and Smith actually tied for the win in Group 'A' and, as they had identical times, the tie-breaker went to the driver who was fastest on the opening stage, and that was Smith. I had to win the event to win the title and with that information I started to feel a bit dejected.

But no! Brookes hadn't won. My old pal had been jumping for joy for *ME!* Malcolm *knew* I had won and he came running up to the car, opened my door and said:

'We've won'

'What do you mean, we've won?'

'You've won,' he said, ***'You've won!'***

My winning margin on the Audi Sport Rally was a mere four seconds from Pat Doran. Ken Wood was 3rd, and Timo Salonen was 4th (but of course his score did not count in the Marlboro/Autosport Championship). In 5th place was Bill Barton in his Metro 6R4, and 3:40 minutes behind me, in 6th position, was a hero of mine, a true legend of special stage rallying, the great Roger Albert Clark on one of his last competitive outings.

Not only had Ken and I won the Audi Sport Rally, we had just won the British National Championship – by a single point (which equated to those four seconds....) but all this was subject to road penalties!

It didn't get much better than this. Yes, I had won it with Ken Rees, but it was all thanks to his co-driving skills, Malcolm Wilson's enthusiasm and encouragement, and especially to Gartrac and the Dave Bignald and his team, and of course, the MG Metro 6R4. Although it wasn't the most reliable car of its day it nevertheless got me through the series and I'll be forever indebted to it. It *was* a very special car, but winning the National Series was a very, very, very close call, and I'll allow Ken to explain exactly why:

'When we got to the end of the stage the Finish Marshal gave me a slip of paper which I honestly did not read. I just put it in my door pocket. I had relaxed and that was almost our downfall. We had held back and waited to see what Pat

Doran's time was on that last stage and this had taken up a fair bit of our time allowed (before penalty).

'Eventually, to make sure we could get to the final control in time, we left in a hurry. After about four miles though, we encountered some major roadworks that blocked the road. I had been following the roadbook and hadn't a clue as to our actual whereabouts, and we still had about four or five miles to go, with limited time to 'clock-in' or face road penalties of ten seconds for every minute late.

'I suddenly realised that the paper I had been given was a route diversion note, so I just said to David.

'I don't know where to go!'

'We could see the hotel in the distance as there was a big Audi balloon high in the sky above it, so I just said to David:

'Head for that balloon. We have to get there!'

'We went over kerbs; we went up one-way streets the wrong direction; we did everything to get there on time. Then we picked up another rally car and followed him in. We arrived right on our due minute; the clock had just entered 58 minutes when I saw the finish ramp ahead but I couldn't see the control, and that was the crucial bit. I asked the marshal who told me:

"Oh that's in the hotel, down the hallway."

'I got out of the car and ran as fast as I could and managed to put my timecard onto the timekeeper's desk with only ten seconds to spare! If I had been 11 seconds later we would have been penalised ten seconds of road penalties, and that would have displaced us from 1st place in the overall classification and we'd have lost the title!'

I'd won three events outright and MG Metros won six of the seven events. Only the quickly driven Opel Manta 400 of Bertie Fisher stopped the whitewash.

Over the season, the individual event winners were:

Citroën Winter Rally	Malcolm Wilson/ Nigel Harris	Metro 6R4
Skip Brown Rally	Malcolm Wilson/ Nigel Harris	Metro 6R4
Granite City Rally	David Gillanders/ Ken Rees	Metro 6R4

Manx Rally	Bertie Fisher/ Austin Frazer	Manta 400
Kayel Graphics Rally	David Gillanders/ Ken Rees	Metro 6R4
Cumbria Rally	Steve Whiteford/ Dave Adams	Metro 6R4
Quip Forest Rally	Ken Wood/ Peter Brown	Metro 6R4
Audi Sport Rally	David Gillanders/ Ken Rees	Metro 6R4

Happiness was....

...winning the Marlboro/Autosport British National Rally Championship in 1987.

Teetotal

In November, Gladys and I arrived at a very plush hotel somewhere in London in time for the annual Dinner and Awards Presentation of the 1987 Marlboro/Autosport British National Rally Championship. John Horton, the renowned Motor Sport Management Consultant, was the Master of Ceremonies, but anything other than that I just can't remember. I cannot even recall in which hotel the function was held

156

because it was that kind of night, a night that I am not at all proud of.

This photograph was taken of Ken Rees and myself on the Dyfnant stage of the Audi Sport Rally in 1987.
Photograph: Martin Hirst.

I had had a whole year of winning rallies or being very highly placed; I'd won three of the events outright, including the Granite City Rally, and had podium places on most of the other rallies that year. I failed to finish once, or perhaps twice, simply because of mechanical problems, but when the car didn't break down I would generally be in the top six, but mostly in the top three.

I'd made many a presentation before where I stood up and delivered a speech; I thanked everybody from the marshals to the organisers, plus the sponsors and my team and co-driver, and I'd been word perfect each and every time. Everybody seemed to realise that I was quite good in front of a micro-phone, in front of a camera, and good to talk with sponsors. I thanked all the right people at the right time – until, that is, my notorious night at the Marlboro/Autosport Awards Pres-entation….

Unfortunately for me, the organisers conducted the presentation 'back to front' which meant that the awards cere-mony was *after* the meal and liquid refreshments. I think they commenced the presentation around 11pm, but by then, I had drunk almost a half bottle of fine Chivas Regal Whisky. I was absolutely drunk, and to use a North East of Scotland expression, *'I was guttered!'* In fact, I hadn't a bloody clue where I was. I was that bad. The presentation went on and on and on, and suddenly I heard the following words, and they should have been some of the nicest words I could ever have wished to hear:

'The Marlboro/Autosport British National Rally Champions for 1987 are... David Gillanders and Ken Rees!'

Much applause followed as I got up and staggered to the stage to merrily sway beside John Horton (not that John was swaying). Gladys watched all of the drunken speech in disgust, then left the ballroom. I was sick all night in the bathroom, and I must say, I think we almost had a divorce because of my state of inebriation. She was very disappointed in me as I was so out of control.

Seemingly, I got up onto the stage and proved what a Scotsman wore under his kilt. I don't remember this, but I do remember taking a bucket of champagne ice which I subsequently tipped over Horton's head, and I also tied the microphones in a knot. I had been jumping up and down on the stage so much that I fell through the floor and I also chased a waitress round the tables. Ken Rees couldn't hold me back and I even slurred out a really bad joke which I refuse to repeat here.

What I said about my team, my sponsors, the series, the event sponsors, the championship sponsors, I haven't got a clue, but I do have a vague recollection of Ken physically pulling me off the stage and getting me up to my room (well, the *door* of my room to be precise) and I have to thank him for that.

I woke up next morning and at breakfast everybody in the room was chatting happily away to each other, but when I appeared there became a deathly hush – there was a very embarrassing silence and they all looked at me. I asked myself, *'Why is nobody speaking?'*

I'd made such an ass of myself. I spent the next two or three days apologising to everybody, to the people at Austin

Rover, to the people at Dunlop, to the people at Marlboro, to the people at Autosport, to the people at Mintex (the brake people), and to John Horton, and to all of my sponsors, and especially to Ken Rees and my wife, Gladys. Did they forgive me, well, yes, they did, because I bent over backwards, unreservedly, and I said to each and every one of them:

'Guys, I'm an ass, a total ass. Please, do not take this as being the normal David Gillanders.'

I had drunk so much whisky that the smell of it today makes me gag. If someone were to pour a nip and place it in front of me right now, well the smell of it would take me straight back to that night in 1987. I almost killed myself drinking so much of *'the cratur'* in those days.

Gladys and I flew home (she didn't divorce me) but the flight was a nightmare; I felt very ill then, and for many days afterwards, so much so that I made a vow that I'd never touch a drop of the stuff again. In fact, I have been teetotal ever since, and I need to put on record that I honestly, sincerely, profusely, and unreservedly, apologise to everyone who was at that awards ceremony. I brought shame on myself, my wife, my co-driver, my team, my sponsors, my sport and also my country.

I was saddened to learn that John Horton had suffered a heart attack on February 22, 2016 and had passed away four days later.

Wings and things: 'C670 JSU' flat out on the 1987 Kingdom Stages Rally.

Photograph: Jack Davidson.

Roger Clark had been persuaded to come out of retirement for the 1987 British National Rally Championship – the same series he had previously dominated in the early 1970s – and I considered it to be a privilege to compete directly against him, with equal machinery. I was, by this time, pretty competent and a 'known force' in national rallying, but Roger, well, he was truly world-famous, and in my eyes, (and many others, I would suggest) a true legend of the sport and one who had been honoured by the establishment with an MBE in 1979.

A flashback as to how I remember Roger Clark in his Ford Escort. He's seen here in Inschriach Forest on the Scottish Rally with Jim Porter in 1970. Photograph: Jack Davidson.

Prior to 1987, I had always looked over my shoulder to see who had been snapping at my heels, but from that point onward, Ken Rees and I found that we had actually stopped looking behind; we only looked to see who was in front of us, if indeed there was anybody, because both of us had become supremely confident in our abilities, and we went into each rally with the belief that we could, and should, win each and every event. We felt that we could challenge for the top position every time and that came over in the way we handled ourselves.

I believe it was Dave Bignald who actually changed my attitude about various things; before we joined forces, rallying was purely a hobby for me, but by 1987, I had become a lot more professional in my outlook.

Dave said to me:

'You can win this championship.'

He even said that I had been the best driver that Gartrac had ever had; I wasn't the quickest, but the best. There is a real difference. It's easy to get quick drivers, who might be brilliant, but often go off the road, and to use the old adage, *"to finish first, one must first finish"*.

I had the attitude that where I could drive at a crazy speed, I could, and sometimes did, especially if I really felt good about myself, and in a rhythm. However, I always drove within my limits. I tended to drive at 'nine-tenths' rather than over the limit at 'eleven-tenths'. At 'nine-tenths' I was in total control of everything and if something along the lines of a safety note proved to be incorrect, or even if an instruction from Ken was wrong, I still felt that I would be able to drive well within my capabilities. I became quite good at it.

Anyway, at the start of the first event in the 1987 series, Ken said to me:

'Hey, Roger Clark has entered.'

*'Roger Clark? **The** Roger Clark? What's he driving?'*

'A Metro 6R4'

'G'way...'

Roger Clark, as you may have gathered, was one of my heroes. I remember him in Ford Escorts, usually driving *"Sideways to Victory"*, just like the title of his excellent auto-biography that was edited by Graham Robson. Roger visited the Granite City Rally many times and indeed won it from 1971 to 1975 (he might have won it for a fifth time in 1974 had the rally not been postponed because of the national fuel crisis). He was untouchable, first in the Ford Escort RS1600 Mk I car, then latterly in the Ford Escort RS1800 Mk II version. In his day he could beat all the Finns, and won the RAC Rally twice. Now he has another 'RAC' event named after him: The Roger Albert Clark Rally! Sadly, this Legend of the sport died, aged only 58, on January 12, 1998.

He was what I always wanted to be, although I never looked upon myself as this 'Champion' guy. I have just been lucky, very lucky in fact. On this particular event I was either car '1' or car '2', and after about five or six stages I arrived at a service area to get the car re-fettled and to allow Ken the opportunity to ascertain the times of the opposition.

Me? I would happily ponce around, have a chat with the spectators, or Dave Bignald. I used to bring the car in when all it really needed was a wash. Maybe that's why Gartrac thought I was the best driver they'd ever had… If I happened to bash something it was really very rare. The mechanics loved me. All they had to do was wash the car, tighten it back up, put it back together again, check the levels, put on a set of tyres, and send me on my way again. Some guys would come in with the back wheel hanging off, the front wheel sporting an unusual camber angle, or have a windscreen missing, a crinkled roof, and panels that certainly didn't leave the show-room in its original condition, but that wasn't me. I brought the car home spotless, figuratively speaking, most of the time.

I had started to relax a bit with a cup of tea and a sand-wich, when Ken returned with some news:

'We're leading by 28 seconds.'

It might not have been 28 seconds, as I really cannot remember the actual details, but once I had been given that sort of information after four or five stages, to me, that was the rally over, because with a gap of almost half a minute, barring a puncture, and/or mechanical disaster, I could drive at that speed all day, and the rest of the field would have had to catch up. I didn't have the need to go any faster; and I certainly wasn't going to go any slower, but with around 28 seconds in hand, I felt I was already at the metaphorical finish line. I don't think I was being big headed about it, I was 'there'. I had calculated that and I had a gap between me and my opposition, so I would have thought to myself, *'That's fine. I've only got another 60 miles to go. It's a done deal!'*

But then I had a thought, and asked Ken:

'By the way, how's Roger Clark getting on?'

'Oh, he's 15th or 16th.'

'That cannae be right.'

'Yes, look at his times; you took ten seconds off him on one stage, and then 20 seconds on the next.'

'There must be something wrong with his car.'

So, out of curiosity, I went towards Roger's 6R4 and by that time, I was quite well known in rallying circles, so people would stop and ask me how I was doing. When I found his car the mechanics were all working on it and Roger was at the rear, so I went round and asked him:

'Mr. Clark,'

(Well, I didn't know him at the time):

'How are you getting on?'

He looked at me, and it was obvious he hadn't a clue as to who I was until he looked down and checked the name on my overalls:

'Oh, I'm doing alright, thank you.'

'Have you any car problems?'

'No.'

'How are you enjoying the 6R4?'

'It's different to what I normally drive.'

Then we had some general chat:

'Are you running a 4:1 differential?'

I asked him that because Gartrac had provided me with a very special car, built specifically for acceleration. I had a unique differential in mine because Gartrac and I had been working on this car for quite some time and had honed it to its optimum performance. We knew just how to make the 6R4 work. I didn't go for a top speed such as 130 miles per hour. I only went for a maximum of 90 or so, but the gearing I had meant that instead of going from 0 to 100 mph in 12.8 seconds, I could get up to 90 in around ten. Given that rallies are all about getting round and out of the corners quickly, that option suited me best. Every exit, every corner, every rally, I was much, much quicker than the majority of the other drivers. When I asked Roger what differential he was running, he simply responded:

'I haven't got a clue.'

'Well, you do need a better differential.'

Concentration; Determination; Application.

Photograph: William Brown.

Roger really didn't have a clue as to what was on his car, so I nipped round and spoke with one of his engineers, and this guy did happen know my name.

The engineer really liked me talking to him because he wanted to ask me all about my car. I gave him a download, as they say, and he was amazed that I was so open about it, but I'd nothing to hide. I said that he should really speak to Dave Bignald at Gartrac as he would willingly help. The great Roger Albert Clark made his decision to retire not long after his Metro outings, although we did compete against each other one more time.

The results of the 1987 Championship were:

1st	David Gillanders	140 points
2nd	Trevor Smith	139
3rd	Russell Brookes	134
4th	Graham Middleton	124
5th	Roger Clark	117
6th	Bill Barton	108
7th	Colin McRae	106
8th	Ewan Brewis	105
9th=	Ken Wood	101
	Frank Meagher	101

Happy Days....
Winning the 1987 Marlboro/Autosport National Rally
Championship, and trophy:

Chapter ELEVEN

PROTEST IN THE TROSSACHS

Although I had won the British National Rally Series in 1987, I also came very, very close to winning the Scottish Rally Championship too. I only lost out on my home series after Murray Grierson submitted a protest on the Trossachs Rally, the final event, and the stewards upheld his complaint (and rightly so, I have to say).

On special stage events these days there is a ban on the servicing of rally cars outwith specifically designated locations. In the early days though, it was a free-for-all in the nearest lay-by, or on the nearest suitable verge, or in the nearest garage, or the nearest car park, but on that particular Trossachs Rally, Dave Bignald suggested that our team ought to hide a service crew somewhere, just in case I happened to encounter any problems.

I cannot remember the particular stage, as one forest had begun to look like every other one, but I did have a problem on the first test: I managed to knock off a front corner of the 6R4 against a tree and was then driving a three-wheeler, but unlike my father with his 3-wheel Morgan, I doubt if it would have taken me all the way to Harley Street. This effectively put me out of the event, but when we got to the end of the stage I turned right. The marshal asked me:

'Where are you going?'

'I'm just going to drive along the road, I'm out.'

However, I knew full well that about a mile up the road, on the left hand side, there was a house with a big garage, and in that garage were a friendly bunch of people… I managed to get there and Gartrac duly repaired the car and thereafter I drove to the finish with the aim of being in the top five to win the championship.

Three wheels on my wagon. As can be seen from the image above, there was a fair amount of damage sustained on the first special stage.

I had already come from last position (on stage 1) to 7th place overall, and had passed a lot of cars on each of the stages. Stage after stage after stage, we were light years quicker than anybody else on the rally and this was proven when I actually passed five cars on one stage alone!

I got to the finish without further mishap and found out that I had actually done just enough to become the Scottish Champion, but the Clerk of the Course, a nice chap although I forget his name, approached me and said:

'David, there is a problem because Murray Grierson has protested. He has accused you of receiving illegal service on the event. Did you?'

The Clerk of the Course then added:

'We can take this to the RAC Tribunal if you wish. I believe they (the protestors) can't prove it, but look at me straight in the eye and tell me that you did not illegally service your car. If you do say that, I think you will be the Scottish Champion, because nobody can actually prove the accusation.'

I had not been the Scottish Rally Champion before and the temptation was absolutely huge, but just then the Clerk of the Course asked again:

'So what are you going to do, David?'

'I serviced illegally.'

Well, what else was I going to do? I couldn't take the title on a lie. I couldn't live with that, but anyway, my drive – and it *was* one of the best drives of my career – showed that I *was* the best. But would I have objected and protested if the boot had been on the other foot? Probably, yes. I would have done exactly the same thing as Grierson.

Ken Rees added:

'I think David and I had a very successful partnership and, like he said, we almost won the Scottish Championship that very same year as well, but rather foolishly, he put it off the road. He had seen Ken Wood off the road and possibly lost his concentration when all we really had to do was sail through to the finish, but we had to have the (illegal) servicing done and we cannot blame Murray for putting in his protest.

'Altogether, I enjoyed my visits to Scotland. We must have done a rally every other weekend in 1987.

'As a person, David is fantastic, but you can either like him or loathe him. He has some good friends in Scotland, but many people don't like him because he is outspoken. Some of the things he says are in a jocular manner, but others take what he says seriously and can be offended. I never had any problem with him although I did sometimes cringe when I heard him say some things to people. He could joke with other drivers, but he could also rub up people the wrong way. Murray and David were public enemies in the forests, but put them in the bar later and they would be the best of friends.

'We were on the top spot a few times and David was very funny with his speeches. He is well spoken, but you have to get to know him and understand his sense of humour. He says exactly what he means and he doesn't beat about the bush. This can upset some folk, but, as long as it's truthful that's fair. However, if I'd only met him the once, I'd have gone away thinking, 'Well, you're not a very likeable guy,'

'I spent a lot of one-to-one time with him and that was great; he knew he needed me and he knew I needed him. We never fell out and I was really impressed with him as a driver and the way he quickly got to grips with the Metro 6R4 and how he took on the established names of the sport. He was as quick, and often quicker, so if he'd taken it all a bit more seriously earlier on, I think he could well have been one of Britain's Best.'

Into Africa

Thankfully, there were no protests when I competed on my only overseas rally. That was in 1988, when I took a trip over the equator to compete on the Castrol International Rally in South Africa, thanks to the invitation and arrangements of none other than Tony Pond. He had previously competed on the event at least five times, and twice won it. He finished it twice in 2nd place and was very much involved in the event at the time. Because of my time in MG Metro 6R4s, (like him), and because I was the reigning British National Champion, Tony made the following suggestion to me:

'Why don't you come over and do the Castrol Rally in South Africa? You'll get paid!'

'Paid?'

I questioned again:

'Paid?'

Well, that really was music to this Aberdonian's ears and so I flew to Johannesburg and met all the guys from Team Toyota South Africa. They gave me 'LPW 656T', a Corolla (although that particular model was called a Starlet in the UK). They also gave me a large Afrikaner co-driver by the name of Leon Joubert.

It was a big event and really quite long. 'The Star' at the time was Sarel van der Merwe, but it was Serge Damseaux who actually won the rally in his Toyota Conquest. I started the contest and basically just plodded along, but lo and behold, found myself in the top ten, maybe even inside the top five at one point, and I thought to myself:

'This is pretty easy.'

The roads were very wide and straight, and in days of old, apparently, they used to stop mid-way through the stages and refuel. At the time I competed there, the indigenous people would simply set up camp on the roads overnight in this, the largest man-made forest in the world. It had something like 10,000,000 trees in it (although I didn't count them) and was located in the Gauteng Province, by Johannesburg. Of course, I had to find the road where some locals had bedded down for the night…

In the UK, we have 'Opening' and 'Closing' cars. One is used to open the stage and other to close it, because generally speaking the forests in Britain are on private land and mainly belong to the Forestry Commission.

With Leon Joubert in the Works Toyota Corolla on the South African Castrol International Rally in 1988. Photograph: Courtesy of Roger Swan and David Pearson (www.motoprint.co.za).

However, in South Africa, and because this rally was so big, the first competing car through was the *only* warning people would get of the event's arrival. That was damned dangerous, actually, and I, for some unknown reason, just happened to be first car into the forest …

I do remember that I had been flying through this particular section when Leon shouted out to me:

'Be careful up there. Be careful.'

So I slowed down.

'Why do you slow down?'

'Well, there are people in the road.'

Obviously, I slowed down, but I am not sure the other drivers did. Anyway, I finished the event and Team Toyota kindly gave me and Gladys a few days' holiday afterwards in one of the holiday camps there. It was fabulous, and I'd go back there given half a chance. I loved South Africa. I thought it was great, the people were nice, Toyota were superb, and I was with Gladys, and a team-mate Tony Pond, a legend, so it couldn't get much better than that.

Sadly, I learned that Tony had passed away on February 7, 2002. I remember, back in 1978, he had broken Ford's dominance of the Granite City Rally, by taking the then British Leyland Works Triumph TR7V8 to a debut win in 1978 with Northern Irish co-driver, Fred Gallagher.

Tony Pond had a roguish charm and a deadpan sense of humour but he passed away at the age of only 56. A sad loss to his family and to rallying.

Unfulfilled Potential

I don't think I reached my true potential in motor sport. I actually think there was a bit to go, but I packed it in at the end of 1995, and retired at the top of that particular tree. That was more or less the end of my motor sport career, but I actually wish I could go back to 1990 as I felt then (and still do) that there is so much more still to achieve. I never really stressed myself out whilst driving, and very rarely did I come to the end of a stage and think to myself:

'Christ! We were lucky in there!'

A lot of guys would come out and say:

'Wow, we'd a huge 'moment' in there!'

I never had any of that.

Colin McRae, now, well, put it this way – if I had been in third gear, he would have been in fifth! He would have been on the limit all the time, but I never got to that level. Thinking back, though, I could have gone quite a bit faster had I had the benefit of Nicky Grist co-driving for me earlier in my career. I would have also learned more about the cars I was driving from a technical point of view; I should have tried to understand them because I think I would have been able to drive them better. Basically, I should not have been so bull-headed about things.

Colin McRae made a statement once, and it was one that I could easily relate to. It was about the testing of cars – he didn't do a lot of it. He would simply drive faster on the day, but allegedly, Carlos Sainz, the Spanish double World Rally Champion, would test all the time, on all surfaces and in all weathers, and have a reference book on the car. Let's say on the second day of an event, it started to rain, and rain really hard, Sainz would have a 'setting for rain' so he'd get the mechanics to change the car to these settings, including the suspension, castor angles, camber and the tyres, from hard to soft, dry to wet, and so on. But if it suddenly became bone dry he'd revert to his 'bone dry' settings.

Colin would simply adapt his natural driving skill to reflect the conditions prevailing at the time. In other words, he would keep the car much as it was, but simply drive faster, or slower, as conditions dictated.

I'm not saying I was like Colin McRae. I'd never, ever dare to say I was like him, but I would do the same sort of thing. I wouldn't change the car, I'd change me! However, I really wish I had learned more about the technicalities of the car when I was younger.

However, I began to learn and understand a lot more about the workings of a car from the tyres and wheels up through my close association with M-Sport *(see Chapter 25)*. I also believe that if the World Rally Championship were to be deemed as 'level 1', and the European Championship considered as 'level 2', I think, therefore, that I would have thought myself to be at 'level 3', albeit at the top of 'level 3'.

The RAC Rally in 1986 was part of the World Rally Championship and that, I think, just serves to prove my point. I could have gone faster – I was up to 8th in that event before the engine blew. Was my performance a fluke? Probably, but, if I could compete on the RAC Rally, arguably one of the toughest rallies in the world (back then anyway), without pacenotes, *and* manage to get as high as 8th, then I might well have had the potential to finish in the top ten of a World Championship event.

I think I had the potential, but would I, or could I have maintained that level of performance? I don't know. In fact, nobody will ever know.

I was happy in the MG Metro 6R4, and I could drive it to nine tenths of its maximum performance. There was no need to go ten tenths because then I'd have crashed. I could drive it all day at nine tenths and never get stressed out, so with a bit of luck I might just have scraped into the aforementioned 'level 1'.

There can be no real comparison between the rally cars from the 70s, 80s and the 90s, compared to today's World Rally Cars, cars such as those prepared and run by Malcolm Wilson's M-Sport at Dovenby Hall near Cockermouth, in Cumbria. They cannot really be compared, other than they had four wheels then, and four wheels now, but nowadays the drive is through all four wheels. For example, I could go out today and buy a standard Subaru from my local Subaru dealer, an S3 from an Audi dealer, or a Volkswagen GTi from a VW dealer, put a sump guard on it, and any of those would make mincemeat of most of the cars I drove in the last century. Any of these current cars would beat the socks off my rally pre-pared Escorts, and Volvos.

It's like saying my Mini Cooper S was quick, but if I look at the modern rally car, and I've been very fortunate to drive both the old and the new, especially the M-Sport Ford Fiesta, there is absolutely no comparison. I found the Fiesta to be a stunningly quick car. From only 1,600cc it produces 300 brake horsepower and around 490 pound/feet of torque. That's incredible. The engine lasts forever, insomuch that I could take one and compete in the both Scottish and British Championships and never even have to service it!

The engine, transmission, suspension and brakes can pretty much last a whole year nowadays with somebody like me driving, but a World Rally driver, well, he would be considerably harder on the car than I ever was. As I said, there's no real comparison with the cars of then and now, especially if judging their performance, and of course, the cost. A Group 4 Ford Escort in my day cost around £20,000 and a Group 'B' MG Metro 6R4 about £55,000, but a WRC Ford Fiesta nowadays would set you back by something like £350,000, depending upon the specification.

I would say that my international career was fairly limited insofar that I only ever competed on one foreign event, the aforementioned Castrol International Rally in South Africa, but I often competed on the home internationals, such as the RAC, the Welsh, the Burmah (which was run in Scotland), and Scottish rallies.

Rhythm and Blues

In 1988, Colin McRae just pipped me for the Scottish Rally Championship, driving not one car, but four: over the season he had his Vauxhall Nova, a Nissan 240RS, a rear wheel drive Peugeot 205, and also a Ford Sierra RS Cosworth. On that year's Trossachs Rally, the final event in the series, I made one little mistake and got out of the rhythm and suffered the blues. It was a really annoying error and I crashed. Once again, it was on the first stage. I had a Ford Sierra 4x4 whereas Colin was in a two wheel drive Ford Sierra Cosworth, and we were in conditions that were more suited to a four wheel drive car.

We spoke at the start, and I said to him:

'Colin, you've no chance. It's very icy and slippery.'

Three quarters through the first stage we reached an open left corner – I can see it now – where there was a big ditch on the left, but rather than simply keep on the road, I decided to ditch-hook and drop a front wheel into the ditch to effectively hold the car back from launching itself off the road on the right hand side. The trouble was there was a tree stump in the ditch, and of course I hit it.

Bob Wilson and I started at number '1' on the 1988 Autofit Stages, and finished number '1', though the 6R4 looked a bit secondhand by the end of this stage.

Trying hard on the Trossachs Rally, perhaps too hard.... Photograph: Jack Davidson.

The impact pulled the bottom suspension arm out and forced my retirement from the event and this handed the title to Colin who was, nevertheless, a worthy winner. It also gave me a seven year itch for the title which I would continue to scratch until 1995. I have since asked myself this question a thousand times:

'Why didn't I stay on the road?'

I had traded times with Colin throughout that year, and it was very generous of him to say in his book, *"The Real McRae"*, that *"Gillanders was an experienced guy with a good track record"*. But could I, would I, dare I, compare myself with *"The Real McRae?"* Not a chance. Colin and I had one thing in common, and that was the fact that we were both rally drivers, and both Scottish.

On the hot and dusty Scottish Rally in 1986.
Photograph: Sandy Topp.

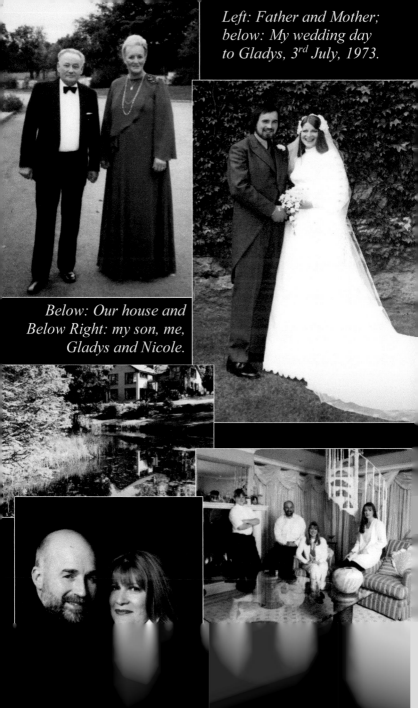

Left: Father and Mother; below: My wedding day to Gladys, 3rd July, 1973.

Below: Our house and Below Right: my son, me, Gladys and Nicole.

Studio Images of Nicole,
Amelie and Finlay by
Simon Club Photography
(www.simonclubb.com).

Fishing with Nicole and David.
Right: David Jnr.

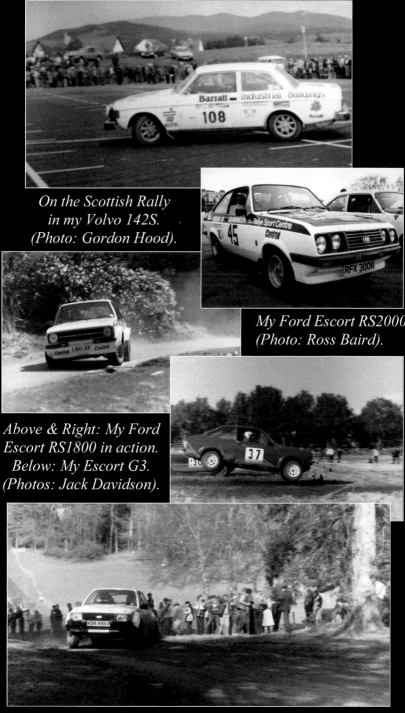

On the Scottish Rally in my Volvo 142S. (Photo: Gordon Hood).

My Ford Escort RS2000 (Photo: Ross Baird).

Above & Right: My Ford Escort RS1800 in action. Below: My Escort G3. (Photos: Jack Davidson).

On the Blair Castle Stage.

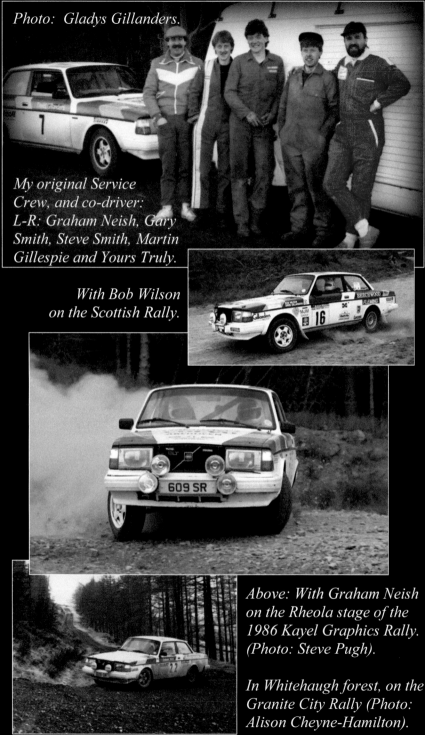

Photo: Gladys Gillanders.

My original Service Crew, and co-driver: L-R: Graham Neish, Gary Smith, Steve Smith, Martin Gillespie and Yours Truly.

With Bob Wilson on the Scottish Rally.

Above: With Graham Neish on the Rheola stage of the 1986 Kayel Graphics Rally. (Photo: Steve Pugh).

In Whitehaugh forest, on the Granite City Rally (Photo: Alison Cheyne-Hamilton).

Flying high in the F-15.

Over Skibo Castle. (Photographs: Courtesy of the USAF).

Above: Centre Spread from "Autosport".

Left: On the Snowman Rally. (Photograph: Ken McEwen).

On the Citroën Winter Rally. (Photo: Courtesy of Scott Brownlee).

29 OCTOBER 1987 95p

AUTOSPORT

DOWN TO THE WIRE!

IN COLOUR: AUDI SPORT RALLY ◆ FORD'S WELLINGTON
A GP PREVIEW ◆ FORD FESTIVAL GUIDE

In the pink!
Photograph:
ys Gillanders.

icing the front
covers of three
motor sport
magazines.

MARCH 1988   ISSUE No. 19   PRICE £1

Wheelbase

Lancia Delta HF integrale
Cartel Rally Report
Snowman Rally Report

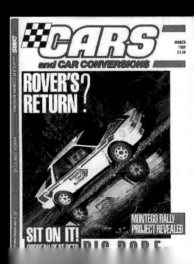

MARCH 1989 £1.40

CARS
and CAR CONVERSIONS

ROVER'S RETURN?

MONTEGO RALLY
PROJECT REVEALED

SIT ON IT!

*My hired Subaru RXT
on the 1987 Scottish
Rally with Ken Rees.
(Photo: Jim Sutherland).*

*Leaning nonchalantly on
one of the Land Rover
Experience vehicles,
Simon Cobb and me.
(Photograph:
Gladys Gillanders).*

*Above: My Ford Sierra
RS Cosworth on the
Snowman Rally
with Bob Wilson.
(Photo: Ken McEwen).*

*Above: My 'Pop, Bang,
Whiz' Ford Escort RS
Cosworth with Stewart
Merry on the Granite
City Rally, 1996.*

*At M-Sport with
Graham Neish and Ross Baird.*

Colin McRae's natural ability and aggression and speed behind the wheel put him in a different league altogether. He was in a different class.

In fact, he was World Class.

There were certain events I'd compete on and within the first three or four corners I'd think to myself, *'This is easy.'* The gear changes had been perfect; I had attacked the corners at perhaps ten miles per hour quicker than I would have normally have done, and everything had flowed perfectly. I could do that if my head was in the 'right' place, and if my feet and arms were in the 'right' places. If the sound, and the smell of the car, in fact, everything, was feeling 'right', and if I wasn't making any mistakes, then that's what I would call rhythm. Colin mentioned this in his book too. Once into that rhythm I became unbeatable. I can think of perhaps a dozen events that I distinctly remember where, yes, there was the rhythm, but definitely no blues.

I had that rhythm (and blues) on the RAC Rally in 1986 though. The rhythm lay in the fact that I got the car up to 8th place overall, but the blues came when the effing engine effectively effed itself! I cannot think of any other sport with such highs and such lows, although there are bound to be many other activities where such a wide range of emotions are shared.

Kicking up the dust on the 1988 Jim Clark Memorial Rally.
Photograph: Eddie Kelly Motorsport Photography.

There was no need to go ditch-hooking on that Trossachs Rally. Under normal circumstances it might have made the corner slightly quicker, but only by a miniscule amount. To this day I still don't know why I did that. If I had actually stayed on the road I would have won the championship. I lost the title on the Trossachs Rally in 1987 and it was déjà vu on the Trossachs Rally in 1988. I'll definitely steer clear of the Trossachs in the future. That was a real disappointment to me.

As I mentioned much earlier in this book of mine, I often participated in the speed hill climbs at Fintray, near Aberdeen. I used it mainly as a 'fun' day out, in between rallies, but in 1988 it was also one of the last times I'd have an MG Metro 6R4 on tarmac, so what better event that the National meeting on June 26.

Magnificent Metro

My record-breaking run, June 26, 1988.
Photograph: Jack Davidson.

My final ascent at the Grampian Automobile Club's hill climb venue brought another class record. I made the tricky ascent in 29.72 seconds in the ex-Works Lombard RAC Rally Metro 6R4, 'C99 KOG' that Malcolm Wilson used in 1986.

As can be seen from the photograph overleaf, I had knocked the entire front end of the car off at Combine Corner by clattering into the bushes on an earlier run, so my record-breaking run was done with a denuded car. I remember that incident. The car just got away from me when I was about halfway round the bend; it started to understeer itself into the undergrowth, but I thought I'd just power it through the shrubs because I had it shod with off-road tyres. If truth be told, I really couldn't be bothered to change to racing tyres... I kept the power on and thought to myself:

'Ach well, sod it,'

(or words to that effect):

'I'll come out of the bush eventually.'

But I didn't: I ran straight into a bloody big bush of rhododendrons. It was pretty much a case of 'hot brain, cold tyres syndrome' and a stupid mistake to make.

'Oh, bother!' (Eddie Kelly Motorsport Photography). I took this (earlier) photo of Gladys with the 6R4.

Chapter TWELVE

___

FROM THE SUBLIME TO THE RIDICULOUS

In the late 1980s I definitely felt that I was going up a level, what with winning the British National Rally title and then experiencing the skills of some top notch co-drivers. But not only that, I also had another incredible incident when, fresh from enjoying the 410 brake horsepower and incredibly 'light' power-to-weight ratio of my MG Metro 6R4, of just over one ton on the weighbridge, I savoured the 695 horse-power and incredibly 'heavy' power-to-weight ratio of a British Army Chieftain tank weighing in at 55 tons.

Although I thoroughly enjoyed the massive power of the Chieftain, I also had to endure the lack of power of the MG Montego before I managed to score an incredible result on what was a very controversial Tour of Britain.

The Chieftain

Early in 1988, I was invited by the top brass of the British Army to visit the Bagshot Testing Grounds with the specific aim of demonstrating my MG Metro 6R4 to the troops, and to give them a blast in the car, if you'll pardon the pun.

The Bagshot Testing Grounds in Surrey covered an area of land near the M3 motorway and was owned by the Ministry of Defence. It was previously known as the Military Vehicle Experimental Establishment but has since been renamed as the Royal Armament Research and Development Establish-ment, or R.A.R.D.E. The tracks covered an area of around five square miles where all sorts of military vehicles had been tested and developed, and where the army also carried out their rifle and high explosive missile target practice. The army also used the dense heath and sandy tracks at high speed, but not as high a speed as Ford, who also used to use the location to test their rally cars.

Like many a good James Bond film, I was taken in by helicopter and escorted by two Lynx helicopters, but at least I wasn't 'arrested' on this particular escapade... But on the way in I also happened to notice some tanks trundling about in the background....

I took the 6R4 out and gave some of the guys a run in the car. It was good fun, but after a while we stopped for lunch, and, well, you'll know me by now, I thought to myself:

'Nothing ventured, nothing gained.'

I asked a question:

'Any chance of getting a shot in one of these tanks?'

'No problem, Sir.'

I think it was a Chieftain Tank that I had my eyes on. The latest model had been built with a jet engine because the old one had a bus motor, which, when started, created so much smoke that it would have alerted the enemy, and that certainly wouldn't be very clever in times of conflict.

Anyway, I got to drive the tank and had some good fun with it: I went through water, I went through bushes, and I was told that if I wanted to, I could fell a tree! But, I found it a little bit scary at 40 miles per hour given that I was hurtling a machine that weighed so much. The real fun, though, came when I got to the firing range and for that I had to move into the gunner's seat, but to do that I had to lie on my back to look through a periscope.

That's where I saw a television screen with built-in crosshairs, and in the distance, a white transit van. I 'locked' the crosshairs onto it, but before I could fire the very clever machine asked if I wanted high explosive or armoured piercing shells. The choice was for 'soft' or 'hard' targets. For a target such as 'White Van Man', I just had to have the high explosive kind, and so, choice made, there followed a few mechanical clattering sounds as the selected shell was taken from the magazine and inserted into the breach.

Before long the whole process was locked and loaded with a high explosive shell. I then pulled the trigger and, *'BANG!'* That was the end of 'White Van Man' some two to three miles away, but there wasn't any real skill it. I simply put the crosshairs on it and pressed a button, but it would be a fabulous tool going down the motorway aiming at all the white vans for all that…

"I'm warning you, pal, one squeak and I'll put this thing into first gear!"   *Photo: Courtesy of the British Army.*

I wouldn't like to be a tank driver because I found it very claustrophobic, especially with all the armour around me. But just think about it if, for example, there were Apache Helicopters on the attack because they would undoubtedly have armour-piercing shells, and they would wipe out the tank occupants very quickly, as happened in the first Gulf War against Saddam Hussein. These were the main battle tanks of the day and they were all wiped out. In days of old, maybe it was *the* thing, but it seems to me that the helicopter has now overtaken the tank as a weapon of choice.

There was one point on the course we were driving along when the Commander suddenly instructed me:

'STOP! You have driven into a minefield.'

'What? How do you know?'

'We have some imaginary minefields, Sir, but don't panic. The 'enemy' only has detonators, so all you have to do is reverse back the way we came.'

When I started to reverse I must have turned the controls a wee bit because there was an almighty *'BANG, BANG!'* and two explosives went off. The Commander, in rather a laconic manner, said:

'Oh well, that's the tank dead!'

The modern tank has a steering wheel and is easier to drive, whereas the old version was more like a bulldozer with levers.

The Chieftain FV4201 was the battle tank that the British Army used in the 1960s, 1970s and the 1980s. It was a development of the Centurion tank and for it's time it was thought to be the most formidable main battle tank in the world. It had a crew of four, and was just over 35 feet in length (including the gun). The engine used was a Leyland L60 diesel with multi-fuel compression ignition, and it could reach a road speed of 48 miles per hour, or 19 when in cross-country mode and had a 120 millimetre rifled tank gun which could fire off ten rounds per minute for the first 60 seconds and then six thereafter. It also had Browning machine guns.

I could metaphorically blow off 'White Van Man' in the Metro 6R4, but with the Chieftain I could physically do it!

From the sublime to the ridiculous

It was definitely a feeling of going from the sublime to the ridiculous when I moved on from the MG Metro to the MG Montego. Honestly, one car was fantastic, but the other was fatally flawed. Part of the problem (as well as the benefit) was the fact that I was sponsored by British Car Rental, and the man in charge there was a fellow called Paul Batchelor. He said to me late in 1987:

'David, we need to have a new car for next year and I think you should drive a Montego.'

The reasoning for this was that the MG Montego was the biggest earning rental car they had, so I agreed:

'Yeah, ok.'

I have to admit I was pretty subdued in my response, but nevertheless I asked Gartrac to build the Montego with 6R4 suspension underneath, both front and rear. It was front wheel drive – and it *was* fantastic – or *would* have been had it not been for the engine. I had to run what was called a 'K' Series engine, a standard power unit intended for the Rover 2000 model in 1988. I had also suggested they slot in a 6R4 engine under the bonnet and couple it up to a four wheel drive system, or install a Ford 2-litre BDA engine under the bonnet and drive it through an axle at the back, but all of those suggestions were poo-poo'd because Paul said:

'That wouldn't be in the spirit of the game. It has to be front wheel drive, but don't worry, it will be the best front wheel drive car you've ever driven!'

I never got the chance to drive it before the Granite City Rally in 1988 and, with the number '1' on the car (as the previous year's winner of the event), everybody looked at 'E666 UOW' with a high degree of anticipation. The officials too, pored over it at scrutineering when they had to ensure its compliance with the regulations and safety equipment, but I never drove it there or back. Ken Rees, my co-driver did that. I only got my hands on the car on the Saturday of the event.

After we'd left the start, we headed towards the forest at Bennachie, the special stage which followed the slopes of the 528 metre peak. On the way there I said to Ken:

'We'd better open this thing up and see how it goes.'

I'll never forget his response:

'How the mighty have fallen!'

We got onto a dual carriageway section of the A96 and the reason for this salutary sentence from Ken? Well, there was a Peugeot 205GTi on the outside lane and he left us for dead, so I said to Ken:

'There's obviously something wrong with this thing. It's running only on two cylinders!'

We got to the stage start and everybody, and I *do* mean everybody, was looking at it. I remember it well, because it was a stunning looking car, and it was beautifully built.

The Start Marshal shouted:

'3-2-1-Go!'

But *'Go'* it wouldn't. I had dropped the clutch but it wouldn't, or couldn't, even spin its wheels. There wasn't enough performance to 'light up' the front tyres, or pull the skin off a rice pudding!

"Don't Cut!" That could have been the instruction from Ken Rees, first time out in the MG Montego on the Granite City Rally in 1988.   *Photograph: Sandy Topp.*

We somehow got to the top of Bennachie (well, the top of the road section in the forest, not the actual summit), and then I remembered Sir Isaac Newton's old adage of *"What goes up must come down"* and I thought that there just *had* to be an improvement. There was: it was quite quick down the other side because obviously, gravity took over. It handled really well and I'd give it 'ten out of ten' for that because it was a rare (good) handling thing, but the performance? Well, the exact phrase of wording is probably unprintable!

The Austin Rover *'K'* series engine was not exactly fit for purpose because it was vastly underpowered, but amazingly, somebody recently phoned me up to say that they had found the car and that it had been, or was being, rebuilt. But hey, that car was ridiculous, and it was embarrassing to debut it on my home rally.

*The MG Montego **was** a good looking car, as the above image shows from the Gartly Moor Stage of the Granite City Rally. Photograph: Duncan Brown.*

On the '88 Cambrian Rally.

Photograph: Tom Chisholm.

Above: The nut behind the wheel!

The Office.

Rover 'K' Series power plant – a misnomer if ever there was.

Photographs: Jack Davidson.

Above: A devil of a registration for the MG Montego.

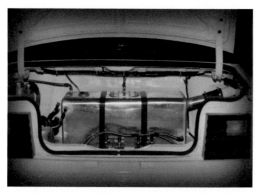

The dry sump set-up in the boot. This was designed to provide the oiling system for the internal combustion engine, only it didn't combust...

Frustration!

Photographs: Jack Davidson.

Chapter THIRTEEN

THE MOTLEY CREW

I've had a motley crew of co-drivers over the years, I really have, but they've all been excellent in their own way. Take Graham Neish, for example; he and I grew up together as chums, and we built our cars together. As far as I was concerned he was a 'Rock' in the sense that nothing could shake him, and he was a good mechanic, so if something broke he'd fix it – a really handy skill to possess – and he was an 'ace' at changing wheels, again a very useful skill.

I'd say that Welshman, Ken Rees, was undoubtedly the most professional co-driver I have had in the hot seat, mainly because we won the British Championship together, although Ken and I didn't have the same friendship that Graham and I had. He was altogether more professional in the sense that being a co-driver *was* his job *(and he handed me my gloves at the start...)* whereas with Graham the sport was purely a hobby. Both wonderful guys but totally different.

I did quite a few rallies with Ross Baird in my first Volvo, 'PRG 1M', then in two of my Escorts, 'RFX 300R', and 'LBO 2P', and I have to say that that episode in my life was also a lot of fun – as you may have picked up from some of our exploits in the earlier chapters.

Ross, I have to say, has been instrumental in helping me to get this book published as well.

I also had Bob Wilson and John Bennie in the co-driver's seat many times, and both were equally as good as co-drivers, although I have to say that Bob and I didn't have the best of relationships. I'll let Bob explain about that aspect of our working partnership:

'Early in January, 1988, I received a phone call from David asking if I'd be interested in co-driving for him in the

Scottish Championship that year, but could I bring some sponsorship with me? I was interested and I did bring some funding, but with David there was no friendship as such; his requirement of me was basically to plan the event, turn up, sit in the car, point the direction of travel, read the maps (there were no legal notes at that time), record the times, complete the event, wait for the prize-giving, and then go home.

'I'd maybe get call from him a week before the next event and as such I felt as though I was pretty much a tool for the job. I suspect he only asked me to co-drive for him because of my considerable and intimate knowledge of the forest stages in Scotland, particularly those on the Snowman Rally which we won twice. I also have to say that I got annoyed when, at the finish of a rally, even if we had won it, he would have already packed up his bags and started out on his way home. As a result, it was left to me to apologise to the organisers and sponsors for his absence, and then thank everybody on his behalf at the prize-giving.

'In saying that, though, I honestly think that David was among the top three or four drivers I have had the privilege of co-driving for. In my opinion, the best behind the wheel was actually Dougie Riach (until he ran out of money), then Jimmy McRae, and also Donald Milne (who would take me to the title in 1991). There was also James Rae (the 1970 and 1972 Scottish Rally Champion from Perth) and of course, David. I'd say that David had the luck, the contacts and the money to buy the right kit, but he also had the ability, and nobody can take that away from him.

'Despite partnering David nine times in 1988, we failed to win the Drivers' and Co-Drivers' titles. David had to wait until 1995 to achieve his lifelong ambition and I have to say he thoroughly deserved it.

'The MG Metro 6R4 was an unbelievably quick car and when David asked me to organise a test session in advance of our first stage event together, the Snowman Rally in 1988, I used my list of contacts and organised the outing in Milbuie Forest on the Black Isle. I arrived in the early afternoon after everything had been set up and I was offered the hot seat for a test run. There was around six inches of snow with 'tram lines' from the earlier runners out testing and it was difficult driving conditions. Nevertheless, David took the Metro and accelerated hard along the dead straight road, heading towards an eventual 45 degree left hand bend, and I thought to myself, 'We're never going to get round...', but we did.

'The car had incredible performance, fantastic agility and unbelievable stopping power; it could turn on a sixpence and David could certainly drive it. I admired him for his ability behind the wheel and also for what he actually achieved, but maybe the cool relationship that we had emanated from the early 1970s when I was asked to navigate him on a road rally. On that event, which started and finished somewhere near the town of Banchory, I made a complete and abject mess of the navigation and of course he wasn't best pleased about my efforts. He 'wisnae a happy chappie' and he didn't like it at all, but in my defence, I was new to the area and I had never rallied there before. In addition, I had no knowledge of the roads or indeed the organisers and their preferences or unique peculiarities of route instructions.

'There was perhaps another reason that David took me on as his co-driver, and that was the sponsorship I mentioned earlier; for years I received generous funding from my employer, the building company, Morrison Construction. I first worked there as a Quantity Surveyor and ended up as Contracts Director based in Inverness. This also gave me some degree of influence over advertising and marketing.

'I remember that Snowman Rally. We won it from a hard-charging Donald Milne, but I also think we'd have won the championship that year except for the fact that I couldn't do the Granite City Rally with David as he'd been contracted to utilise Ken Rees' skills in the MG Montego. Not only that, but David couldn't use either of his MGs (the Montego or the Metro) on the Scottish Rally because both cars were inelig-ible, so he had to resort to competing in the Volvo 240T.'

Bob continued:

'As David has already mentioned, we **had** to beat Colin McRae to win the Scottish Championship on the Trossachs Rally in 1988, so I suggested to him that we hide en route to the first stage.'

I took my Volvo 240T out for an airing on the 1988 Scottish Rally with Bob Wilson.

Photograph: Fergus McAnallen (www.rallyretro.com).

Above:
Round the hairpin in Cardrona.
Photograph: Tom Chisholm.

The stages could be sometimes smooth, but sometimes rough.
Photograph: Richard Murtha.

'I didn't want us, as car number '3', to enter the forest on our scheduled time and in our numerical starting sequence because that would have meant that we would have been clearing much of the ice-covered roads and letting everybody else know our time too. We did hide, but so, apparently, did the crews of cars '1' and '2' so, in hindsight, we obviously didn't hide for long enough, and instead of going through the stage as the ninth or tenth car, we ended up going in about fourth...

*'Less than two miles from the start, on a very icy 45 degree bend, we slid off the road and got stuck on top of a tree stump. There were lots of spectators about at that point, but nobody waved us down to warn us of the particularly difficult conditions at that corner, and after our excursion no-one rushed to help us back onto the road. All of the people watching obviously wanted Colin to win, but **if** we had been able to get the spectators to help, and **if** we had been pushed back onto the track and **if** we had finished the rally we might have won the title.*

*'However, '**if**' is the biggest word in rallying!'*

My Toyota Celica GT-4 in Devilla Forest on the 1989 Scottish Rally. Photograph: Frank Love (www.raceandrally.co.uk).

I couldn't agree more with Bob about the biggest word in rallying. It has been used a lot, especially in terms of results during the years 1989 through to 1992. They were barren, apart from a single victory on the Snowman Rally (with Bob again in 1989), but I'd say they were interesting from a car perspective because I used four different models from three different marques, and had the services of five co-drivers. I had the Ford Sierra RS Cosworth in 1989 with Bob, but it was Ken Rees who accompanied me in my Celica GT-4 on the Scottish Rally.

On the Glenurquhart Stage with Bob Wilson on the Snowman Rally in 1989.

On the Gartly Moor Stage with Ken Rees during the 1989 Granite City Rally.

Photographs: Duncan Brown.

202

Chapter FOURTEEN

CONTROVERSIAL TOUR

A newspaper in Scotland said it all:

"Lanark's Jimmy McRae leads a Scottish 1-2-3 in the 1989 Autoglass Tour of Britain."

But did it say it all?

'No it did not!'

The paper also said that:

"After a gruelling seven days and 2,200 miles around Britain and Ireland, the tour ended with a 27-lap race at Brands Hatch in Kent. Already 20 minutes ahead of his nearest rival, Aberdonian, David Gillanders, Jim McRae coasted to third place (on the final event) to take the overall title. McRae had a faultless run to victory – a win he considers the finest of his career."

The top four final placings were:

1	Jimmy McRae	7 hr 9 min 58 sec
2	David Gillanders	7 hr 31 min 58 sec
3	Robbie Head	7 hr 34 min 55 sec
4	Roger Clark	7 hr 35 min 23 sec

I remember seeing the first Tour of Britain in 1973, a 1,000 mile competition which was won by James Hunt in a Chevrolet Camaro. I thought the format of the event actually looked like a lot of fun, and it suited me in that it comprised races, rally special stages, hill climbs and also autotests – and I'd done most of these disciplines already.

It had a touch of everything, so when the event was held in '89, with Autoglass, the windscreen replacement company, as the main sponsor, it attracted Jimmy McRae, Roger Clark, and Formula One racers, Derek Bell and Johnny Herbert. I self-funded my effort and rented a suitable car from Mike Little Preparations in Carlisle. It was there that I got my hands on a whale-tail two door, rear wheel drive, Group 'N', Ford Sierra Cosworth. In its standard form, it produced 300 brake horsepower, had a different gearbox, a limited slip differential, and a roll cage, but the suspension units, as per the event regulations, had to stay as standard.

It did have slightly stiffer coil springs (which were allowed with other stuff like that) but generally, the car had to retain most of the standard kit. I also secured the services of Ken Rees to co-drive again.

The top ten from the list of entries were:

1	Johnny Herbert	Ford Sierra Cosworth
2	Derek Bell	Vauxhall Astra GTE
3	Jimmy McRae	Ford Sierra Cosworth
4	Dai Llewellin	Ford Sierra Cosworth
5	John Haugland	Skoda 130RS
6	Nick Adams	Ford Sierra Cosworth
7	Trevor Smith	Ford Sierra Cosworth
8	Nick Hodgetts	Ford Sierra Cosworth
9	David Gillanders	Ford Sierra Cosworth
10	Roger Clark	Ford Sierra Cosworth

There was also a trio of quick drivers behind us in Graham Middleton, Chris Lord, and Robbie Head, the latter co-driven by Campbell Roy. Four years later I would secure the services of Campbell for a few rallies in 1993 and you can read his account of our time together in the next Chapter.

A rough outline of the Tour of Britain route showed that it started in Cardington, Bedford, thence to Cardiff in Wales and the next day to Liverpool and onto Holyhead for the midnight ferry to Ireland. From there we did a (short) circuit of Ireland with an overnight halt at Dublin Castle.

Jimmy McRae excelled on the (long) Circuit of Ireland Rally which he won a magnificent seven times. This included two fantastic hat-tricks, the first between 1980 and 1982, and the second trio from 1987 to 1989, so any attempt by me to try and beat him would have been absolutely futile. He also won it again in 1985. But I have to ask why he didn't win it in 1983, 1984, and 1986?

We then headed towards Glasgow for a night's stay before heading south to Leeds, and the following day from Yorkshire to Ipswich. The final day was from East Anglia to Kent and then to Brands Hatch, the racing circuit.

Blazing Candles! On the Autoglass Tour of Britain, 1989.

I had a good car and was in the top six most of the time, partly due to the length of the event, where some of the cars either dropped out or suffered from mechanical maladies. Gradually, I crept up the leader board and then Ken Rees said to me:

'You know, we could win this.'

'Oh, hardly.'

But then, having thought about it, we both agreed:

'If we just keep going, we can win this.'

We were beaten by Jimmy McRae in his Cosworth, and Roger Clark's car all but broke down on him. In fact, I remember passing Roger on the circuit at Brands Hatch because his engine had blown up, but even so he was still classified as 4th in the results.

Nevertheless, 2nd place overall was a fantastic result for us, especially after a whole week of motorsport. It was a very long way to go in a car, round Britain and Ireland, and had every discipline in it. It's probably too expensive to run it nowadays but it was fabulous and I thoroughly enjoyed the event. It had everything, and both Ken and I were over the moon with our result. I'd taken out everybody, bar Jimmy, who was a very difficult guy to beat. On the Circuit of Ireland stages, he *was* unbeatable and much more experienced too.

However, one of the mechanics told me that the post-event scrutineers had conducted a check of Jimmy's car and reckoned that it had failed. This meant that there was something wrong with it. I thought to myself, *'So what?'*

I was happy with my 2nd place finish, but then, Mike Little himself came over to me and said that although he would *not* protest, I could if I wanted to. Mike didn't want to (protest) because he had a good working relationship with Ford, and he did not want to be seen as a troublemaker. But if I protested, and this was upheld, I could be classified the winner.

Mike said:

'If you want to protest, there's a damn good chance you could win the Tour of Britain.'

'Why would I want to win under a protest?'

I say that because, to be fair, I either win or lose on my own abilities, and Jimmy was much further ahead of me anyway. If I'd won it under a protest it would have emphasised that I wasn't the quickest and that I would only have won because of a technical issue. *"Rules is rules"*, as they say, but I was never like that. This attitude was borne out of the result of the 1987 Trossachs Rally, and with it the Scottish Rally Championship title, when people accused me of this or that. I just took it on the chin; I either beat the rest or lost to someone else.

I didn't know that, allegedly, Jimmy's car was technically non-compliant and this meant that his Sierra Cosworth was better, or at least faster, than mine. It had modified rear suspension, with different bushes, and the benefit (and I stress, unknown to Jimmy, I believe) was probably worth a good couple of seconds a mile over the period of however many tarmac events we competed on, and we were on a lot of tarmac courses on the tour.

The net result was that I was beaten by around 24 minutes, yes 24 minutes, and I had more or less accepted that until Jimmy came up to me and said:

'David, I hope you're not going to protest?'

'Jimmy, why would I want to protest?'

His response took me by surprise, and I refuse to reiterate it in this book because I still admire everything that Jimmy has done in the sport. My response, when someone *tells* me to do, or not do something, can often lead me to act in completely the opposite direction, so I said:

'You know something, that's enough. I will protest.'

I wasn't going to be told what to do by anybody, so I put the protest money down, all £1,000 of it. The entire presentation of awards was stopped there and then and the television crew had to return home. The whole thing was hung out to dry for two to three months, until I went to the sport's governing body's offices with my lawyer. I'd never been to a court like that before and was, I guess, much like a criminal court, but held in the MSA's new offices in Colnbrook, Berkshire.

My case came up and my lawyer said:

'My Lord, this is a very simple case, and I am going to show you two items of vehicle suspension, one from Mr. Gillanders' car, the other from Mr. McRae's.'

My car's suspension had the rubber bush type, and was solid, but my lawyer managed to physically pull apart the bush from McRae's car. It was alleged that his team (and I stress yet again, *not* Jimmy himself, I believe) had cut the bush in half and inserted a steel brace in contradiction to the requirements of the regulations.

But then a funny thing happened. In my experience, any issue which renders a car *"illegal"* results in that car and crew being disqualified from the event, just as I was disqualified from the Trossachs Rally, but instead of Jimmy being thrown out he was penalised only for the Brands Hatch race, and that merey knocked two minutes off his time. He was penalised merely the amount he had won the race by, because Jimmy's team, allegedly, had said that that particular bush had been inserted in error and had only been used during that Brands Hatch race.

Even deducting this penalty from the Brands Hatch event, Jimmy was still declared the winner, although I considered myself to be, without question, the moral victor. In saying that, though, I would not have liked to have won because of another person's disqualification.

That's the power of a car manufacturer, and their advertising, because, to all intents and purposes, I was just a talented amateur, whereas Jimmy McRae was a professional. It looked to me as though the result had been decided that he would win, come hell or high water, but in the real world he should have been excluded.

The thing is: would I have wanted to win like that? No, I would not. That's not my way; I would always want to win in a straight fight, and Jimmy would probably have beaten me in a straight fight without all this aggravation anyway, but it was the way I was approached that set me off. I had been ecstatic with my 2nd place before all of the controversy, but the whole affair left me with a really bad taste.

My view is this: if something is done wrong, or is against the rules, an individual receives the 'belt' as a punishment (as I was given the 'belt' at school all those years ago), but if there has been a proven contravention of the regulations, then disqualification should follow.

I have nothing but admiration for Jimmy and what he has done for motor sport, but frankly, a token penalty was a pretty pathetic punishment. But remember, Jimmy McRae, the five times British Rally Champion, a true legend in the sport, was driving for Ford's Rallye Sport (RS) set-up. RS was a huge name in the sport at the time and Jimmy's car was a fully sponsored Works car, whereas mine was a privately funded effort. It was a disappointing end to what was a fantastic result, and although my protest was upheld, we lost! We were still 2nd. I didn't expect to win, and as I have already said, I wouldn't have liked to have won the event through a protest.

And so ended the Case of Gillanders v McRae.

And so ended my partnership with Ken Rees too.

Cardiff Ken

I got to know Cardiff Ken a lot. A person does when two people share a car for that length of time because they build up a trust and dependency upon each other. I found out that Ken had been a driver before he switched seats. Apparently, he had driven Ford Escorts and Hillman Avengers back in the 1970s until the accidents outweighed his wallet.

He used to own a domestic appliance business coupled to a pair of retail shops, but rallying was his life and after our efforts together I was delighted that he got a call from Prodrive in 1990 to help them on the RAC Rally with Ari Vatanen's entry. He was retained in 1991 and 1992, when he got a phone call from Jimmy McRae who asked him to fly to Greece to co-drive for him and to make gravel notes for his son, Colin, and from that point in time Ken became a full time rally man. He thus gave up his business and shops and commenced what was to become a World Record in the making.

Ken did every event as part of Colin's team, then the same for Juha Kankkunen after McRae moved on, but he never thought he would become a World Record Holder himself. The statistics show otherwise: from Greece in 1992, through until New Zealand in 2012, he found that he had covered every single World Rally Championship event continuously. It transpired that he had participated in 280 events and travelled around the world an incredible 20 times!

Chapter FIFTEEN

_____

CELEBRITY CO-DRIVERS

I've had some co-drivers who have been equally as good as the aforementioned ones in my book, but I have had others who couldn't read a map, or a road book, and some who were sick because reading with the head down in a rapidly moving car on a rough, undulating surface is not for everybody, but I have had some very well known co-drivers as well.

For the International Scottish Rally in 1990 I used a Subaru Legacy RS and secured the services of one such 'celebrity' co-driver, the former ARG motor sport supremo, John Davenport, and I think he would be best placed to relate our experience together:

'Many years had passed since we last met, but David called me and asked me if I would like to co-drive him on the Scottish Rally. By this time, the 6R4 was no longer being used and some slick salesman called David Richards (why does everyone in this story have to be called David?) had sold David a Group 'N' Subaru Legacy RS. It was in this remarkable machine that we took on the world, and finished 12th overall and 4th in the category.

'I remember two outstanding things about that rally. Firstly that David evidently knew how much punishment a modern rally car could absorb. He simply astounded me by not lifting off for what I would have thought to be rally-terminating bumps. We had done our 30 mph recce to make pacenotes in an Isuzu 4x4 in which we had literally felt all of these hazards and also carefully noted them, but David certainly knew better.

'The second thing I recall is that the rally had been delayed for some time in the area around Carron Valley. It was a hot day and with the windows down and engines off, all

the rally crews presented a nice meal to our invertebrate pals. It was then that David discovered a truly wonderful thing about rallying in a Group 'N' car. He put up the windows, started the engine and turned on the air conditioning to its coldest setting. The midgies, thinking that winter had come a bit early, either died or disappeared.

'It was bliss, absolute bliss.

'Since then, though, our paths have only crossed on the telephone but, it's only fair to point out that Aberdeen is long way from Wiltshire and, as the song says, "Don't get around much any more".

The Subaru Legacy RS that John Davenport and I competed with on the 1990 Scottish Rally. Photograph: Fergus McAnallen (www.rallyretro.com).

A different kind of horsepower on the Jim Fleming Stages at Ayr Race course.

Photograph: Sandy Topp.

I had a Ford Sierra RS Cosworth 4x4 in 1991, and participated in the odd event, including the Jim Fleming Stages that
year. I managed to persuade Ken Rees to sit beside me again,
but for a single event only, the Audi Sport Rally in 1991, I
had yet another Welshman in the left hand seat. Incredibly,
Nicky Grist actually volunteered his services! When he co-
drove for me on that event he was a Works Co-Driver for
Ford and Malcolm Wilson, so it was quite a feather in my cap
to attract an individual of his calibre.

Nicky and I became friends in 1989, during the recce for
the Scottish Rally that year; I was there with my regular co-
driver, Ken Rees, but I'll let Ken's compatriot explain all
about what happened one evening:

'I first heard of David when a good friend of mine, Ken
Rees, began to co-drive for him in 1986, and also during the
National Championship the following year. I was playing
around in the same rallies around that time, but of course he
was battling head to head with the likes of Alistair Sutherland
and that's when I really came into contact with him the first
time. Back then, of course, David didn't know me from Adam;
I wasn't a star in the rally world at that time; I was just a
young boy setting off.

'David has that marmite kind of personality, but for me
it's a very sweet marmite indeed because I just love the
straight-talking, fun-loving, character that he is. I'll always
remember that 1989 recce on the Scottish Rally because it
was ever so funny. Everybody who was present thoroughly
enjoyed the interlude.

'We had been staying in a lovely hotel in Gatehouse-of-
Fleet in Dumfriesshire, and at the time I happened to be co-
driving for David (Dave) Metcalfe in a Vauxhall Nova GTE.
The GM Dealer Sport Team was also there with Malcolm
Wilson and Ian Grindrod, as well as Mitsubishi Motors, who
were there with Pentti Airikkala and Ronan McNamee in their
Galant VR-4. Well, one night, my God, David just took poor
old Pentti apart. So much so, that the big Finn just had to get
up and go to his room! David was just so full of life and
hugely entertaining that day. He was just having a 'go' at

Pentti with friendly banter and putting him down as well. But Pentti couldn't handle it. He just had to get up and go...

'No matter what he tried to come back to David with, it just didn't work for the Finn, as David responded with even smarter, even funnier answers. We were all in stitches, and it was very, very memorable indeed.

'I had not done that many recces before that, but it was, quite literally, one of the best recces I have ever done, and much of that had to be down to David and his effervescent demeanour.

'The Audi Sport Rally was based in Telford in 1991, and David had a Group 'N' Ford Sierra RS Cosworth 4x4. We ended up 5th overall and my old driver, Dave Metcalfe, partnered by Ian Grindrod, finished 4th in a Nova GSi. Colin McRae and Derek Ringer were in a Subaru Legacy RS and finished 3rd, and Russell Brookes and Neil Wilson were in a similar car to David's and were 2nd. The winners, though, were Dai Llewellin and Mike Corner in their Nissan Pulsar GTi-R.

'But (after the Audi Sport) the memories of the event were just so funny. Instead of him concentrating harder and making sure he did the job right, he was calling me for everything, and it was so, so funny. With David it was all just fun and games. He was a good driver but he wasn't really willing to let himself go, like a lot of good drivers out there that just don't want to, or aren't willing, to commit themselves to push for the next level. However, I think on that rally, we actually did have some good fun although I pushed him harder than perhaps I would have done normally, but in fairness to him, we did go very well on that event.

'David can make friends and colleagues cringe with some of the things he says, but that is a quality I admire. David just says what he thinks. Probably there is a filter in there some-where, but where? The filter is not as thick in his mind, as that in of a lot of other people's minds. He tells you as it is. I have always enjoyed David's company, and I feel I'm a much better person from knowing him, having rallied with him, and socialised with him, than not to have known him at all.

213

'He is just one of life's characters, and certainly one of life's funny guys.'

I had already entered the Audi Sport Rally in Telford, Shropshire, close to the Welsh border, on October 19, and planned to drive a Sierra Cosworth 4x4 when the telephone rang. It was Nicky Grist, who said:

'Listen, David, this next event (the Audi Sport) that you intend to do, who's your co-driver?'

'Oh, I just take anybody just now as I don't have a regular co-driver.'

'Let me co-drive for you.'

I had to question him:

*'Why on earth would you, a top world championship co-driver, want **me** to drive **you**?'*

'I want to prepare pacenotes for the RAC Rally.'

'Pacenotes?'

*'Yes, I'll co-drive **and** also make pacenotes.'*

That's how good he was!

We arrived at the car park by the start and I noticed that the spectators were there waiting for us to arrive. I couldn't believe all the adulation: everybody wanted an autograph, but I found that they only wanted *his* autograph, not mine... Everybody wanted *Nicky's* autograph because *he* was of world championship standard, and I wasn't.

Anyway, we headed off to the start of the first stage, and Nicky asked:

'What tyres are we on just now?'

'Black!'

'Soft?'

'Hell, I don't know.'

'Well, this is a 25 mile stage coming up, so we want hard (compound) tyres.'

'We've got what we've got, and they're staying on.'

We got to the stage start and he said to me:

'Ok, just drive normally, as I know the first stage.'

We got to the end and he quietly asked:

'That was fine, David. Can you go a bit quicker?'

'Not really.'

'But we need to go quicker.'

214

'I don't want to go any quicker.'
'We can go a lot faster, David.'
'Really?'

*'Oh, David, we can go a **lot** faster. Now, in this next stage I want you to listen to every word **I** say, and do as **I** say. It's not what **you** want to do, but what **I** want to do.'*

I thought, well, we're good friends, Nicky and I, and I trusted him, so I said:

'Well, ok, let's do it!'

There was me, competing with a world championship co-driver who was about to compete on the forthcoming RAC Rally beside one of the top rally drivers in the world in Malcolm Wilson. So why would I argue with him? This is the guy who would go on to become Colin McRae's co-driver.

We reached the start of the next stage and Nicky said:

*'Now, David, just do as **I** say.'*

I replied:

'Remember, if I go off it's your fault!'
'You won't go off.'

I forget which stage it was, but it was one of those stages which had l-o-n-g rights, l-o-n-g lefts, and flowed. If the bends had tightened up in the middle and I had been committed to a particular line, then I would have crashed, because normally I'd go into such a long left or right and have the car slightly upset, or nervous, so that the rear of the car was always a little bit out of line. That would have allowed me to induce a greater degree of oversteer and get out of any difficulty should the road suddenly tighten, but Nicky wanted me to actually *drive* round these corners because it was much, much faster.

I remember going into these corners and he said:

*'Ok, just keep it in fifth (gear), keep it, keep it. **Do not** change down, **don't** change down.'*

We (somehow) got to the end of the stage and found that we were comfortably 20 seconds faster than anybody else. My right leg was bloody well trembling because I wanted to take it off the throttle and I physically had to force myself to keep it down.

At the end of the stage I said to Nicky:

'Nicky, I can't do any more stages like that.'

'David, that was a much better effort.'

We certainly did very well on that rally.

I'll let Nicky explain a bit more about our escapade:

'I'll always remember going into the Dyfi forest complex high in the Cambrian Mountains, somewhere between Dolgellau and Machynlleth, and telling David:

'David, we are now in the Gartheiniog stage, and there's one particular section in here where we'll enter what we call the 'ski-slope'. When we get onto this 'ski-slope' it is downhill. It's about one and a half miles long, and it's absolutely flat out from start to finish. I don't want you to lift at all. I just want you to keep your foot flat to the floor, but David said:

'I don't like the sound of it... I don't like it at all.....'

'Listen, it's flat, I'm not here to make you drive round like an old woman, I want to get the best out of you, and this is effectively why I want you to keep it flat.'

'Anyway, we started, got to a hairpin right, and I then said, 'OK, we're now on the 'ski-slope'. Remember, it's flat (meaning flat out in speed) all the way until I tell you to stop.'

'Well, we were going down this hill, on a forest track, in a Group 'N' specification car which probably carried a considerably higher top speed back then, compared to what a Group 'N' car does nowadays. We were driving at a speed of somewhere between 125 mph and 135 mph and he was saying to me all the time:

'You're an effing twat, effing this, and effing that',

'I just kept on saying:

'Go on, keep it going...'

'But David just kept on muttering:

'Effin hell, this is madness!'

'This is what he was doing instead of concentrating on keeping the car on the road. He was cursing me all the way down this hill because it was just a step too far for him. But it was so memorable, and then I said:

'Brake now!'

'At the bottom of the 'ski-slope' there is a corner where, in 2005, Malcolm Wilson's son, Matthew, and his co-driver, Scott Martin, had a really bad accident in their M-Sport Ford

Focus. Both of them suffered really serious physical injury, so, the 'ski-slope' was not a place for the faint-hearted. It had to be treated with respect.'

That was Nicky's viewpoint on the event and it certainly crossed my mind that there was a big difference between me and the World Rally Championship drivers. I was driving at a different pace. I only had to win the British Championship, not the World Championship, and I was happy with the pace I could maintain.

Although he no longer competes, Nicky remains in motor sport, mainly because in 2006 he was approached by the Italian owners of Stilo helmets to become their sole distributor in the UK. Through this he set up Nicky Grist Motorsport, based in Pontrilas, in Herefordshire. He also started a co-driver's academy for young co-drivers to help develop their skills to become experienced, skilled co-drivers.

Photograph: Colin McMaster, McKlein Photography. (www.mcklein.de).

Nicky Grist, on the right, was instrumental in getting me to the next level. This photograph shows Colin McRae and Nicky on their last event together – in 2006.

Nicky didn't win the World Rally Championship for co-drivers, but I'll let him take up that point:

'It's true, I didn't win the World Rally Championship although I did help Juha Kankkunen to win it. I think that winning championships is nice, but is it really important? Probably not, but, I do think that good competition is all about competing, not necessarily winning. That's the way I look at it when I look back at my motor sport career. I have absolutely no regrets. I look at David, and yes, he's been the British National Champion and won a lot of rallies, and when he does something, he does it to the full. He's lived the life that probably 95% of the people in the UK would have liked to have lived.

*'Doing this piece has also reminded me that I have started a book myself – a Talking Book – now **that** would really suit David! His character would suit a talking book, but there'd be an awful lot of bleeps in it....'*

In my opinion, a good co-driver has to be a most level-headed individual. He or she really does. In fact I would say that a co-driver is the most under-rated person in a car although it's the driver who gets the accolades. But, without a good co-driver, the driver is nothing. The 'Office Manager' has to be punctual, has to be brave, and has to be able to handle all sorts of conditions.

The co-driver has to keep an eye on the time in the car, right up until (and during) a service halt. He, or she, then needs to work out the time allowed for the service crew to make sure there is enough minutes to complete the required work on the car and then head out of the service area in a timely manner, while the driver, me, well, I would keep out of the way until my co-driver came chasing after me and said:

'David, five minutes to get in the car, please.'

I would climb back into the car and hear my co-driver's calm, reassuring voice talking to me through my headset all the time. This was because the MG Metro 6R4, in particular, was so incredibly noisy that we had to get ear defenders and intercom. And over the intercom, my co-driver would (or could) get it wrong, or I'd mishear and/or I'd get a corner wrong, and we'd both get a terrible fright.

So he (and I say he, because all my co-drivers have been male) has been the most under-rated person in the car and he deserves everything and more in the way of praise that I could, and can ever, hope to give.

Yet another Welsh Co-Driver!

In 1992, I had yet another Welsh co-driver *(just how many more of them are there?)*. This time it was another good friend of Nicky's, and this one came in the form of a larger-than-life chap called Howard Davies.

Although Howard and I only competed on a handful of events, he was great fun in the car and could talk the hind legs off a donkey, so you can imagine what it was like being inside the car with me behind the wheel and Howard in the hot seat!

The marshals didn't have a chance…

Howard is probably better known for his co-driving of Gwyndaf Evans (Elfyn's father) to the British Rally Championship title in '96, and more recently as a sports reporter for the Welsh language channel, *"SC4"*, but I'll let this effervescent Welshman recap our encounter:

'I don't know quite how I ended up co-driving for David, but I believe that Malcolm Wilson was involved somewhere along the line. I know there was some talk of me getting a Nissan Primera Estate Car in the deal somewhere, but that all went belly up for some kind of reason. Nevertheless I agreed to go and do the Granite City Rally with David in 1992, and as I've said before, control wasn't the sort of word I'd use to describe anything that David Gillanders did in life, or on a rally, really, nor in speech! But, in fairness, I was pleasantly surprised on the 'Granite' and we got on very well together although it all went a bit pear-shaped when we picked up a puncture in Clash-in-dar-roch.'

I laughed at his excellent and very deliberate attempt at the pronunciation of 'Clashindarroch' and responded:

'That's a lot better than my attempts at pronouncing the names of some of the Welsh forests!'

Howard laughed, then continued:

'Yes, and we did kick (Murray) Grierson's backside which was the most important thing, although Alistair McRae, David

Mann, and Robbie Head beat us to the win. Nevertheless, I think we still got pissed afterwards if I am not mistaken.

'David then invited me to go to the Isle of Man for the Manx Rally and I must say I was filled with some trepidation, especially when he didn't turn up on the day we were supposed to do the recce. It wasn't M-Sport then, of course, it was 'Malcolm Wilson Motorsport', and John Steele drove me round for half of the recce in an Isuzu Trooper, and when David did turn up we drove round the stages twice, but by 3 o'clock he'd had enough and said:

'Stuff this (or something similar), let's go to the pub.'

'As I mentioned, I was filled with trepidation going into this rally because I knew the car was a bit of a beast and a real handful; I don't think the differentials were as soft as they could have been and I recall the first couple of stages being akin to a rocket being launched down a lane.'

I agreed with Howard: it was a difficult car to drive.

Then he continued with his reminiscing:

'I remember we started a stage somewhere and went over a bump and almost immediately into 45 (degree) left and right hand bends. It was very slippery down the hill and we went round a straw bale and up to a T-Junction then onto a long straight towards a roundabout at the top. I think we changed gears from 1st into 2nd, 3rd, 4th, 5th, and then 'BANG!' I think David was delighted!'

I was. I was over the moon.

'The gearbox had gone and it was certainly terminal. We couldn't carry on so it was back to the bar, wasn't it? The Isle of Man wasn't overwhelmed with posh hotels, but I have to say that David's people managed to find a very posh one right on the sea front. And we'd a few more beers that night as well.'

I remember it fondly, and agreed: it seems to me that all we did was to get drunk rather than go driving! Howard then reminded me of our effort on the 1992 Granite City Rally:

'I have a picture of David and myself on the Granite in my office at home – it's been here for years, still up on the wall – showing us in the blue and white Sierra RS Cosworth 4x4 when we finished in 4th position overall. So, to be fair, David

has made rallying in the UK a lot more colourful, and it would be a sadder place without him. You could definitely hear David Gillanders coming, long, long before you saw him! He has probably put a few individuals' backs up, but at the end of the day, I think they probably deserved it.'

I took Howard as my co-driver a few times because he's a bit of a talker himself, and it was good to have him in the car for the entertainment value alone.

I think Howard agreed:

'We did have a bit of a craic, didn't we?'

Half the time, though, I couldn't understand Howard's Welsh accent, but funnily enough I ended up winning the British Rally Championship with a Welsh co-driver in Ken Rees, as Howard commented:

'What a guy! An amazing guy, still going, and he's still networking. What a chap, still buzzing about. He's some boy, isn't he? Fantastic!'

I would bump into Howard again in 2017....

Co-Driver to the Champions

An opportunity presented itself in 1993 for me to secure the excellent co-driving skills of Campbell Roy – the co-driver to the champions, well Scottish Champions if I want to be precise – and so I jumped at the chance, although I can't remember how it all came about. I'll let Huntly's famous co-driver reiterate some of our time together:

'Like Malcolm Wilson, when I heard that the title of David's book was going to be, "David Gillanders – I do all the talking!" I too, laughed out loud, and then commented that the title sounded most suitable because he is a great raconteur and good at embellishments. He's also excellent at adding in bits in that maybe didn't happen, although all will undoubtedly have their origins in a true story. Nevertheless, he is absolutely brilliant at telling his stories.'

But the stories ***did*** happen. ***They're all true!***

Anyway, Campbell wanted to continue:

'David's attention span is not great and his memory fails him. In fact my memory fails me as well, because neither of us

can truly remember all the events we did together. I do recall one that was based in Glenbranter, on the shores of Loch Eck in Argyll, so I'd say it was probably one of the Argyll Stages events, but which year, I don't know. I don't recall doing the Granite City Rally in 1993 but the records show that David and I started as car 8 in a Ford Sierra RS Cosworth 4x4 and finished in 2nd place only 33 seconds behind Murray Grierson and Stewart Merry in their MG Metro 6R4. And, obviously, we competed on the Snowman Rally as Jim Sutherland's photographs confirm. That was in 1993 before David actually acquired his Ford Escort RS Cosworth.

'The reason I do remember the event in Glenbrantner was because of an incident that happened to us that day. We had picked up a puncture on one of the long stages in Glenshellish and I noticed that the calibrated clocks were 'out' by 10-12 seconds – the start clock was wrong and (unfortunately), I mentioned it to David, by stating:

'Look that clock's wrong.'

'Ah well, get the stage cancelled. That'd be great!'

'I suppose that's the co-driver's job so I submitted a query and when the stewards checked the timepiece they found that it was indeed 'out' by more than the tolerance allowed, but as it was the longest stage of the rally I really felt sorry for the organisers. They cancelled the test.

'I tend not to hold onto any results of the Scottish Rally Championship events, but I remember that incident quite well as David was quite chuffed given that he'd lost a great deal of time with that puncture. To get the stage scrubbed was great news for him.

'Memory is such a strange thing. I cannot remember just how or why I came to act as his co-driver two or three times. I think David must have asked me although I don't actually remember him speaking with me about it. It must have been around the time I would have been co-driving Robbie Head in the midst of the British Rally Championship in the Michelin Pilot Escort Cosworth, which was (at the time) a Malcolm Wilson Motorsport car – the boss was driving the other one – though his was in Group 'A' specification and Robbie's was in Group 'N'. Both were in the same colours and David, I

222

guess, would likely have been around during the time of some of these events, so in all probability he might have asked Malcolm about being on the lookout for a co-driver for a few events. I'm sure that's how it came about.'

I have known Campbell since the early 1970s when he was active in road rallying in the north east of Scotland, and when he also won the Tour of Mull Rally twice as a co-driver. He was obviously a talented individual in the hot seat, so I filed that information for the future. However, I digress, so it's back to Campbell's memoirs:

'David, I felt, was full of self-confidence; he talked a great game before the event, and he talked even more after the event (in the bar where so much wheeling and dealing would go on in between pints). He was always supremely confident in his own ability, and not without reason, I would have to say. He wasn't a world beater, and I'm sure he'd admit to that (or maybe he wouldn't), but in terms of natural ability and car control, in the Scottish series in particular, he was right up there with the best of them. Obviously, he won the British National Championship but maybe that had something to do with having the best car and equipment at the time.

'Or maybe it's something about the Aberdeen Motor Sport Mafia: I have been privileged to co-drive for a trio of them, namely David, Donald Milne and Brian Lyall. All came from backgrounds where they could afford the best of equipment, but of the three, though, I maintain that David was undoubtedly the most natural driver.

'David could easily rub a lot of people up the wrong way with his quick comments, and arrogance (which I suppose is a good word for it), but once a person got to know him properly he could be great fun to be with. I don't honestly know if the bravado was a cover for insecurity or what, but he certainly told great stories, was good fun to be with, and I especially remember being in his company for various recces on events and in numerous hotels with Malcolm and his team. David was always the life and soul of the party at the dinner table so he was good value as far as that was concerned.

'I cannot remember any incidents or 'moments' on any of the rallies I did with David, but what I do recall was his

demeanour, his funny stories in the bar, and his superb ability to tell them that springs to mind. His confidence came over well in the car too; yes, he was an aggressive driver, but he had the car control to match. Some drivers (who shall remain nameless) would have me on the edge of my seat when I acted as their co-driver, but David came over as being able to cope with any sort of situation behind the wheel.

With Campbell Roy on the Monaughty Stage of the Snowman Rally in 1993.   *Photograph: Jim Sutherland.*

'I won't rank David, but I have co-driven a number of Scottish Rally Champions at one time or another. David, though, wouldn't be at the top (and he wouldn't expect to be) because I sat beside Colin McRae of course. My only thoughts were, when asked to contribute to his book, that he must have been scraping the bottom of the barrel given that I only co-drove for him a few times. I wasn't a regular part of his motor sport career.

'In Scottish Rally Championship events, before and after David himself had won the title, I sat alongside Colin McRae, Murray Grierson, Donald Milne, Brian Lyall and Raymond Munro, as well as with Jimmy Girvan (with whom I won the title twice) and more recently, Euan Thorburn.

With Campbell Roy on the Monaughty Stage of the 1993
Snowman Rally. Photograph: Jim Sutherland.

'*However, I think my main claim to fame is the fact that Ian Grindrod and I are the only two co-drivers to have co-driven for the entire McRae rallying dynasty, namely Jim, Colin, and Alister.*'

It could easily be said that Campbell has had a pretty intensive motor sport career and after our few events together he went on and up to another level and thence to his biggest involvement in motor sport, that of being Manager for Colin McRae.

Me? I was still striving for the title of Scottish Rally Champion, but at least I believed I now had a car capable of achieving my goal....

Chapter SIXTEEN

SOMEONE STOLE MY HELICOPTER

It's difficult to slot this particular chapter into strict chronological order, and the reasons will become clear during the reading of the next ten pages. However, many of the incidents in this story happened in the early 1990s.

My passion for flying was such that I flew in a helicopter for a number of years. I clocked up many hours of flying time in the machines and even 'owned' one for a time. I loved every moment of it, but despite this I was always genuinely apprehensive, and very much respectful of them. I also felt that helicopters appeared to be under-powered, and there were always a lot of considerations to take cognisance of, and act upon: there was always the likelihood of inclement weather, and I continually kept a keen pair of eyes open for the likes of electricity pylons, wires, trees and buildings, especially during take offs and landings. I was always aware of variable wind speeds too.

Things can happen really quickly in a helicopter, and the pilot has to keep on top of it all the time. There have been too many instances of motor sport people involved in helicopter incidents, such as the chairman of Prodrive, and former WRC co-driver in 1981, Dave Richards, and also former Scottish Rally Champions, Murray Grierson and Donald Milne. Donald crashed in his helicopter but less than 24 hours later he had taken out his MG Metro 6R4 and won a rally.

Richards, Milne and Grierson all survived, but sadly, Colin McRae perished in his helicopter accident. This one is probably the most widely known of all, and sadly it also claimed the lives of Colin's young son, Johnny, and two family friends, only a few hundred yards from Colin's home in Lanark. His passing was a huge, huge loss to the McRae family, the other families involved, and to motor sport. I miss Colin a lot.

When I flew in my helicopter there was always a safety pilot, a co-pilot in other words, but if the pilot became tired, I'd hear the words:

'You have control.'

And hope to God that he'd actually be listening. But if something had gone wrong there would have been no coming back from it. Nevertheless, I still love to fly.

I did have a few close calls in my helicopter though: we once had to land on a golf course because of bad weather and when on the final approach and didn't notice some telephone wires. Thankfully, these were missed by around 50 feet or so, a tiny margin, really. In my flying days the helicopter also encountered engine problems and we once had to land in the middle of nowhere with low fuel warnings.

The website, *"www.scottishgolfview.com"* stated that two of the sport's top golfers, Tom Weiskopf and Steve Elkington, were flown in to conduct a clinic at the Kings Links Golf Centre in Aberdeen in 1992. The website, however, did *not* mention that I was in the aircraft, nor did it mention that (according to Gladys who was waiting for me inside) we only just missed the high perimeter fence by a few feet.

We had collected both the American and his Australian playing partner from the home of golf, St. Andrews, and flown them to the Aberdeen links-side venue, but on the approach to the landing site, we hadn't actually taken into consideration the wind speed. We had been travelling at around 90 knots (about 100 miles per hour) and as we approached the site the co-pilot said:

'I think you should be throttling back now.'

'It's under control.'

Well, that was a mistake, and we just managed to land inside the perimeter at precisely the moment a gust of wind slewed the tail round. It was at a critical point and the speed *was* too fast, but we got down. What the website failed to mention was the fact that Weiskopf and Elkington were not flown back out by the co-pilot, but returned to St Andrews with the proper pilot at the controls....

*I would have had more photographs of my helicopter
if it hadn't been stolen!*

Photograph: Derry Taylor.

However, this story probably started around 1989, when a guy by the name of Paul Bennett came to Aberdeen from New Zealand. He was introduced to me by Donald Milne, another helicopter fan, and he took with him a new Hughes 500 Helicopter (the same kind that appeared in the film, *"Black Hawk Down"* where it was called *"Little Bird"*). This particular helicopter was extremely agile and the best way I can illustrate it is by suggesting that if a Jet Ranger helicopter was a Transit Van then a Hughes 500 would have been a Ferrari. It was a very quick, fancy, four-seater, with a jet engine. Its maximum speed was 152 knots, (170 miles per hour) and it had a service ceiling of 16,000 feet.

I had my 'Gillanders Motors' garage in the Bridge of Don at the time and I befriended him and gave him a job. He, rather ironically as it later transpired, also helped the police with their 'eye in the sky' patrols and stuff like that. He became my pilot and I gave him a large sum of money to pay off his VAT bill, and for that I took a share of the helicopter. We flew the helicopter all over the country; we went testing with it, and of course, we went to motor sport events in it. But one day he failed to collect me, and as I had to get to Wales for a rally, I was forced to put my Plan 'B' into operation and rush to catch a scheduled flight.

I managed to win the event, though. I came home the next day, but there was still no sign of the helicopter although later that afternoon I received a telephone call:

'Hi, it's Paul here. I had to take the helicopter down to Kidlington Airport in Oxford, to get it serviced.'

I smelled a rat.

'Paul, look, whatever is wrong, please don't do it. Whatever it is you're doing, we can sort it out.'

It later transpired that he had (allegedly) stolen the helicopter although I had been under the impression that it was his machine, and I had a share in it by this time. It simply disappeared and I had little option but to go to my local police station in Aberdeen where I lodged a 'Lost and Found' ticket.

The policeman found it really funny:

'Sorry, what have you lost?

'A helicopter.'

'You've lost a what? You've lost a helicopter?'

It took a while to get the message through.

Some time later I received a phone call from the Metropolitan Police in London and they asked:

'Sir, we believe you have been dealing with a person called Paul Bennett and we have noticed that your name has cropped up. This gentleman is an alleged crook and there are quite a lot of people still looking for him. Can you tell us what has happened?'

I explained, and about three or four months later I took another call from 'the Met', saying that Bennett had just landed in America with 'my' helicopter. He had shipped it to the USA but then assembled it overnight and illegally flew away from inside the dock area. He was chased through Manhattan by the NYPD helicopter, which he managed to lose. It sounded as though it was like a scene from a Hollywood blockbuster.

A further call from Aberdeen City Police explained the latest US adventure by Bennett. It was alleged, that he had flown the helicopter over the Miami State Penitentiary and lifted a Columbian drug baron out on the skids. The drug boss, I believe, was killed by the guards and the aircraft was riddled with bullets, but Bennett disappeared into the Everglades, a vast, 1.5 million acre natural wetlands on the southern tip of Florida. It was presumed that he had crashed, never to be seen again.

I thought that was the last I would hear of Bennett and the helicopter......

A couple of years later I received a telephone call from Toyota South Africa. One of the guys had actually remembered that I had rallied with them a few years previously. Anyway, the caller asked me:

'Have you got a brother?'

'No.'

'Well, there's a guy here going by the name of 'David Gillanders', and he is flying a Hughes 500 helicopter. He's doing Safari runs. Is he a friend of yours?'

'No. But I know exactly who he is!'

Bennett had used my logbook which I had left in the helicopter, so I got hold of my old friend, Jim Robson and asked him to go over to South Africa and without too much difficulty he found him. I got in contact with the police and they asked:

'Well, can you get him to the UK?'

The South Africans had, by now, actually impounded the helicopter and kept it, so that was it well and truly gone, but Bennett *was* put on a flight back to the UK. All did not go well. Soon after the flight had taken off, he jumped up from his seat and started to shout:

'I'm being kidnapped!'

The pilot returned the aircraft to Johannesburg.

Eventually, the authorities put Bennett onto a second flight to London, and there he was locked up. Amazingly, though, he got off on a technicality under English Law. The intent was to have him subsequently tried under Scots Law – which is different from that in England – but before a transfer could be made, Bennett made an excuse to use the toilet, 'did a runner', and disappeared.

About ten years later I heard from the police again:

'You're not going to believe this, but the film star, Russell Crowe, has just had his helicopter stolen in Australia, allegedly by Paul Bennett.'

Over a decade later a New Zealand website carried a story that on Tuesday, February 17, 2015, Bennett and his partner had been caught and arrested in Sydney Harbour, Australia. He made an appearance in court and entered a 'not guilty' plea to a charge of receiving stolen goods. The pair had been on the run for years, Bennett, in particular, from allegations of fraud, theft, a suspected shooting (causing fatal injuries), arson, embezzlement, and also sexual assault.

The same website also claimed that they had stolen a $145,000 ocean-going yacht from the Bay of Islands in New Zealand, but following some inclement weather, they were forced to limp into Sydney with a broken mast. The website mentioned that there was an outstanding warrant for Bennett's arrest dating back to 2003.

Allegedly, the crucial breakthrough for the police came from a teenage sailing enthusiast who had spotted the yacht at anchor in rough water. The teenager thought that this was very unusual because nobody, normally, would drop anchor at that point. Then he realised that it could be the yacht he'd seen advertised as stolen on '*www.livesaildie.com*' and so he contacted the website personnel who verified that it *was* the missing yacht. It was a relief to the multiple government agencies who had long been in search of the fugitives.

There was a further allegation that Bennett had stolen a $250,000 helicopter from a New Zealand helicopter firm, the director of which had earlier offered a reward of $50,000 for information leading to an arrest. You can imagine that the same director was *"thrilled to pieces"* when he heard that Bennett had been arrested.

Bennett, or whatever his real name was, operated under numerous aliases, and is alleged to have defrauded many people, businesses and organisations of something in the region of $6 million.

There's no doubt about it, the six million dollar man could really fly, and he proved that several times. One such incident happened when Aberdeen's BMW Garage Owner, John Clark, oilman, Klaas Zwart, and myself, got Bennett to fly us to Silverstone for the Grand Prix weekend one year. The three of us were due to race in some of the supporting events.

Unknown to us prior to take-off, there was a problem with the R/T. In other words, the radio telephone didn't work! This meant that we could not communicate with Air Traffic Control. The three of us were a bit puzzled as to why Bennett had been flying at a very low level, but apparently his intention was to fly below the radar, and thus avoid detection.

When I think about it, if this had happened in today's political climate, we could have been shot down as terrorists! We hedge-hopped all the way to the circuit in North-amptonshire and upon arrival, Bennett located the helipad, right in the middle of the complex. He put it down on top of the 'H', slap bang in the middle.

However, the minute we landed we were surrounded by four security cars, and as soon as we climbed out of the aircraft we were taken and separated from each other. John Clark was put in one car, Klaas Zwart in another, Bennett in yet another, and I was placed in the final car. We were all whisked away for interrogation and were each asked independently:

'Do you understand why we have brought you here?'

'Is it because we haven't been able to communicate with Air Traffic Control?'

'Not entirely, although that does have a bearing on the matter. The main reason is the fact that your actions could have cancelled the Grand Prix because the helipad you have landed on is the special FIA designated pad for emergencies!'

Meanwhile, true to form, Bennett had asked to use the toilet, and he immediately ran all the way to the helicopter which he then started up and flew away! This left John, Klaas, and me to face the music. Thankfully, we were released when we managed to prove that we were only the passengers and were about to race at the circuit.

Some time later, Bennett rang me and arranged to pick us up in a field north of Silverstone, to allow us to return home, and that in itself was fine. What was not very fine, however, was the fact that we were very low on fuel. Bennett spotted a filling station on the M6 near Preston. He suggested we drop in and fill up with diesel, to which I queried:

'Diesel?'

'Yes, diesel is alright as long as I keep the engine running. We'll get a few pops and bangs after we leave, so be prepared for that.'

So we popped down and joined the queue behind the trucks, hovering only a couple of feet above the ground behind an HGV. Bennett certainly was a brilliant pilot, and to see the expression on the face of the lorry driver immediately in front of us was priceless! I could see him looking in his mirror, and his expression of disbelief was in itself a picture! Everybody in the petrol station took photographs of us, and then, when it was our turn, I jumped out and the helicopter hovered up to the pump with the blades still spinning. I filled the tank and nipped in to pay as Bennett hovered slowly out. Once clear of the petrol station we ascended and turned and headed north towards Aberdeen. Apparently, the entire incident was featured in one of the national dailies down south, but I haven't been able to track a copy to illustrate it here.

It struck me later that Bennett (or whoever he actually was) could have had the book thrown at him and his licence rescinded by the licensing authorities, the Joint Aviation Authorities (in Europe) or their enforcers, the Civil Aviation Authorities (CAA) in the UK…

If only he'd had a licence in the first place!

The saga continued, though. He managed to win a High Court action in London to block his committal for trial on fraud charges, following the release of evidence after the lifting of a Government *"Gagging Order"*.

Previously, some Public Interest Immunity certificates prevented the disclosure of information for security purposes, but, at the time of writing, he still faces the possibility of other charges pertaining to the alleged theft of *'my'* helicopter from Aberdeen as Grampian Police still has an outstanding warrant for his arrest.

Bennett claimed that he had been working for the CIA, the American Central Intelligence Agency, and had been illegally snatched from South Africa. He asserted that he had been taken against his will to the UK and the legal profession agreed that there had been *"procedural impropriety"* in the way he had actually been brought into Britain. The authorities quashed his committal for trial.

It was alleged that the South Africans had decided to deport him as an illegal immigrant via Heathrow in London, and coupled with crucial evidence, the Justices made their decision. They backed Bennett's claim that he was a victim of collusion, allegedly between the British and South African police. However, I have a feeling that this story will run and run, and run….

A bit like the man himself…..

Chapter SEVENTEEN

SCOTTISH RALLY CHAMPION

My final rally car was a truly fabulous Ford Escort RS Cosworth, and it was with this car in 1995 that I finally managed to win the Scottish Rally Championship. I bought it from Malcolm Wilson and had it professionally built by his car preparation business on the edge of the Lake District, in Cockermouth, Cumbria.

I was fortunate to receive a donation of a complete power train (the complete transmission and back axle) to use in the car. This came from Quaife Engineering of Sevenoaks in Kent and the gearbox and axle created a bit of a stir once it was installed because everybody else in rallying at the time used Ford equipment for their Fords.

The Ford Escort RS Cosworth on the daunting Rest and be Thankful stage of the 1993 Perth Scottish Rally. Dougie Redpath was my co-driver on that event.

Photograph: Sandy Topp

Keeping clear of the ditches on the Corrie special stage of the 1993 International Scottish Rally.
Photograph: Jim Sutherland.

I cannot remember exactly how and when I came across Rod and Michael Quaife, the father and son team who owned the business, but I did know that Quaife Engineering initially made gearboxes for motor bikes. One day, Rod, Michael and I and I had been conversing and I happened to mention to them:

'I'm building a Ford Escort RS Cosworth.'

To which they enquired:

'Would you use one of our sequential gearboxes?'

'Wow! A sequential gearbox? Yes. I'll try that!'

Motor Bike gearboxes, as many folk may know, are all sequential, but at the time this was very unusual in a car. Quaife, however, built this special gearbox for my Escort Cosworth and it worked really well. It was one of the first sequential boxes in a rally car, but the only downside was that it didn't have was an indicator light to identify which gear I was in and that was a wee bit of a problem. I remember one time when I had been pressing hard in the forest at over 100 mph and I suddenly wondered: *'Am I in sixth, am I in fifth, or am I in fourth?'* I simply didn't know.

The old gearboxes with the 'H' type configuration were fine because with them it was blindingly obvious, but it wasn't so crystal clear on a car with a sequential gearbox without a gear indicator light. In layman's terms the sequential box was a gearstick which I would pull back to make an up-change, or push forward to effect a down-change. And with the gearing designed for quick acceleration, I would pull back every couple of seconds until I was in top gear, all the way up to fifth, or sixth gear, and then I would simply push forward in a series of rapid movements to come down the box to the required gear.

Pressing on in the Ford Escort RS Cosworth.
Photograph: Graeme Howard.

Nowadays, the sequential gearboxes have numbered indicators, like '1', '2', '3', '4', '5', and '6', but I didn't even have an orange light for 'neutral' which would have been handy. Even more modern is the paddle shift where the left flap (located just under the steering wheel by the indicator stalk) is used for down-changes and the right flap (located just under the steering wheel by the wiper stalk) for up-changes.

I really enjoyed that car and I got on very well with it, but in the heat of battle, on a very long stage after maybe 20 or 25 kilometres, I would forget where I was in the gearbox, as I would have been going up and down the gearbox faster than the stock market in the middle of a recession!

In hindsight, it would have been nice to have had an indicator much earlier, but eventually Quaife did install one on the dashboard, but remember, this was early on in the product development, and they still didn't have the 'number' of the relevant gear illuminated. Coming down the box, I still had that thought: *'Whoa! Is there another gear to go?'*

If I selected first gear instead of third, the thing would stand on its nose and the engine would scream, *'enough!'* I must have hit first many times, but overall it was great.

Photograph:
Graeme Howard.

The Weldex Rally in 1993.
Photograph: Brian Riddell.

It was Malcolm Wilson Motorsport who built my car because Malcolm hadn't actually started trading as M-Sport in 1994. He was working out of the garage in his house and I still remember going to see him and driving the car for the first time. In addition to getting a new sequential box, I also got a new co-driver in John Bennie. I'll let John explain how our partnership came about:

'Late in 1993, I heard a rumour that David was on the lookout for a co-driver for the 1994 season, so I contacted Scottish motor sport journalist, John Fife, who runs the website, "www.jaggybunnet.co.uk". As the voice behind the Scottish Rally Championship, John put me in touch with David and he and I agreed to do the Snowman Rally. I arrived in Inverness to find what I considered to be an extremely professional set-up, which, of course, Malcolm himself had organised.

'Malcolm was there, along with two of his mechanics, John Steele and Geoff (Jolly) Roberts, but while the boss let John and "Jolly" get on with the technical stuff, he was also there to oversee and evaluate my abilities as a co-driver, and so he stuck a camera in the car to allow him to analyse my performance later.

'So, no pressure then!

'We had a competitive outing and lay 2nd overall, right up to the last stage. However, on that last section, the cross-member broke and we limped out of the forest to get some emergency service by the roadside.

'At that point, John and "Jolly" got to work on the car, with "Jolly" definitely in the not-so-jolly position of lying in an ice-cold burn in February, deep in the middle of winter in the Highlands of Scotland! The consummate professional that "Jolly" was cemented all of my thoughts on the immense knowledge, abilities, and enthusiasm that Malcolm Wilson's Motorsport organisation brought to the scene.'

It had been my intention to contest both the British National and the Scottish Rally Championships, and John and I went from the furthest north location in the UK (with the Snowman Rally) to the furthest south location in the UK (for the Winter Rally) in Bournemouth, which we won. It was John's second event with me and we just clicked on that rally. Everything went perfectly.

I'll let John pick up on that perfect event:

'We had been in the top four or five all day long, and fellow Scot, Raymond Munro, was in the lead. We were only around 11 seconds behind him, with one stage to go, but there gasps of disbelief when it was found that David had taken 14 seconds off Raymond on the last stage, to win the rally by a slender three seconds. Neither Raymond, nor Neale Dougan, another Scottish driver, could believe it! They just couldn't understand where David had got that turn of speed from.

On the 1994 Valentine Rally. Photograph: Graeme Howard.

'The downside was that after I got home to Glasgow, I felt really unwell, and on the Monday I had to visit the doctor who diagnosed chickenpox! You can imagine David's comments when, one week later, I appeared in Stirling for the Scotphone Stages. He wasn't pleased:
'You spotty bugger, you!'

On the Valentine Rally in 1994.

Photograph: Graeme Howard.

Look closely at the front nearside wheel. Only the wheel rim remains after the tyre had been ripped off during the Glenurquhart Stage of the Snowman Rally. It still didn't stop us! Photograph: Jim Sutherland.

'We had a few indiscretions that year but took 2nd place overall on the Granite City Rally. In hindsight, we should have won it. At scrutineering, everything checked out alright on the Friday night, but early on the Saturday morning, I noticed a strange light coming from behind the curtains. When I looked out I saw that about a foot of snow had fallen on the City of Aberdeen and its surrounding hinterland. Malcolm's support team had only one set of winter tyres that we could use, but that was an advantage as most of the other crews had none.

'Erroneously, we decided to hold them in reserve until the notorious Clashindarroch Forest. With regular forest tyres we had some interesting 'moments', one of which was in the Bin Forest, near Huntly, when the rear end of the Escort slipped into a ditch, and then the front followed suit. David, though, just kept the foot down and the acting snowplough eventually popped out of the ditch and back onto the road. Our snow tyres would have been extremely useful there, but we had been keeping them in reserve for Clashindarroch, hadn't we?

241

'The problem was that the organisers had decided that the "Clash" stage could not be run because of the heavy snow and so our master plan failed miserably. Chris Mellors, our main competitor in the National Series, won instead. Mellors, in fact, had a great season, and we arrived at the last event of the national series, the Artemis Equipment Stages in North Yorkshire, close to Chesterfield, and pretty much, in Chris' back yard, so to speak.

On the Snowman Rally.   Photograph: Jim Sutherland.

Below: On the Daviot Stage of the Snowman Rally.
Photograph: Jim Sutherland.

'Basically, it was down to this last event (it usually was down to the wire with David) and the title would go to whoever won on the day. The banter at the start of Langdale, the last stage, between Chris, his co-driver Brian Goff, and David and me was very intense. It was psychological warfare, but it was Chris, with his more intimate knowledge of the stage, who won the rally, and with it, the British title.

'David actually encouraged me to offer my co-driving services to some of the other drivers associated with Malcolm Wilson's car preparation team and I partnered Brian Lyall as a result. Because I partnered Brian on the Snowman Rally, David employed Bob Wilson to co-drive for him in 1995, but as I had won the Winter (Sunseeker) Rally with David in 1994, he invited me to sit alongside him again, and we won that event for the second time.

'That win effectively sealed our partnership although he had Bob with him again on the Valentine Rally.'

With Bob Wilson on the wintry Snowman Rally, in 1995.

I'll let Bob expand on that:

'Early in 1995, David asked if I would co-drive for him again, so we duly entered, and won, the Snowman Rally for a second time. We then competed in another event in the Scottish Championship, the Valentine Rally, but that resulted in retirement with engine failure in Strathyre, a forest near

243

Callander, where we ended up attached to a tow rope. That was the last time I competed with David.'

Bob continued:

'David can be a very abrasive character, and lots of people find him difficult to get on with, but nevertheless, I would like to say "thank you" here and now to him for giving me the opportunity to compete with a quality driver in quite stunning rally cars. We had a few wins together and I'll always remember that, but other than that we are not friends and don't keep in touch.'

Bob was a good co-driver and his knowledge and skills in reading the notes were excellent, but for the Granite City Rally in 1995 I acquired the services of Bryan Thomas (Mark Higgins' regular co-driver) before John Bennie and I got back together for the Weldex Rally, which we won.

Then Steve Harris co-drove for me on the Trackrod Rally and for the final event of the year, I had the Welsh Wizard, Howard Davies, in the hot seat for one last time, with none better to speak about it than Howard himself:

'Ah, well, for some reason David asked me to co-drive again even though he'd had a few others in the hot seat – John Bennie is one who springs to mind. But I was asked (probably by Malcolm) to help David to try and win the ANCRA Championship at the last event, the 1995 Bulldog Rally. We actually finished 2ⁿᵈ to Chris Mellors, but David had to win to stand any chance of taking the championship.

Pushing hard on the 1995 Bulldog Rally.

Photograph: Speedsports (Ruthin).

'What ruined David's chances was a puncture which we picked up in Dyfi (or some other Welsh wood), and we lost a

244

fair bit of time, so it was basically 'all or nothing' when we went through the last stage, Tarenig. I vaguely remember going through there at very, very weird angles where we had some very big 'moments', but it wasn't to be, and we finished behind Mellors.

'David, from the previous time that I had co-driven for him, had progressed to the aforementioned Ford Escort RS Cosworth, and this sported a very big, long gearlever which looked something like the handlebars off a motor bike. He told me it was a sequential gearbox, and when he changed gear it travelled about a foot and resembled the pulling of a one-arm bandit machine in an fun arcade!

'David confirmed that it was the very first sequential box made by Quaife, I remember that. He was the first to have the innovation, so it was quite interesting to see its development. I also recall that the car was a lot softer and much easier to drive than the Sierra when I last partnered him on a rally. He'd obviously developed it with Malcolm Wilson and worked very hard on that.'

It was a crazy year, but at least with John Bennie, we had a relationship that would provide a dividend for me and a stepping stone for him; I'll let John explain further:

'We stayed as a partnership for the remainder of the year. All in all it was a successful season and we secured maximum points on the Scottish Rally, then picked up a handful of national championship points on the Isle of Man event, and were 3rd on the Kerridge Rally. But, on the Jim Clark Memorial Rally which was held in the forests that year, we drifted too wide on a square left (90 degree corner) and dropped into a deep ditch in Keilder. Unfortunately, we found that it was a very deep ditch from which there was no immediate escape. It would go down to the wire (yet again) to determine just who would win the championship!

'Chris Wagner, the quick Quattro driver from Thornton-hall in South Lanarkshire, just had to finish in a half decent position on the last event of the 1995 rally season, the Weir Stages in Dumfries, to win the Scottish title. It was a straight fight between Chris, John Baird, and David, but I think the pressure got to Chris and he dropped a minute on the first

special stage. Rather than calmly claw back the time, he took the 'maximum attack' route, and this led to him visiting the vegetation, from which even the renowned four wheel drive traction of the Audi failed to extricate him. He retired, right there and then.

'Following Wagner's retirement, it was 'game on' so we had it all to play for. I suggested to John Steele and "Jolly" to leave out the spare wheel and go for lightness because every second would count. David and I managed to get into 3rd place overall and this was just enough for him to finally secure his first Scottish Rally Championship title after 25 years of effort.

'I have had a habit of helping drivers to win titles, but my patience was rewarded when I won the co-driver's title in 1997 with Brian Lyall. I would actually go on to win two more National Championships, both with Marcus Dodds, in 2000 and 2001.

'David was over the moon in 1995 though. He was delighted to capture the title he'd long aspired to win. People who have never chased a championship before might not understand the effort and concentration needed to reach – and maintain – such a high level of personal commitment over an entire season. It really is incredibly hard.'

John is spot-on with his statement about commitment, but in addition to having a good co-driver it was essential to have a top quality car and Malcolm Wilson Motorsport certainly provided me with one in my Ford Escort RS Cosworth. It was an extremely well built car, and Malcolm used the engine from a Ford Sierra Cosworth. It was painted in bright red and yellow colours and was so beautiful that I didn't want to take it into the forests. That gave me a flashback to the days of my Mini Cooper S, when, on my first special stage event, the Granite City Rally, I actually slowed down on the straights as I didn't want to mark the bodywork with flying gravel, stones, and rocks.

Pop, Bang, Whiz!

I called the Escort my 'pop, bang, whiz' car. It had anti-lag, and it was fantastic because I'd not had anti-lag before (remember the Volvo which I had to spool up, about one and a half seconds before each corner?). I'll let John explain how I was introduced to this:

'We were lazing about in the lounge of the hotel that was hosting the rally headquarters of the Kayel Graphics Rally in South Wales, when one of Malcolm's mechanics brought the car down to the entrance just before 7 o'clock in the morning and said to David:

'Oh, David, we've got a new switch in the car.'

'For God's sake......'

*'David, you'll **have** to learn how to use it otherwise you'll get one hell of a scare in the middle of the stages.'*

The mechanic continued:

'When you get to the start line for the first time, and receive the countdown, you need to flick this switch on. I'll show you: I'll take the revs up to 7,000 rpm and this is what will happen whenever you take your foot off the loud pedal (which the mechanic did). It will go, (and it did go):

'BANG! BANG! BANG!'

'And all hell broke loose.... A lot of the car alarms had gone off in the car park.'

'Everybody was asking:

'What the hell's happened? What's going on?'

'It was hilarious.'

I helped Malcolm with a few of his development ideas and this was one of them; what this engine did was throw fuel into the turbocharger. It meant that there was no turbo lag, but of course on the overrun, it created a tremendous report:

'BANG!'

I used to play with it all the time in the forest because I enjoyed making it pop and bang:

'Oh, I loved it.'

I drove it flat out until I lifted off momentarily, and then put the foot back down, again:

'BANG!'

I loved it, but I blew out the exhaust so many times that people kept asking:

'Why's your car so noisy?'

I never told them I was playing:

'BANG! BANG! BANG!'

Of course, cars don't do that nowadays because the manufacturers have long since moved on. They all have anti-lag, just like the modern Ford Fiesta that Malcolm Wilson's current business, 'M-Sport', developed for the World Rally Championship, but back in 1995, my 'pop, bang, whiz' Escort sounded absolutely wonderful.

As John alluded to, the entire 1995 season was a tight affair between Chris Wagner in his Audi Quattro, John Baird in his Nissan 240RS, and me in my Cosworth. I had Bob Wilson for two events, but for most of the year, John Bennie was in the 'hot seat'. Although I won the driver's title on the tie-break from John Baird, it was his co-driver, Martin Forrest from Aberdeen, who won the co-driver's title that year. The record book definitely shows that a pair of Aberdonians won the Scottish Rally Championship in 1995. Aberdonians, we certainly were, but we had competed in two different cars!

It would be easy to put two and two together, but on this occasion the two plus two equation would equal five, because Martin never co-drove for me. It was just pure coincidence that he secured the title of Scottish Rally Champion Co-Driver at the same time that I won the drivers' title.

Having co-driven for both Brian Lyall and myself, John wanted to compare us as drivers and as individuals.

I had to laugh.....

John said:

'I have been privileged to have been part of two winning teams, with David initially, and then with Brian Lyall. Both are similar individuals, both are loud and brash, and both were excellent drivers, although I'd say that David was the more natural whereas Brian learned his craft. David spent the majority of his career with map men and driving on sight whereas Brian based much of his success through the use of pacenotes, or safety notes.

'David is also misunderstood; from the outside he is loud and brash, but he's really quite a shy person. In my opinion, the gruff exterior is there to protect himself. To really get to know another person, you have to spend a lot of time with that individual, and I really got to know David because I had a lot of one-to-one time with him in his rally car. He is fun to be with when he relaxes in close company.

'I will be forever grateful to him for giving me a stepping stone in the sport, going from being a clubman, and maturing into a semi-professional co-driver. It let me earn a living from the sport for a decade. I enjoyed my time with him and the doors that he opened for me, so I was really delighted that he finally achieved his ambition of becoming the Scottish Rally Champion.'

Yes, I really was over the moon given that after 25 years of trying I had finally managed to win the Scottish Rally Championship.

The 1995 Scottish Rally Champion.
Photograph: Speedsports (Ruthin).

I had been very close to winning it eight years earlier (in 1987) but as has been mentioned, Murray Grierson protested me on the Trossachs Rally; I had gone close again in 1988, until I went off on the Trossachs Rally – it *had* to be the Trossachs, didn't it? I virtually handed the title to Colin

249

McRae that year, so it was very fitting, and a great honour that he, as the newly crowned 1995 World Rally Champion (and the youngest winner in the history of the series) presented me with the Scottish Rally Championship Trophy.

I was honoured when Colin McRae handed me the trophy, because I virtually 'handed it' to him in 1988! Photo: Courtesy of the Scottish Rally Championship.

Colin had something special that made me want to be just like him; he had a carefree attitude which I admired. I remember, one year, he and I were at Goodwood with Ford, and everybody there, and especially those of us in the sport, knew that he was world class, but none of us actually realised at the time just what sort of impact he'd have on the sport.

In between runs, Colin and I decided to nip out of the paddock and go for what we thought would be a relaxing walk. We had been chatting away to each other, but after a few minutes I happened to look behind and was amazed to see about 50 or 60 people trailing us, well him, really, so I asked:

'What's that all about, Colin?'

'I don't know, but they're always there...'

'What do you mean, they're always there?'

'Well, they want my autograph.'

I looked back every now and again and the crowd had increased to hundreds.

Even when Colin was the World Champion, back at home in Scotland he could still be found at local events; he would end up 'mucking around' with everybody else because he wasn't an aloof, super-character. He was just like us, only much, much faster!

He was unique.

Favourites

The modern national one-day rallies comprise a mere 40 to 45 miles of forest stages, but I'm an old-school rally driver, and therefore biased in favour of 90 plus miles of forest tracks over the likes of some famous special stages, like Culbin, Devilla, Fetteresso, Kirkhill and Tentsmuir, that can no longer used for one reason or another. I consider them 'classics' in their own right, and as I have rallied a fair bit I do know a lot about them. It's a great pity that they cannot be reinstated.

I believe that the Scottish Rally Championship has hosted, and still hosts, some of the best stages in the world. They are perfect for testing the speed and skill of the drivers, and when winter comes in and there's snow and ice, this further enhances their abilities, so I would definitely, and quite categorically, state that the Scottish Rally Championship made me the kind of driver I was.

I admire and look up to Ari Vatanen, the Flying Finn who won the 1981 World Rally Championship. Ari first visited the British Isles by taking his Opel Ascona SR into the lead of the International Scottish Rally in 1975, despite damaging every single panel on his car, such was his commitment and speed.

Ari certainly made a big impression on me and many others, and definitely the landscape on more than one occasion, but he almost died in a huge accident in Argentina in 1985, when his car, a Works Peugeot 205 Turbo 16, somersaulted at over 120 miles per hour. He was airlifted to hospital where he took almost 18 months to recover from his life-threatening injuries. He eventually recovered and went on to become an elected member of the European Parliament and served therein for ten years.

'Can you imagine me becoming an MP?'

'No, I didn't think so!'

Ari's WRC winning co-driver, Dave Richards, went on to found Prodrive, and in 2005 was honoured by being made a Commander of the British Empire (CBE) for services to motor sport. However, in the late 1980s I persuaded him to build a Group 'N' Subaru Legacy for me to drive on the International Scottish Rally. That was the event that I got John Davenport to partner me, and from that single request to Richards, I believe Prodrive went on to sell more Group 'N' Subaru rally cars than the more powerful Group 'A' versions.

I admire Walter Rohrl, the 1980 and 1982 World Rally Champion, mainly because the German could drive an Audi Quattro like nobody else, although it was the legendary Hannu Mikkola who turned the Bavarian manufacturer's revolutionary four-wheel drive concept into a proper rally car. And, of course, I really looked up to Roger Clark. He changed the face of British Rallying with his then unique sideways style of driving. Vatanen, Rohrl, Mikkola and Clark drove on 'blind' events, without pacenotes, so I'd say that these four, and numerous other drivers from that era, gave me something to aim for.

I like special stage rallying because it is one of the few sports where ordinary clubmen can compete against the best, the world champions of the sport. They might not have the same car, the same budget, the same skill set, but nonetheless they compete on the same event.

My favourite rally car has to be my Volvo 240 Turbo, although easily the best car would be my MG Metro 6R4. That really was something else! My Volvo, though, was the car that got me the route into the Metro 6R4; without my 240T I would not have had the four wheel drive car. It's as simple as that.

I was once asked what my favourite motor sport discipline was, given that I have competed in Autotests, Autocrosses, Sprints, Hill Climbs, Road Rallies, Races and Special Stage Rallies. The interviewer thought that this was rather a silly question, given my history and involvement in rallying, but I responded:

'That's not such a stupid question.'

Obviously, I have a bent towards rallying, and I think there is something very special about both the driver and co-driver combining to fight against the elements because they do not actually immediately see who they are up against. In some of the other branches of motor sport there is somebody racing front and rear, and often at the side, so you know what and who you are trying to beat. In rallying, it's the crew against the clock, and an ability to have the mental capacity to retain the time in your head and know if you've got five seconds here, or five seconds there. You cannot visually compare yourself against the opposition unless you catch up with somebody who has maybe had a problem, or just been off, or is dreadfully slow.

You can see the oppositions' times, but you wouldn't know if they were struggling, or if they'd had a puncture. I have a penchant for rallying, but if someone asked me to look at motor sport overall, then I'd have to say that I really like the superbikes, and the Isle of Man TT in particular. It's scary as hell, but these guys are the real gladiators.

A Sponsor's Dream

I believe I was a sponsor's dream. You're laughing; I can almost hear it, even from these pages! But I really thought I was better out of the car than in it most of the time. I understood branding, and still do. I understood how to speak to sponsors, and still do, and how best to speak with customers, and still do – remember, I was a car salesman. So how do I reach my conclusion?

For example: if I'd stopped for a service halt in the middle of a rally, and happened to be sponsored by Shell, Dunlop, English of Bournemouth, Ford, or British Car Rental, and Gartrac, then invariably the sponsors would, at some time or other, bring along their customers to see the action and savour the atmosphere.

I then had to remember that I was sponsored, not only to drive the car, but to talk to people, *(I'm good at talking...)* so in a rally I might have had a 20 minute break or an hour's stop at a lunch halt and at that point I'd notice a busload of people arrive. The passengers, in the main, would have no idea of the strain I might have been under at that point in time. I could have been leading the event, or I might have had a gearbox, engine, or a suspension problem, or I might have been driving a car with a fault which I knew could eventually enforce my retirement from the rally. I might even have had an oil leak from the differential, an engine that was low on oil pressure, or perhaps a radiator problem. My brain would constantly worry about what's coming next...

I'd be there to compete, but as far as a sponsor was concerned, I had to be good with them and their guests. Generally, I was good for sponsors. They liked me and I liked them.

I think the Scottish and British Rally Championships are both very tough to win. In my day there wasn't just one Metro in Scotland; there were at least a handful. Ken Wood had one, Andy Horne had another, and so too had Murray Grierson, and Jimmy Christie, plus myself. There were the English Metros in the British series too, so it wasn't as though I had the only four wheel drive car. Donald Heggie had ended his association with Ford and moved into an Audi Quattro, so the competition was pretty intense and it was far from a foregone conclusion that I would win any of the individual events, far less the overall championship.

In '87, there were up to 25 drivers who were capable of winning the title at the beginning of the season, but nowadays there's only two, or maybe three. The events back then comprised around 100 miles of special stages so there was a greater chance to break down or go off. The Metro was unreliable, but it was quick, and while it was fun to drive it had its problems, notably the gearbox, cambelt, and fuel rail issues, as well as front differential maladies. It certainly wasn't bomb-proof from a reliability perspective.

A modern rally car, like the M-Sport WRC Fiesta of today *is* bomb-proof, I kid you not. I have driven both the Works Focus and Fiesta rally cars and found them to be extremely tough machines. You would not believe how tough they are. You simply would not believe it!

Professional Aggression

In the days of the MG Metro 6R4, and the year I won the Granite City Rally, it cost in the region of £10,000 per event, but Gartrac had managed to accrue all of the necessary funding from sponsorship. The great thing was that when I did the British Championship, the car was returned to Gartrac after each event for a rebuild, before they brought it to the next rally. This basically meant that I drove a 'new' car on each and every event. All I did was get my overalls, helmet and gloves.

It was a tough life, but somebody had to do it!

Life was sweet: I was a professional in every sense other than being paid to do it. I didn't get any monetary benefits, but I was a professional in the sense that my car was completely and professionally maintained before each and every event, as well as during the competition. I'd still be somewhat scared, though, to put an actual figure on the money I've personally spent on motor sport.

Occasionally I'd get angry behind the wheel if, for example, I was being held up after catching somebody in a stage (like I did with Russell Brookes), and especially so if the driver didn't move over (like Russell Brookes). Let's say I could get a little bit agitated. I've had words with other drivers at the end of a stage but I never physically fought with any of them. There were a few occasions where I wanted to rip somebody out of a car, but I never lost my temper.

Chapter EIGHTEEN

LAND ROVER: THE BEST 4X4XFAR

I needed something to occupy myself after I finished competing at the end of the 1995 season. I had also sold Gillanders Motors in November that year and hadn't a clue what to do, so Gladys and I took a few days off to recharge the batteries.

We decided to spend some time at Skibo Castle. Although the beginnings of the castle date back to 1211, the bulk of the castle is from the 19th century. At that time, it was the home of the Dunfermline-born industrialist and philanthropist, Andrew Carnegie, but it currently operates as the Carnegie Club, a members-only hotel and country club with beautiful views overlooking the Dornoch Firth, north of Inverness.

In 1982, Skibo Castle was sold by the Carnegie family to Peter de Savary, an English Multi-Millionaire and entrepreneur.

I went to the castle many times, but on one particular occasion I thought to myself:

'It's so beautiful here. It's a fabulous place and out of this world, with the golf and the spa, as well as fine dining, but there's got to be other things to do as well?'

So I made a suggestion to Peter de Savary:

'Why don't we do an off-road course?'

'What's that?'

'It's the tuition of off-road driving skills in suitable 4x4 vehicles, like Land Rovers, on the lovely terrain around the castle.'

Anyway, me being me, I picked up the telephone and gave Land Rover a call:

'Hello, this is David Gillanders speaking.'

This introduction obviously meant damn all to the person on the other end of the line.

'Who?'

'David Gillanders. I would like to run some Land Rovers at Skibo Castle.'

The answer from the individual at Land Rover was as forthright as it was negative:

'Well, we don't know who you are; we don't know what Skibo is; and so you've no chance! Not a chance!'

It sounded final, but *'Not a chance'* rankled with me so I went back to Peter de Savary and he said:

'Well, that's the end of that.'

With Peter de Savary outside Skibo Castle.
Photograph: Courtesy of Peter de Savary.

BMW had just taken over Land Rover, and at the time, the Germans had a very able employee by the name of Wolfgang Reitzle. He was destined to become head of Ford's Premier Automotive Group, and thus oversee their Jaguar, Volvo, and Land Rover marques and it was pure coincidence that Herr

Reitzle arrived at Skibo Castle on one of the days that I happened to be there. Pure luck.

At first, I had no idea who this pleasant German was because he had been sitting on his own over breakfast, but after some pleasantries we soon started talking about cars, and I found out who he was, and his position within BMW, so I said to him:

'You know, it's a pity that your company won't allow me to run Land Rovers up here to do off-road driving.'

'Why won't they do it?'

'I've no idea. I made a phone call and ...'

'Who would do it?'

'Well, I would do it.'

'But you're a rally driver!'

'Yes, but I'm sure I could make it work.'

That was the start. He went back to Land Rover and within two weeks there was a visitation of Off-Road Land Rover people in the grounds of Skibo Castle. They drove up north (on the roads) in their Defenders and then drove round the whole estate (off the roads). I showed them roughly where all the tracks would be located, to which one of the representatives responded:

'Yes, well, it certainly has possibilities, but you can't be a Land Rover instructor – you drive too fast! You're a rally driver!'

*'I **used** to be a rally driver.'*

'You could never be an off-road instructor.'

'Try me!'

I challenged them.

'Try me!'

They took me to stunning Eastnor Castle, nestling in the Malvern Hills in Herefordshire, and there they put me through my paces. They *really* put me through my paces there because they wanted me to fail. I *know* they wanted me to fail, but I passed and became an off-road instructor in a Land Rover Defender, driving at five miles per hour instead of the 105 miles per hour through the forests as in my previous life.

I enjoyed it, and it became part of my life because it was a complete change. I got some Land Rovers taken up north and started doing some driving round Skibo Castle with both the Defender and Discovery models.

Then I started the business as 'The David Gillanders Driving Academy with Land Rover.' It went on for many years and the roads became better, trenches were dug deeper, and burns and rivers were traversed. The almost vertical drops were conquered and it became a truly spectacular experience in a spectacular setting.

Riding along on the crest of a wave.... tackling a burn on the Skibo Castle estate.   Photograph: Gladys Gillanders.

Gladys, who's long been interested in photography, became the unofficial off-road photographer at Skibo Castle, but first of all I taught her to drive a Land Rover Defender. Then I asked her to go forward onto the off-road course to stop at certain locations en route that were good for photographs. As the guests came by we would tell them that we had an official photographer placed at specific locations. She took photographs of everybody, and that included a number of celebrities too.

With Dawn French and friends at Skibo.

Photograph: Gladys Gillanders.

I was at Skibo Castle for all of nine years and built up quite a relationship with the folk there, in much the same way I got on with the people at Land Rover. I worked on a few things for them, especially when JLR commenced preparations to launch their new model Range Rover. The 'P38A' was the old one (so named after the office building in which the Development Team was based), but this was the new model in the year 2000.

I happened to be with Land Rover one day and out of curiosity I asked one of the company representatives:

'Where's the launch going to be held?'

'Italy, or somewhere sunny like Spain.'

'How good is this car?'

'Oh, it's outstanding!'

'And its off-road ability?'

'Off the charts!'

'So why launch it in Italy or Spain? Why not launch it in Scotland in the middle of winter?'

'You know something, that's not a bad idea.'

Accordingly, I went back to Peter de Savary and said:

'Listen, Land Rover is thinking of taking over Skibo Castle in 2000, for three or four months. Would that be acceptable?'

'Yes, we'll do that.'

We prepared all of the routes in time for Land Rover, who came north early in the year 2000. No Millennium Bug was going to stop this, and so the Press Launch for the new Range Rover was held at Skibo Castle. We had what felt like 600

Jeremy Clarksons over a period of nine weeks – plus, of course, Jeremy himself. It was fabulous; the launch ran like clockwork after the Press Pack arrived at RAF Kinloss, the military airbase near Forres, where the Nimrod reconnaissance aircraft were then based.

The media touched down in a private jet and, drawing upon my experience from my Volvo trip to Altafjord, I arranged for the Press Corps to be met by a cordon of armed security personnel and police dogs. If you have reached this far in my book then you'll know exactly what's coming…. Well, they were duly 'arrested' just as they disembarked, and bluntly asked:

'Why have you landed here? This is an active military base. You should have landed at Inverness. You can't land here, so get into the back of these vehicles!'

The Press were 'persuaded' to climb into the back of a number of Land Rover Defenders and then they were driven off in convoy. It was like a relic from the past as they headed towards one of the original arched blister wartime hangers, the type of hangar that was covered with earth and grass to camouflage it from the air. The journalists were herded from the Land Rovers and motioned to enter the rather dilapidated building with its rickety and rusty front door. It creaked loudly as it slowly opened. Nobody spoke….

The media were aghast when they discovered that behind this facade was a lovely rosewood reception area. Land Rover had turned it into a six-star facility! It was here that the Master of Ceremonies gave his presentation, and after this, the showroom doors sprung open to reveal ten, brand new Range Rovers, each sitting at an angle, with an instructor alongside every one.

Ten journalists were actively encouraged to get into the cars and take them out the back door. They were instructed to turn immediately to the right, and drive *over* the hangar! I got them to do this because there was a new Land Rover innovation called 'Hill Descent Control' and this was a great test for it. In fact, it was the perfect test.

The Press then spent a day and a half driving over some of the most beautiful parts of Scotland, right up to Skibo Castle itself, going through various rivers, ditches, and over tracks en route. It was absolutely fabulous and a total success, or was, until we got about three quarters through the launch when I was called over by the Land Rover boss, who said to me:

'David, we've got a problem.'

The problem was Jeremy Clarkson, and this was because somebody at Land Rover had actually loaned him a car prior to the Launch and he'd gone shooting with it. Unfortunately, he had managed to get himself stuck in a field and he'd to get a Toyota Land Cruiser to tow him out. Land Rover's main concern was that this was going to be Clarkson's story of the launch of the new Range Rover. I knew Jeremy, so I was given the task of looking after him for the day. I went over to him and we jumped into the car, but then he said to me:

'I don't want to do any of the scheduled route. I want to go straight to Skibo, and I'll do my story there because I know what I'm going to write about.'

I thought to myself, *'Oh, bother!'*

Anyway, Jeremy and I drove along the main road and when we reached roughly the halfway point between Inverness and Skibo Castle, he stopped the car, turned round and said to me:

'See that field over there? We'll drive in there.'

He let me take the wheel but I knew exactly what his intentions were. We opened the gate and drove in. This was not a field that Land Rover had hired and therefore we were not supposed to go into it, but we were there, and well, who was I to argue?

Very conscious of what Clarkson's cunning plan was, I made sure that I prepared the car properly by disconnecting the normal drives and putting it in 'low', and with all of the preparations done, and suitably organised, I simply drove in and went right up to the top of the field and stopped; then I drove back out, and said to him:

'Where do you want to go next?'

'Is this a special car?'

'No.'

'Can I drive it?'

'Sure.'

So he drove it back in and went up to the top of the field, where he turned around and then came back out again. Then he asked me:

'Why did I not get stuck in there?'

'Remember, you have to first make sure that you disconnect this, and disconnect that before you drive off-road.'

I gave him specific details of the actions required to go off-road, to which he replied:

'Nobody told me about this!'

'You cannot just drive off-road straight away; you have to make a few adjustments first.'

Clarkson tried it again, and he went right to the top of the field and then back down again. When the next issue of the *"Sunday Times"* was published, the last paragraph of Jeremy Clarkson's report simply stated:

"New model Range Rover: undoubtedly the best off-road car in the world!"

That saved the Launch as far as I was concerned, and I suspect Land Rover thought that too.

It might seem difficult to believe, or even accept, that I actually taught both Colin McRae and Dario Franchitti how to drive! Of course, I didn't teach either of them how to control a World Rally Car, or an Indianapolis Race Car, but what I did teach them was how to drive a Land Rover 4x4 properly because I certainly couldn't have, and certainly wouldn't have, imparted any basic driving skills to them, but when the opportunity arrived to educate them on the intricacies of off-road 4x4 (slow speed) car control, I jumped at the chance because of my huge respect for them both.

I would also like to emphasise that although they were both leaders in their fields, indeed champions, they applied their professionalism to this off-road experience and took it extremely seriously, both proving to themselves that they had excellent skills and at the same time respected my task as a Land Rover instructor.

Colin, of course, was well known to rally folk and he was indeed a household name in the UK, and all over the world for that matter, but to many folk, the name, Dario Franchitti, is almost as famous, especially in America. The Bathgate-born racer (a relative of another famous West Lothian racer in Paul Di Resta), was a three-time winner of the Indianapolis 500, and four-time winner of the IndyCar Championship in the USA, a far cry from the Central Belt town only 13 miles from Ingliston where his father first raced in Formula Ford.

Land Rovers in Action

For the longest, toughest, roughest event in the World Rally calendar, somebody in M-Sport made a suggestion prior to the Safari Rally:

'Why don't we use Freelanders as recce cars?'

The consideration was that Land Rovers were ideally suited to the Kenyan terrain, so the manufacturer decided to loan a number of them to M-Sport for Malcolm Wilson's engineers to turn them into suitably prepared recce cars. The V6 engine was retained as standard, but the brakes and suspension units *were* changed, and of course a roll cage and other motor sport safety features were added.

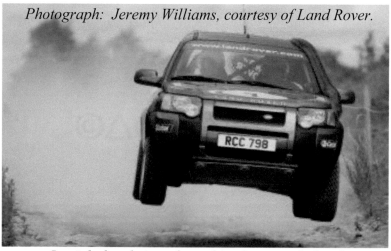

Photograph: Jeremy Williams, courtesy of Land Rover.

It might be obvious from this photograph, but I really enjoyed testing the M-Sport-built Freelander.

In addition, the seats were changed out and lower replacements installed to replicate the view through a Ford Focus instead of that of a much higher 4x4. Colin McRae had signed up with M-Sport and when he and Nicky Grist made the recce pacenotes they would have visually felt that they were driving in a Ford Focus, not a Freelander 4x4. The speed, however, was considerably slower to allow the co-driver to make the said notes.

After these particular cars completed the Safari recce it was alleged that Colin had said:

'I'd like to buy one of these cars; I tried to break the one I had but I just can't!'

The Freelanders were brilliant on the Safari recce, but afterwards they became redundant and as such lay around Dovenby Hall for a long time because neither Land Rover nor M-Sport could use them for anything else. Malcolm Wilson's team had moved over to Volvos for use as recce cars and as a former Volvo car dealer, I understood that.

I had been working with Land Rover for some time and happened to mention to the bosses there that these cars were just sitting at M-Sport doing nothing, and so we took one of them, the flying Freelander on the previous page – the one you see trying to emulate an F-15 – and gave it a facelift. They took the wings off and made it look like the latest model Freelander for marketing purposes, but underneath it was the same old indestructible Land Rover Freelander.

During one particular testing session at Land Rover's proving ground I got the feeling that this was the most capable Freelander in the world; it could take everything I could throw at it, and then some, and so I used one of the other V6 cars on the 2003 Pirelli British Rally Championship events. My job was to open each of the special stages and act as the Spectator and Safety Control vehicle following an agreement with Land Rover and M-Sport.

I had a 30-minute start on the competition cars and, to stay ahead, I needed a vehicle that had both high performance and reliability and the Freelander fitted the bill perfectly for that. For my Opening Car duties I was given a different co-driver for each event, but on top of that the car also had a seat installed in the back for a different member of the press per rally. Initially I thought that this was quite a good idea, but

then again most of the media suffered from travel sickness...
and I was sitting right in front of them!

The organisers also gave me a big speaker so that I could
talk *(I do like to talk)* to the spectators and advise them that
the rally cars would be along in 30 minutes, but I would also
ask them to move if I felt they were standing in what I
considered were dangerous locations.

The sport, and often the driver, gets the blame if a
spectator is injured if his (or her) car goes off the road, but
look carefully at this photograph below:

Some dangerous spectating on the Scottish Rally in 1970
as 'Dan' Grewer negotiates a corner in his Volvo 121.
Photograph: Jack Davidson.

Quite often a firebreak can disguise the fact that the road
could veer off to the left (or right) and should a driver arrive
at a corner far too fast (it can happen...) then he or she might
simply elect to drive up the firebreak rather than to try and
negotiate the bend. What do you think might have happened
to the two spectators standing there if 'Desperate Dan', aka
Colin 'Dan' Grewer had misread the road and headed up the
firebreak? And if the driver should try and take the bend but

end up clattering into the pile of logs, what do you think might have happened to the individual perched on the top?

Spectators *have to* take ownership of their own safety – that applies to the media, officials and competitors too. I do have sympathy for the families of the bereaved from the 2013 Snowman and 2014 Jim Clark rallies, but any person, in any capacity, going into a forest to be a part of, or simply watch a car rally, **must** be fully aware that:

Motor Sport is Dangerous!

Spectator and Safety Control in action….
Photograph: Courtesy Land Rover.

Anyway, I did every event in that championship, which started with the Pirelli International Rally in Gateshead, Tyne and Wear. This was then followed by a further six events which comprised the International Scottish Rally, the Jim Clark Memorial Rally, the Manx International Rally on the Isle of Man, the International Ulster Rally in Northern Ireland, the Trackrod Rally in Yorkshire, and also the Tempest South of England Rally.

I loved it. I know it wasn't fast but we opened up the exhaust so that the V6 sounded a lot more 'angrier' than it actually was. It wasn't ideal that it was automatic, but it was a whole lot of fun, and many people admired and loved it because they could hear the car (and me too, probably) coming for miles. They thought the rally had started! I loved every minute of it, and so did Land Rover – they thought it was a great advert.

Man of action........
Photograph: Courtesy Land Rover.

Bahrain

In 2005 I was introduced to Martin Whitaker, the former head of Ford's European Motorsport Programme. His role for the 'Blue Oval' covered both Formula One, and the World Rally Championship, and to manage the latter discipline, he outsourced the company's WRC efforts to M-Sport, owned and run by Malcolm Wilson. It could well have been his links with Malcolm that led to Martin inviting me over to Bahrain.

Bahrain is a small island country situated near the western shores of the Persian Gulf and Martin asked me over to have a look at an Off-Road Course.

He said to me:

'David, we have just built a Hummer Course, and I'd like it if you would come over and have a look at it please because I value your opinion.'

The Hummer could be described as a giant Sports Utility Vehicle, and although it was originally built for the United States Army as a High Mobility Multi-purpose Wheeled Vehicle (HMMWV), although most people might know it as a Humvee.

I flew to Bahrain, looked at the site, and said to Martin:

'You know, Martin, this is a fabulous course, but Land Rovers could handle this, all day and all night.'

'Really?'

'Y-e-e-e-s! Land Rovers are really good.'

I organised Land Rover to hold a Press Launch in Bahrain, and arranged for some new Discovery models to be flown over. The scene was amazing – the Hummer guys were there with their Humvees which had been set up with sump guards and huge off-road tyres. It made them extremely aggressive looking machines, but then I arrived with a squad of bog-standard Land Rovers and we simply drove over the course! The Humvee guys couldn't believe it; they were blown away by this demonstration.

After this we did some off-road driving in the desert and filmed there with a number of Range Rovers. We also went to Dubai, and in particular to *"Big Red"*, a giant sand dune known locally as Al Hamar. It got its 'Big Red' moniker from its height of 300 feet which is more than three times the height of the Broad Hill in Aberdeen where I first did a bit of off-road driving. It puts the sand dunes beside Donald Trump's golf course at Balmedie (to the north of the Granite City) well into perspective! The red element is because of its high iron oxide content.

'Big Red', in black and white...

The organisers had also planned a Pro-Celebrity Race, and Martin Whitaker turned to me and asked:

'David, would you like to be in it?'

'Hell, yes!'

This was prior to my triple heart bypass operation because I was totally and blissfully ignorant of my condition at that time. Martin then responded by saying:

'Ok, I'll put your name down. We'll invite Sir Steven Redgrave, the five times Olympic Rowing Champion, and the American singer songwriter and actor, John Legend, as well. And we'll get a few more folk, like Tiff Needell and Martin Brundle to come along too.'

I simply had to wait until the date of the event.

Chapter NINETEEN

BREAKFAST WITH "BARBARELLA"

I have tried to keep every chapter in strict chronological order, but it has not been easy because some of the incidents actually happened around the same time, just like this particular one and the previous chapter. This particular one was only over a couple of weeks whereas my time at Skibo Castle was over a decade, so bear with me if it sometimes feels as though I have gone back in time.

Yachts

It was July, 1997, and I'd been having a chat with Peter de Savary in Skibo Castle when the conversation got round to yachts of all sorts of shapes and sizes, and he said to me:

'Do you fancy going over to the United States to enjoy the experience of racing a yacht?'

I didn't take long to respond:

'I've never done that, and I'm not a good swimmer, but I'll certainly have a go.'

The "Northern Light"

There was a regatta off Newport, Rhode Island, and Peter was in the process of assembling a crew for a former 1970's America's Cup yacht. The one I was to sail on, was, funnily enough, called the *"Northern Light"*. I say, 'funnily enough', because *"The Northern Lights (of Old Aberdeen)"* is arguably the most famous song about my home town, the City of Aberdeen.

Anyway, I found out that the crew of the *"Northern Light"* could really drink, but because I was teetotal by this time it therefore fell to me – it was my job – to drive the team bus. I arrived at the Yacht Club, a beautiful place and a venue for seriously heavy hitters. I parked up and the crew got out but, unfortunately, I had to park the transport a distance away from the entrance and by the time I got back I found that I was on my own. I couldn't find my team anywhere because they had already eaten and simply wandered away. I hadn't had any breakfast, so I picked up a tray, joined the queue and waited until it was my turn to be served.

There was a lady just ahead of me who had started to order but she suddenly turned round and exclaimed:

'Oh dear, I've forgotten my tray.'

So ever the gentleman, I said:

'Och, join me, I've got a tray. Just order your food.'

We found a table and chatted about the sailing for a wee while, but then I noticed this guy looking at us. He was about 100 yards away and had a camera with a bloody great lens attached to it. And he was pointing it straight at us! I was dressed in my Carnegie tartan outfit, which Peter had organ-ised, and I thought I looked really, really smart, so I thought to myself:

'This outfit is very photogenic ... ...'

I looked over again, and this time there were around 50 or 60 photographers all staring, and clicking furiously away. In fact there was an army of them so I said to my breakfast companion:

'Excuse me, this is very rude, and I'd like to have my breakfast before I get my photographs taken....'

She looked at me, slightly puzzled, so I said:

'They'll just have to wait a minute, excuse me.'

I got up from the table and wandered over to where the paparazzi were and said to them:

'Guys, I know that I'm part of the team that's going to win, but please…'

However, they ignored my pleas and pushed me to one side; instead, they started to focus on my dining partner, so I sheepishly returned to the table and said:

*'Look, I'm a bit embarrassed here. I think it's **you** they're taking photographs of.'*

'Hmmm… Maybe.'

'So, who are you?'

She was really sweet about this because she knew I was absolutely clueless as to her identity. She said:

'I'm married to Ted Turner.'

The penny dropped.

'Oh, you must be Miss Fonda, Jane Fonda?'

I hadn't a clue that I had been enjoying breakfast with film star, Jane Fonda. We got on great and had a long chat after I found out who she actually was. She was really lovely.

I don't think there can be anyone on the planet who doesn't know who Jane Fonda is, although I didn't know myself to begin with, but perhaps the poster overleaf might explain. I can confirm that she starred in the 1968 spoof sci-fi film, *"Barbarella"*. It was therefore little wonder that it was she, not me, who was the magnet for the media, and there was I, unknowingly breakfasting with a Superstar, and preening myself for my adoring paparazzi at the breakfast table…..

Poster courtesy of Paramount Studios

After that we got onboard our boats. Miss Fonda went onto Ted Turner's yacht and I went onto Peter de Savary's. Our two yachts were the only vessels capable of winning the best of three races.

At that point the excitement level rapidly dropped off: these yachts were not quite in the same league as speeding rally cars, but they *were* different! Their speed *(speed?)* was about four or five miles per hour (it felt more like four or five hours per mile...) and we had to cross imaginary lines to start and finish.

Ted Turner, or to give him his full title, Mr. Robert Edward Turner III, the media mogul and philanthropist, was, at the time, the largest private landowner in the USA, and that's a *big* country!

Turner won the first race, and we won the second, so it was all down to the decider. There were a lot of boats in the regatta, but the two ocean-going yachts were much faster than the rest, so you can imagine just how slow the others were going! Turner had what is called a spinnaker on his yacht, but we didn't. A spinnaker is a large three cornered sail, usually set forward of the mainsail of a racing yacht when running before the wind, at the sharp end of the boat. Apparently, there was a gentleman's agreement that Turner's team would not deploy their spinnaker, but nearing the end of the last race, when the two yachts were neck-and-neck, around 100 yards apart, and just when the race was up for grabs, I started to think:

'Wow! Maybe we're going to win this.'

Suddenly, however, Turner deployed his spinnaker and took off like a rocket to cross the finishing 'line' and thus win the race.

We tied up, but I was furious, so I said to Peter:

'You'll have to do something about this, Peter. He's a cheeky bastard. It's all wrong.'

'Oh, David.....'

Peter's voice trailed away to nothing.

I was incensed at what I considered to be ungentlemanly conduct and Peter could see that, especially when I suggested:

'I'm going to have it out with him.'

'Well, you can if you want.....'

I waited for Turner to come off his boat, but he didn't appear, so I eventually headed back to the yacht club thinking that was that. However, I suddenly remembered that I had left my jacket on Peter's boat so I decided to nip back to the mooring to fetch it. Both yachts were moored side by side and to reach the *"Northern Light"* I had to walk over the deck of Turner's yacht. I found my jacket and was on my way back, crossing over Turner's boat again when suddenly the door opened and out stepped Robert Edward Turner III.

'Ah, Mr. Turner, how are you?'

I was ignored. Why would he want to speak to me? Nevertheless, I said:

'I was on de Peter de Savary's yacht and we'd have probably won that last race if you hadn't deployed your spinnaker.'

Still no response.

'Tell me, what was that big red thing that came out of the front of your boat? That great big balloon thing that suddenly appeared.'

Remember, I'm not a sailor, not then, not now, and probably not ever, but it did solicit a response:

'What do you know about yachting?'

'Nothing whatsoever, but I do happen to know what a gentleman's agreement is!'

'Jesus Christ!'

That certainly lit the blue touch paper, and he roared up immediately, but just then, his lovely wife appeared behind him and said:

'Oh, David, how nice to see you..... Ted, this is the gentleman I had breakfast with.'

Phew! Imagine that: me 'having a go' at Ted Turner.

How ridiculous was that?

We all went to the prize-giving at night and Peter's team each got a glass tankard award, but Turner's Team received a gold Rolex watch each. I was seriously pissed off with that.

Competitive, I am.

For those who are interested in the detail of such things, the *"Nothern Light"* was built in 1938 and is a class 12 metre yacht with a very spacious deck layout complete with a large hand crafted cockpit area made from mahogany wood; the seating was comfortable and finished off with highly polished brass fittings. It was all very impressive, and it was topped by an incredibly high spruce mast, all 91 ft of it. The interior was just as beautiful with an enclosed private area and seating for all onboard, along with a beautifully equipped galley.

It was excellent, but I wanted something much faster.

'Much faster....'

Chapter TWENTY

FLIGHT OF THE F-15

The timeframes of this particular chapter, and the last two episodes, are very much interwoven, but to tell all three as a single storyline would have been unnecessarily complex. Accordingly, I made the decision to write them as three separate chapters; one on the British icon (the Land Rover), another one on the American icon (Jane Fonda) plus a third one, this one, on how I got the fantastic opportunity to fly an F-15 jet.

My relationship with Land Rover had blossomed, and within two years of setting up the off-road courses at Skibo Castle the car manufacturer asked if I would assist them with other tasks. Of course I said, yes, and so, one day in 1997, they asked me to go to RAF Leuchars which, at the time, was an air force base located a few miles from the royal burgh of St. Andrews, in Fife.

My 'job' that day was to meet and greet a Very Important Person and his guests because, by this time, I had become the individual that Land Rover turned to if they needed someone to look after their V.I.P.s in Scotland. The primary intent of this particular V.I.P. was for him and his guests to play golf on the 'Old Course'.

I, and two of my colleagues, took three of the P38A Land Rovers, more commonly known as Range Rovers, to the RAF Base so that the entire party could be transported as they desired. I had all three vehicles lined up when a private Lear Jet landed. The party disembarked, led by an American by the name of Jerry Weintraub. He was a Hollywood film producer but I later found out that he had been the Chairman and Chief Executive Officer of United Artists for a time. He was initially a talent agent and it was he who spotted future stars of the time. One such star was John Denver, the folk singer. He also organised large arena concert tours for the *'King of Rock'*, Elvis Presley.

He, as you will have gathered, was a very influential man, and he managed concert tours for Frank Sinatra, among others. He also became a producer of many successful films culminating in the remake of the extremely funny *"Ocean's Eleven"* film in 2001.

But back to the summer of 1997: Jerry Weintraub had taken his party of friends over to Scotland for a long weekend at the 'Home of Golf' in St. Andrews, and after he disembarked, he asked:

'Are you David Gillanders?'

'I am.'

'Will you join us?'

'No, it's not my job; my role is to make sure you are looked after when in Scotland.'

'No, no, I'd like you to join us.'

He insisted. So I did join the party, and we later sat down for dinner and enjoyed a very entertaining evening after the golf. He then asked if I happened to be a member of Skibo Castle because, he said:

'I'd like to play a round of golf there.'

'We can do, but we've got to play Gleneagles first.'

'Alright, but how quick a driver are you?'

'I'm ok.'

I was puzzled by the question, but he also asked:

'But if these three cars went to Gleneagles from this place (St. Andrews), who would get there first?'

'Well, I would....'

How could I possibly have answered otherwise?

He responded quickly, and decisively:

'You drive me!'

Unknown to me at the time, the Americans had taken a bet amongst themselves to see just who would get to Gleneagles first, so we all set off and, of course, I was the first to arrive at the luxury five star hotel and spa in Auchterarder in the heart of Perthshire. He was delighted that he had won the bet.

We played a round of golf at Gleneagles before we headed north to Dornoch and played the course at Skibo Castle. It was brilliant; in fact, the entire weekend was fabulous.

When we finished, Jerry turned round to me and said:

'Listen, David, you have been great. Do you fancy coming down to Pinewood Studios and doing some of the driving stunts on a film? It's called "The Avengers".

'Y-e-e-s-s! It sounds like great fun.'

Three weeks later I was in Pinewood to do the stunt driving in a Mini, but then there was a problem with the stunt co-ordinator. He fell out with me because – well, it's a long story – he wanted to take weeks to do it and I said I'd only an afternoon that I could spare. In the end I didn't do the stunt, so when Jerry arrived he asked:

'What's happened?'

'Hey! These guys are charging you a fortune for doing nothing. I could do this stunt in ten minutes! They want weeks to do it.'

He shrugged.

'That's Hollywood.'

'Well, I don't understand the budget.'

'Look, I'm sorry about that. Can I grant you a wish?'

'A wish?'

I must have looked as if I'd been play acting in Cinderella or something.

'Yes, a wish. If I could give you a wish, for something that you could have that money couldn't buy, what would it be?'

'Oh, that's very simple. I'd like to fly a fast jet.'

'A Lear Jet?'

'No, no, a fighter jet.'

'Hmm. I can do that.'

He picked up his mobile and then said:

'Hang on a second.'

It was more than a second that I waited because he chatted away on the phone for a long time, but eventually he handed his mobile over to me and said:

'Tell the guy what you want.'

On the other end of the line was an American with a slow Texan drawl, and he asked:

'What's he promised?'

'Well, he said I could fly a fast jet.'

'What jet would you like to fly?'

'An F-15.'

'Ok, where do you want to fly it?'

'If you tell me that I have to come over to America, I'll just catch the next flight.'

'No, that won't be necessary. We have Lakenheath in Suffolk, England. We fly F-15s from there.'

'Aye, Right!'

'No, no. It's no problem. We'll be in touch.'

I handed the mobile back to Jerry, then said cheerio. Then I headed back home to tell everybody in Aberdeen, and it was there I said to my friends:

"You are not going to believe this – I've been offered a flight in an F-15 Jet!"

Of course, nobody believed me, nobody at all.

A few weeks later I got a call to go to Lakenheath, an RAF station hosting USAF units and personnel, to meet up with the 492nd Fighter Squadron, part of the host 48th Fighter Wing, also known as the Statue of Liberty Wing, assigned to the United States Air Force in Europe. By this time, I was crapping myself, because this 'wish' of mine was about to come to true.

I was met by the Commander, a lovely guy by the name of Colonel Carl E Van Pelt, USAF. I was driven into the base with Gladys, and the first thing I noticed was the parking space. It was painted white, but it also had my name printed in stencilled lettering.

I said to Gladys:

'Look at this. This is crazy.'

After the introductions, we were escorted into the hanger area and the Commander asked:

'Would you like to see your jet, Sir?'

'S-E-E, Y-O-U-R, J-E-T!'

I'm sure I heard him correctly. So I said:

'Yes, show me my jet!'

So the Colonel slowly opened the door and standing there in the subdued light was a very dramatic looking McDonnell

Douglas F-15E Strike Eagle, worth something around $29 million. Not only that, *my* name was on the cockpit area.

Climbing aboard for the ride of my life.

Pilot: David Gillanders.

It was surreal; it felt as though I was actually living a Walter Mitty dream sequence and I was well aware that the whole episode had been orchestrated by a top Hollywood Producer, but then I met the pilot, François, a 23 year old who had been taken from Fighter Town, USA. He was the guy in the front seat; the guy in the back seat, normally, is called a Weapons Support Officer, (WSO) but I'm not normal, so I wasn't called a WSO.

François (my pilot) and me; and below, kitted out in my helmet and USAF Jacket.   Photos: Courtesy of USAF.

The WSO would usually do about 40% of the flying and the guy in the front, the pilot, would do the rest, including the take off and landing. Between them they would do a lot during a mission, but with me, the guy in the front was going to do all of the flying, or so I thought. The entire mission would be his responsibility and I had the best of the best of the very best.

Our flying partner (in the other jet) was pilot, Brett *"Stretch"* Provinsky. His WSO was a guy called *"Fuzzy"* and both of them were really nice guys. I forget *"Fuzzy's"* surname, and I also forget François' surname, and like *"Stretch's"* WSO in the other jet, my memory is a little bit fuzzy too.

Standing with Gladys beside "My" Jet!
Photograph: Courtesy of USAF.

I did Escape Training, and although my memory is awful, I will *never* forget what the instructor told me:

'*Now, you are in the back seat of the aircraft and the pilot will say, 'Bale Out!' He might say it once; he won't say it twice, because he'll be gone! What you have to do in that situation is pull these yellow handles down here and that's your ejector seat. You will be knocked out as you exit the aircraft because you will pull 12-g as you escape, but you will waken up and then you have to look up to make sure that your parachute has been deployed correctly.'*

I was listening intently to all this, you understand:

'Right.'

But then he said:

'Oh! I forgot to tell you. Don't let go of the handles as you eject because as you leave the aircraft the wind will catch both arms and snap them both off just at the shoulder joints, so you'd have no arms.'

'Right.'

'If the parachute hasn't been deployed correctly pull the red toggle to let that parachute go and get the reserve 'chute out.'

'Right.'

I was quite a conversationalist, you can tell.

'But if some of the chords are twisted, take the knife from your pocket and cut them away.'

'Right, but I've no arms! My arms got snapped off!'

'No, no, your arms won't snap off as long as you lock them into the handles because when you get knocked out you seemingly grip tighter.'

So I thought, *'W-O-W! That is a lot to remember.'*

The next step was to get kitted out and climb aboard this magnificent flying machine and the first thing I did was to remember and pull the pins out of my ejector seat. I had to stick them into a little holder by the canopy and the ground crew member looked in to check that I'd done this. By this time I was wiggling about in the seat thinking to myself: *'Is this thing going to go off by itself?'*

You have no idea what went through my mind.

François taxied to the runway with the second F-15 in

close attendance. These aircraft generally fly in pairs, and we took off in pairs, side by side. What a performance from the two Pratt and Whitney F100-200 afterburning turbofans! It had thrust, using the after-burner, of almost 24,000 pounds per foot, and the F-15 could reach 50,000 ft in 90 seconds...

We flew over Skibo Castle and buzzed it. Overall I did two hours and 20 minutes in this fast jet: we went everywhere and *"Fuzzy"*, in the other jet, took photographs of me having the time of my life. *"Stretch"*, his pilot, wanted a picture of me upside down, so we went upside down, canopy to canopy.

Buzzing Skibo Castle late in the afternoon.
Photograph: Courtesy USAF.

After buzzing Skibo Castle we 'attacked' the bombing range near Dornoch, and then we high-tailed it over to the west coast, past the Outer Hebrides with its magnificent white-coloured and unspoilt sands and out over the Atlantic. I didn't have any time to admire the view as we went super-sonic away from land, beyond the Speed of Sound, or Mach 1, at over 768 miles per hour, (that's around 314 yards per second). That's a hell of a lot faster than my MG Metro 6R4 and light years faster than de Savary's yacht!

285

We returned from our supersonic sortie and flew low level over 'Bal-Mo-Ral' as François happened to pronounce it, but Her Majesty wasn't in her castle in the Highlands.

It was probably a mistake flying low over what could well be restricted airspace, but that's what happened.

On approach to the Tain Bombing Range near Dornoch.
Photograph: Courtesy USAF.

Very soon after that, as we approached Aberdeen Airport, François called up the control tower (and it really would have been fantastic if triple Scottish Rally Champion Ken Wood had actually been at his day job as an Air Traffic Controller at Dyce Airport that day) but he does not recollect it because we never touched down and we were not subjected to landing fees, so as a result any record of me doing a low level flypast at Aberdeen Airport is gone.

The ultimate back seat driver, eh?

Photo: courtesy USAF.

François radioed the following message:

'Aberdeen Tower, this is 'Speed 71'; we are two USAF F-15E Strike Eagles requesting permission to execute a 'PD' low approach.'

'PD' stands for 'Practice Diversion' and every now and then such manoeuvres are regularly carried out by the military at civil airports to ensure that their pilots are familiar with civil procedures just in case they have to use them in a real life emergency, although civil and military Air Traffic Control procedures have many notable differences.

'Speed 71', this is Aberdeen Tower. Why?'

Obviously, the radio telecommunications would have been a lot more technical than this, but François replied:

'Aberdeen Tower, we happen to have one of your citizens onboard and we would like to give him a unique view of the Aberdeen Runway.'

Head in the clouds: Who needs Walter Mitty now then?
Photograph: courtesy USAF.

The ATC again, somewhat disbelievingly, asked:
'Speed 71', did you say you were two USAF F-15s?'
'Affirmative, Aberdeen Tower.'
'Speed 71 cleared for low approach and go-around run-way one-seven, left turn out of the perimeter. Wind at one-three at ten, remain cold.'

Translated, that actually meant that both François and *"Stretch"* were cleared to conduct a low level approach from the north, and Aberdeen Tower advised that the wind was from a north-westerly direction at a surface speed of ten knots (approximately 13 miles per hour). The "remain cold" state-ment referred to the non-use of the afterburner because noise abatement procedures at most civil airports preclude the use of afterburners.

The ATC added:
'Speed 71, we've never had USAF fighter jets over Aber-deen Airport before. We'll shut everybody out.'

This sounded as though it was going to be a lot of fun, but moreso when François stated:
'Aberdeen Tower, there's just one thing.... When we leave the perimeter we have to use our afterburners and it can be very noisy with the potential to cause damage to property.'

'Affirmative, Speed 71. We'll accept any flak coming because we want to see this!'

We flew alongside the River Don to the north and west of Aberdeen, (and, ironically, directly over the Fintray Hill Climb Course) and from there we executed a low level flypast, perhaps 50 or 60 feet off the runway, and saluted the tower in the peculiar way that Americans do. Side by side we flew, and then, with afterburners on we went straight up – it was fantastic!

Apparently, after we made our low level pass and hit the afterburners, there were a fair number of calls to the police over smashed windows in the Blackburn and Northfield areas of Aberdeen…

We then headed south and buzzed Malcolm Wilson's motor sport preparation business in Cumbria. It was just as well that Malcolm had not yet moved into the 'listed' building of Dovenby Hall by Cockermouth before these two F-15s flew over because it might well have listed a bit more after we whizzed past!

It didn't take us long to reach and then pass Wales, and about 100 miles or so from base, François asked me:

'Sir, would you like to fly this aircraft?'

'Y-E-S!'

'Right, Sir. I control the throttle. You have the stick and you have the pedals, but you have no throttle in the back. So I throttle it, you fly it. Do what you like. Throw it around. You have control!'

'I have control.'

I said it almost sheepishly, and I moved the stick ever so gingerly to begin with.

'No, No, Sir. Throw it around.'

'I'm not sure about this.'

That's just what I did. I pushed the stick to the right by giving it an almighty yank.

'Ooyah boy!'

(Or words to that effect).

That scared me.

'Yes Sir, honestly, that was good.'

François called up *"Stretch"* who came in close by, about 200 feet off our port (left) wing, just ahead of us, and he said:

'Follow him.'

Well, he banked to the right, so I banked to the right; he banked to the left, so I banked to the left. I dutifully followed wherever the other pilot went. Then François spoke again:

'Now, he wants to fight you.'

'What do you mean?'

'Let's have a dogfight. An F-15 is alright for 13-g'.

I understood a bit about g-force, or gravitational force to be precise, from an element of that in my various rally cars and my helicopter flying days, but this was something else entirely. In an aircraft pulling a +g manoeuvre, the pilot and passenger (me on this occasion) experienced several 'g' of inertial acceleration in addition to the force of gravity, but especially in a fast fighter jet.

The cumulative vertical axis forces that acted upon my body made me momentarily 'weigh' many times more than normal. Although I could 'feel' all this I still had to look up 'Wikipedia' to get the explanation!

François continued:

'I'm good for 9-g; but you are good for nothing... because you'll pass out long before anything happens, so go for it!'

'Oh, well, damn it. I'll have a go at this.'

'Ok, Sir, 1 – 2 – 3 – Go!'

Honestly, it's like a PlayStation game.

François said:

'He's going to go right.'

So, I just threw the stick to the right and the thing flipped completely over and François shouted over the intercom:

'That's the way to do it!'

The whole aircraft instantly flipped right over and we were basically upside down and on a downward spiral.

'Now pull the stick back, Sir.'

So I pulled the stick back and the thing rolled back up and François exclaimed:

'You've lost him, Sir, you've lost him.'

'Where is he?'

'Look in your mirrors, Sir. He's right above you.'

And there he was, upside down, looking right at me, waving, and pointing as if to say:

'BANG! BANG! You're dead!'

We followed this with an inverted loop, that's a vertical circle where the cockpit canopy faces outwards during the manoeuvre. This drew an extreme negative g-force and I think that François and *"Stretch"* wanted me to pass out. In fact, I am definitely sure they wanted to knock me out – I must have been talking too much! I wonder if that's why they made a video of the flight?

Onto the loop, I pulled the stick fully back, and I was now lying right on my back. You know you're going straight up when you see the instrument gauges going completely haywire, especially the artificial horizon one.

The other F-15 was in front when François said:

'Sir, you need to roll over.'

'Why? I'm enjoying this.'

'Sir, we've now gone past 65,000 feet and soon we'll be classed as a UFO, and we're not supposed to be at this height, but because you're a friend of the 'boss' – well he says you can do what you like.'

I will explain about the *'boss'* shortly.

Meanwhile, I managed to roll over and I got to perhaps 3.5-g or maybe 4-g when I passed out. The video showed my head dropping, unconscious. I *had* stopped talking!

When we landed at RAF Lakenheath I am proud to say that although I was a little green and very dizzy I was able to drive home, although I have to confess that I was still affected for a week or so afterwards.

But it was a great, great experience and one which no money could buy. It *was* indeed priceless, but the reason I got this experience, apart from the initial 'wish' offered by Jerry Weintraub, was revealed when Gladys and I had dinner with Colonel van Pelt who said:

'You know, something, Sir? You are the only British civilian to have flown an F-15 fast jet in the UK, and you are one of perhaps 20 in the world that's ever done it. Your connections are huge.'

'Yes. A guy called Jerry Weintraub.'

'Who? I'm sorry, Sir, I have absolutely no idea who Mr. Weintraub is... You really don't know who organised this for you, do you?'

'If it wasn't Weintraub, then, no.'

Apparently, when Jerry Weintraub handed over his mobile phone to me at Pinewood Studios earlier, it transpired that the Texan drawl I'd heard, and been talking to, belonged to none other than George H. W. Bush, the 41st President of the United States of America! He was a very good friend of Jerry Weintraub's. Unknown to me at the time, President Bush had phoned a friend, Vice President Dick Cheney, and he, in turn, I believe, then contacted the *'boss'*, President Bill Clinton! And it was Bill Clinton who actually signed off on the flight for me to go supersonic in an F-15.

'W-o-w!'

The Eagle has Landed

About three years later, when I was having dinner in Skibo Castle one evening, the door opened and this guy came into the dining room and said:

'Ok. Room's clear, let the Eagle in, let the Eagle in.'

I wondered what on earth was actually going on. I thought to myself, *'What the hell is this?'*

Then in through the open doorway walked President Bill Clinton! He had been playing a round of golf at Skibo and dropped in for cocktails. He went round the room, shook hands and spoke with everybody, and then he reached me:

'Hi, I'm President Bill Clinton.'

Well, you know me by now, so I said:

'I'm David Gillanders, and I have something to say to you, Sir, which I bet nobody's ever going to say to you again.'

I could see he was a bit staggered by this comment. I think what might have been passing through his mind would have been something along the lines of:

'Whoa! You don't talk to me....'

But I continued:

'You actually signed off a requisition for me to get a flight in an F-15 jet.'

'Really?'

'Yes.'

'Did you enjoy it?'

'I certainly did.'

'That's why I'm President Bill Clinton!'

Honestly, he's a lovely guy. A great guy, actually, and it was fantastic to meet him and close the entire episode of the *'Flight of the F-15.'*

As well as making dreams come true for millions of people through the cinema, Jerry Weintraub certainly made my dream come true. He also wrote a book, *"When I Stop Talking, You'll Know I'm Dead: Useful Stories from a Persuasive Man"*. It was published on March 23, 2011, but I am sad to say that this great man stopped talking on July 6, 2015. I have a lot to thank him for.

Chapter TWENTYONE

LOOKING INTO THE ABYSS

I simply cannot remember if I had been playing golf or having dinner on this particular occasion, but one day I happened to be with family friends, Dr. Francis Clark Snr., and Henry Cameron. During the meal, Henry turned round to me and said:

'You know, David, you'll only know how good you are when you look into the abyss.'

I remember that statement, but I thought at the time:

'What a strange statement.'

(Or words to that effect).

As far as I was concerned, Henry always talked in riddles, although somehow, his words stuck in my mind. In 2006, though, I really did *"look into the abyss"*.

I remember going home after the hospital visit that diagnosed my serious heart problem, and as I lay in bed and talked it through with Gladys, I became very scared, really scared, then the thought occurred to me:

'Wow! I'm going to die if I don't get this fixed soon!'

I'd come through everything unscathed so far: I'd had my share of helicopter near-misses; I'd been in the back seat of an F-15 fighter jet; I'd driven rally cars for nigh on 35 years and been upside down in several of them; I'd rally cars that went on fire and I even rolled another one into a river. A life of adventure without a doubt, and I'd done all of those things without a scratch!

But now, suddenly, to be told I could be dead within three months, well, that really was the abyss.

And I was staring into it!

Henry Cameron was right after all.

When a person looks into the abyss – and I don't care who you are – maybe it's something this book will tell you – there will be a point in your life that you too will look into one. After I metaphorically stepped back from the edge, though, Gladys and I became even closer. She became my carer despite everything that she had already gone through with me, and that was a lot. An awful lot…

Nobody would want to marry me because I am just a nightmare to be with, I understand that. I have been the most difficult guy in the world: I'm intolerant, I'm rude, I'm gruff, and I have no patience whatsoever. You could think of 100 derogatory terms and they'd all fit me.

The grumpy, Victor Meldrew character, portrayed by the Scots actor, Richard Wilson, in the BBC's *"One Foot in the Grave"* situation comedy, must have been modelled on me. Meldrew, ha, ha! *I am* Victor Meldrew, and the older I get the *more* 'Meldrew' I become.

I am *so* grateful to Gladys, though; she has stuck by me and with me through thick and thin, and I am forever in awe of her. To go through what she's gone through with me, my heart surgery, the three episodes as they're called, and some other issues is quite something.

The first incident (before I had my heart surgery) was classified as an actual heart attack; that's when my 'oil pump' became blocked in one of my arteries, whereas the other three have been classified as episodes – that's more like my 'electrical wiring system' – where fused electrical signals within my heart had suddenly become completely chaotic. I don't quite know what the difference is, but it's to do with the same thing. Gladys and I often look at each other and I'm sure she thinks:

'Are you ok?'

This is the reason I decided to write my book: I felt it important to put it all down on paper because I think that if a person has reached the age of 65 years, or more, then that person *has* done something with his or her life and the details of that life should definitely be written down for posterity. I qualify on both counts given that I was born in 1950 and I have certainly had what I call my *"Life of Adventure"*.

I *have* done a lot with my life.

But read on, there's a lot more to follow…

Just who is David Gillanders?

I was once asked the question:

'Just who is David Gillanders?'

Well, I suppose I am the only person who can really answer that. I also believe I am the most complicated person you could meet, or ever want to meet. I'm very confident, and yet, totally insecure. I *think* I can do anything, but deep down I *know* I can not, and therefore I try really, really hard to accomplish everything – the hard way.

My driving, for example, wasn't taught because I believe I'm a natural driver. Some drivers *can* be taught, and I've met them, but you couldn't teach *me* anything. I just didn't listen. Whatever I did, I did on my own, so yes, I *am* a natural driver. I'm a bit of a character too, but after my heart issues surfaced in 2006, I think I became a much nicer person. Well I hope I am a nicer person.

I listen to everybody now and think I am much more approachable. Before my health problems I was totally insufferable. Gladys might say I can still be….

But back then I didn't really care, whereas nowadays, I do. I certainly couldn't be approached prior to 2006 and I wasn't nice to live with, but since my triple heart bypass, I like to think that I *have* become a nicer person. Furthermore, I wish I'd been that person all my life, I really do. I believe that my heart issues have completely changed my outlook.

Mind you, I can still talk about myself for ages, although I don't like crowds anymore. I don't mind being in a room with 12 people because I can handle that, but there was a time when I used to get annoyed if I *wasn't* the centre of attention. I don't seek the limelight any more, although I am still quite restless in my mind because I don't think I have accomplished everything that I want to accomplish. There are things I still need and want to do.

In the early days after my heart bypass surgery, I went through the rehabilitation unit in the Aberdeen Royal Infirmary and there the medical staff conducted a fairly extensive introduction; in attendance was a nurse, a psychologist, a cardiovascular clinical nurse and a physiotherapist. They gave me a paper to read and then they interviewed me. A lot of questions were asked and after I had answered them, Cardio Nurse, Dawn Simpson, said to me:

'David, you seem to be a very complicated person!'

'Ha! I am certainly the most complicated person that you have ever met!'

'I don't believe that.'

'You wait and see...'

Three months into the course, Dawn quipped:

*'David, I believe you now. You **are** definitely the most complicated person I have ever met!'*

I *am* a very complicated person.

Pro-Celebrity Race: Bahrain Grand Prix

I was eight weeks away from the 2006 Bahrain Grand Prix when I underwent my triple heart bypass operation, so I said to Dr. Malcolm Metcalfe, the cardiologist, beforehand:

'Doctor, I need to be fit in eight weeks.'

'David, there's no way you will be fit in eight weeks.'

*'I know I'm getting this operation done, but I **have** to be in Bahrain on the racing circuit as I've been invited to compete in a Pro-Celebrity Race on March 2.'*

I think he was resigned to my determination.

'Okay, we'll do extra lattice work at the front'.

During the six hour operation, the heart surgeon, Mr. Bob Jeffries and his team carried out the complex procedure, but when he finished he decided not to close me up with the normal clips. Instead, he fastened me up with wire, so that in the event of a serious accident all the bits wouldn't fall out! The wound, he told me, would be very fresh and there were concerns for the ramifications should I happen to have an accident and get thrown forward in a crash.

Nevertheless, only eight weeks later, I boarded a private Boeing 757 and seven hours later arrived in Bahrain! It was fabulous, and first class all the way. All of the celebrities were onboard and we spent three days there before the race. I had been teamed up with a guy called Gavin Green, the then editor of *"CAR Magazine."* I have known Gavin – a bit of a driver himself – for many years and our plan was share the driving on an equal basis.

However, I had first to teach John Legend how to drive a manual car: the American singer songwriter from Springfield, Ohio, like most others from that side of the pond, had only ever driven automatics, but nevertheless he acquitted himself by being a fast learner on how to operate a gear lever and clutch for this race.

The Pink Floyd drummer, Nick Mason, a classic car and motor sport enthusiast, was also there, as was Status Quo's Rick Parfitt. Other notable celebrities included the Olympic Gold Medallist, Michael Johnson, as well as Emma Parker-Bowles, the niece of Camilla, Duchess of Rothesay. She was there as a motoring correspondent, and Anoushka, the Egyptian singing and acting sensation also participated along with Persian-born racer, Laleh Seddigh.

Each ten-lap race comprised 16 similar cars with the professional drivers (me included) starting and driving the first five laps of the track before changing over with their own paired celebrity for the remainder of the race. The cars were thundering great 415 brake horsepower Chevrolet V8 SS Lumina saloons. To put this horsepower (into novice hands) I thought some semblance of perspective might be necessary, so I looked up the website, *"www.carwow.co.uk"* and I quote therefrom:

"A horsepower is a totally arbitrary measurement dreamt up by Greenock-born, James Watt, (in 1781) when trying to compare the effectiveness of his steam engines against the horses they were replacing. One horsepower was deemed to be the equivalent of one horse lifting 33,000 pounds over one foot in one minute on the surface of the Earth."

But as I was never any good at school, and maths in particular, I'll let you work out for yourself what 415 horsepower equates to!

Anyway, suitably powered up, we all went onto the track and had our practice session the day before the race. My problem was my health, obviously, and the fact that it was 40 degrees centigrade in Bahrain. In Scotland, at that time of year, it could be well below zero, and I'd just had major surgery. I wasn't fit.

'Christ! I really wasn't fit, but there was absolutely no way I was going to miss this opportunity.'

During the practice session on one of the laps I went whizzing down the start/finish straight and about 100 yards in front of me, I had what could be described as a 'heart-stopping moment' when two of the other Luminas had a 'coming together' in front of me. They banged into each other and both started to spin. The old story goes that if someone is spinning in front of you, you aim straight at them, because when you get there they'll be gone.

I had decided to aim for one particular car, which happened to be that of John Legend's, and well, how we missed each other, I don't know. John said he saw me coming straight at him and he later asked me:

'Why didn't you brake?'

So, I told him about the old story and how I aimed for the spot at where he was spinning, expecting him not to be there when I arrived..... But he *was* still there when I arrived! Somehow, I missed him.

I returned from what was an extremely satisfying, but very tiring journey. I was totally knackered.

I had been very friendly with the people at the Bahrain Circuit for quite a long time and had been going there for about a year, once every month, so it was good fun to actually race there.

Overleaf: Try and name the celebrities. Here's a few to help you get started, in no particular order: there's Sir Steven Redgrave Jay Kay, Tiff Needell, Gavin Green, Martin Brundle, Nick Mason, John Legend, Emma Parker-Bowles, Rick Parfitt, Michael Johnson and Simon Webbe along with several others.

The celebrities (and me) at the 2006 Bahrain Grand Prix Pro-Celebrity Race. I'm in the back row, eighth from the left, all in white, and that included my complexion.

David's Angels

There are a number of angels in the Aberdeen Royal Infirmary, but in the Cardiac Rehabilitation Unit there are three angels who are very special to me, namely, Lauren Chalmers, Karen Fyvie, and Dawn Simpson. These three girls became a very important part of my life.

I had been speaking with another member of the Cardio team who mentioned that I needed to take a tablet which had potential side effects. He said it could make me dizzy, but it didn't, so it must be the one hour I have with the girls that makes me dizzy! So, if I get dizzy, it's the girls' fault….

I know that they think I am a bit crazy, but everything I tell them is true, honestly, and I say this now, specifically to Lauren, Karen and Dawn:

'What you girls have done for me I find difficult to put into words and I mean that! I think you have given me huge confidence to carry on with my life. I said I would put this in writing, and now it is.'

A Selfie with three angels at ARI's Rehabilitation Unit.
L-R: Lauren Chalmers, Karen Fyvie and Dawn Simpson.

To me, thanking such angels like Lauren, Karen and Dawn, is very important, because the older an individual gets the more he or she depends upon the National Health Service. I did not go private and I am fed up seeing the NHS getting the bad press it sometimes gets. When I read the newspapers, or view the news on television, there are often complaints about the NHS doing this, or the NHS not doing that. Well, I would like to put it on record that in my personal experience, the NHS and the staff therein, have been exemplary.

I really have been treated wonderfully well and the care, professionalism and support I have had shown to me all my life, through to and including my triple heart bypass operation in 2006, and then my episodes in 2014, 2015, and beyond, has been fantastic. I have found each and every member of the staff in the infirmary to be nothing but professional, and 'my' three angels have been great fun to be with; they have a tremendous appetite for care.

I should have been thrown out some time ago, but now I'm like a local; I can go in and get on with my own fitness regime. My angels have a lovely ability to make people feel relaxed and confident, and I cannot speak more highly of them. Ladies, thank you very much.

I certainly did look into the abyss in 2006, but through the skills of the medical staff in the Aberdeen Royal Infirmary, I lived to tell my tale.

Meeting my Hero

Sadly, one of my rally colleagues did not live to tell his tale, and after his tragic helicopter accident, I attended the memorial service of Colin McRae in his home town of Lanark, on September 30, 2007. It was there that I met my hero at last. No, no, *not* Malcolm Wilson *but* Ari Vatanen! Malcolm's a really great pal and although we were laughing here, it was on a very, very sad day.

(Right): Malcolm Wilson, me and Ari Vatanen.

Photo: Gladys Gillanders.

Chapter TWENTYTWO

THE BIGGEST INSURANCE CLAIM
OF ITS TIME IN BRITISH MOTORING HISTORY

Perhaps I do, do all the talking, but this will come as a big surprise to a lot of folk: I actually undertook some *written* journalistic work after I had my heart problems and one of the publications I contributed to was *"Trend"* magazine in Aberdeen. I conducted road tests for them although I have to say that I was very relieved that the following escapade did not grace their pages.

Left: The front cover of the magazine from October, 2009.

My write-up of the Pagani Zonda is too small to read here, but I show it for illustration purposes only.

My pieces were usually road tests on new or exciting cars and, of course, I found that element of the exercise very interesting, but in saying that, nobody would ever want to let me road test a Pagani Zonda again, that's for sure.

And the reason?

Well, in the month of September, 2009, the biggest insurance claim of its time in UK motoring history was submitted. And, yes, it *was* me who submitted it!

So how did this happen?

A very good friend of mine just happened to own a Pagani Zonda 'S', sports car and because he knew that I had been writing a series of car reports he kindly invited me to drive his car which was worth all of £528,000 in standard form, and his one wasn't standard!

Well, I'll try anything once, so with me at the wheel, we took it onto the back roads between the towns of Ellon and Auchnagatt, to the north of Aberdeen. It felt good to handle and it certainly was quick. Nevertheless, I thought I'd ask the question:

'Why don't we turn off the traction control? I'd like to "feel" this thing really work!'

My trusting friend agreed and so he switched the traction control off, and that's when I really tried out the car, but I hadn't realised that the tyres were a bit beyond their best.....

I only found that out when I came to a particular section of road where the surface, I was told later, was renowned for having farm lorries cross over and drop, shall I be polite and call it 'fertilizer' on the road? Well, this manure became pressed into the tarmac by much slower and heavier passing traffic, and as a result the surface had become exceptionally smooth and very, very slippery.

Maybe that's an excuse, but it's not a very good one, is it? Anyway, I had entered this particular corner at something that certainly wasn't a legal speed on the quiet country road, but because of the smooth, manure-infested surface, the car simply snapped away from me and went straight into an oversteering attitude. I thought to myself, *'No great problem. I'll just drift it round the bend.....'*

But there *was* a problem: the corner itself just kept going round, round, and round, and there came a point on that bend when I thought to myself, *'Hmm. It's either going over the wall at that side, or I need to bring it into this side.'*

And just as I thought that, I caught a glimpse of a field on the left and instantly decided that I'd head into it. What I really didn't see en route to the vegetation was a telegraph pole supported by two great big wire strainers, one of which simply sliced through the bodywork to pretty much cut the car in half! The wire went in at the front wing and tore right through the side of it like a rampant cheesecutter all the way up to the dashboard!

According to the farmer, whom I later met:

'Och I tak a car oot o' there ilky wikk...'

Translated from the Doric tongue, that meant that the farmer had been in the habit of extricating a car out of there every other week! But then he thought about it a bit more and laconically added:

'But nithin' as expensive as this!'

It was a bit of an embarrassment for me, especially (as you can imagine) but we called up a breakdown crew who collected it quickly, got it under cover, transported it off the scene and locked it away out of sight.

After that I went to see Aviva, the car insurance company, and advised their representative:

'I have a car insurance claim to make.'

'Yes Sir. I'll take down some details. Now, what kind of car is it, please?'

'A Pagani Zonda?'

'Sorry? A what?'

'A Zonda. A Pagani Zonda 'S', actually.'

'What's its value?'

'No idea. Maybe around £1 million!'

'S-O-R-R-Y?'

'Yes, I think it is, about £1 million.'

At the time, I didn't have a clue as to the actual cost of such a car, but I knew it had to be expensive because it wasn't the standard car. The flustered representative said to me:

'I'll get the Loss Adjuster to see it, Sir.'

What a Pagani Zonda should look like.....

Pagani repaired the car before it was eventually sold, but near London, on February 11, 2015, the very same car (below) savaged a steel fence in an industrial estate.

Above: What a Pagani Zonda should not look like.......
*This one was **not** down to me!*

The Italian manufacturer of this hand-built supercar came all the way from Modena in Italy to inspect it, and the representative agreed that it had to go back to the factory for a full evaluation, but the really strange thing about this whole episode was that nobody knew that it was me who had been behind the wheel, and Sir Jackie Stewart, of all people, had been named as *"the mystery driver"*. This, I think, was probably because Sir Jackie had previously driven the car at Ingliston, the now defunct racing circuit to the west of Edinburgh, and someone had put two and two together and not reached four on this occasion.

Not that long afterwards I got a phone call from Sir Jackie because he knew that this rumour emanated from my territory of Aberdeenshire. He had been named as the mystery driver by my local daily newspaper, *"The Press and Journal"*.

He asked me:

'David, do you know why I'm getting the blame for crashing a Zonda in Aberdeenshire?'

'I don't know…. Don't ask me!'

Well, I really didn't actually know why he was getting the blame, because the newspapers were camped outside *my* front door and Sir Jackie had been out of the country at the time of the accident anyway.

My friend got the car repaired, and the actual cost to Aviva was in the region of £300,000 but at least he didn't lose his no-claims bonus as I'd made the claim under my insurance. Then he sold it and bought another one, but he sold that one too – long before I had a chance to drive it…..

Did I like it? Yes, I thought it was a great car. Would I buy one? No, I wouldn't because I don't normally go in for that sort of sports car. I'm just not that type of person.

The insurance company confirmed that my claim was the biggest insurance payout for repairs to a private car in Great Britain at the time. I held that dubious record right up to the time that the actor, Rowan Atkinson, allegedly obliterated his McLaren F1 when he crashed it (for a second time) in 2011. The popular star of *"Mr. Bean"* and *"Blackadder"*, allegedly, now holds the record for what is believed to be the largest motoring claim for the repair of a private car in the UK, a staggering £910,000.

'And I wasn't even driving it!'

Pacenotes or Safety Notes?

Would pacenotes have helped me in my driving of the Zonda at that deceptive manure-infested corner? Probably. Pacenotes, which are now officially known as Safety Notes (for those not acquainted with them) are what could be described as an accurate description of a competitive section on a rally. The driver himself usually creates the record (at slow speed) with his co-driver writing down verbatim all of the details prior to the rally itself. Then, during the rally, the co-driver regurgitates the record (at high speed) by talking incessantly and always in advance of the bend, crest, junction or hazard.

I didn't have pacenotes at the start of my rally career; the only instructions I got from my co-driver back then came from the roadbook which more or less described the severity of the junctions or marked a caution where there could have been a 'fresh air' corner, a term used to describe a bend with a large drop to either (or both) sides of the track.

Nowadays, for the Scottish events at least, the crews actually get their notes from the organisers, but they are called 'Safety Notes', not 'Pacenotes'. From my point of view this takes some of the fun out of stage rallying simply because, in my day, everything was 'blind'; my co-driver back then would get in the car and call:

'3-2-1-Go!'

All my co-driver had to do after that was to read the roadbook and give details of each junction, and perhaps call out any cautions so marked, but the speed and the gear round every bend, or over every brow, or dip, or through every junction, would be down to *my* judgement, and although it is faster with the 'Safety Notes' I'd also say that any resultant accident is likely to be faster and bigger too.

I used to drive what I could see in front of me, so if there was a brow coming up in 100 yards and I was doing 100 mph, I'd 'make up' or imagine what was on the other side, and take it flat out. If the road turned right or left after the brow, then it was down to me to make it round the bend.

Although driving faster, the driver nowadays does know where he (or she) is going. Accordingly, there has to be an element of safety in knowing where the road is leading to, even if travelling around 10% faster.

Understanding the notes is a pure skill that the driver 'works into' and when driving on notes the co-driver is reading a corner ahead, or two corners ahead if they are driving really fast, perhaps in excess of 80 or 90 miles per hour. If the co-driver is delivering a section of very tight instructions it's almost an *'and...'* scenario, because he, or she, simply does not have enough time to shout all of the instructions, so the driver gets an *'and...'*

Using notes, the control that the co-driver has over the driver is remarkable, because should the car crash it is the co-driver's fault, it's not the driver's. If the co-driver reads a note incorrectly, or the timing of the note is wrong, it would be assumed that the driver would be able to see that, and correct it, but he could be so intently focused on that (erroneous) instruction in his head that he'd take that note as verbatim and act on it accordingly.

It should be noted that every single entry form has a disclaimer that specifically states that every competitor effectively participates in motor sport at his or her own risk. There is no doubt that motor sport is dangerous: it says so on all the entry tickets; it says so on all the programmes; and it says so on all of the warning signs.

Overall, given the speeds, terrain, and the close proximity of the spectators, I believe we have in special stage rallying, a reasonably safe sport for everybody, although there have been a few more accidents in the second decade of the 21st century, so all of us in the sport cannot afford to be complacent. Each and every one of us, irrespective of whether we are involved in an event as a competitor, or as an official, or simply as a spectator, must realise that:

'MOTOR SPORT IS DANGEROUS!'

Photograph: Frank Love (www.raceandrally.co.uk).

MONTE CARLO OR BUST

Gordon Hutcheon and I became close friends in 2008 although we'd known each other for some time through his Hutcheon Electrical business in Aberdeen. I had also met with him on a few other occasions when we played some rounds of golf because it just so happened that we tended to be in the same golf club at the same time.

I believe that Gordon is a lovely, genuine and very honest man who'd give you his last pound and I like him because he's a very easy guy to get on with. In addition, he's been there for Gladys and me at the right time.

Unfortunately, Gordon became ill around the time I started writing my book and Gladys and I thought about him day and night.

Banger Challenge

Although my motor sport career was behind me, I did actually participate on the *"Monte Carlo or Bust Banger Challenge"*, the ultimate European Banger Rally. This was in 2013, and my co-driver was Gordon (before his illness). We decided that we wanted to make this a worthwhile experience, and as he was the Chairman of the Ball Committee of the VSA (formerly the Voluntary Service Aberdeen), we agreed that our goal would be to raise funds for the Linn Moor Residential School on behalf of the VSA, a major social care charity based on the outskirts of Aberdeen.

The school is located to the west of Peterculter, and our goal was to raise around £6,000 to help children with complex additional support needs, as well as autism, and to hopefully provide them with a better existence.

To qualify for the rally, our 'banger' had to have four wheels and cost less than £250, but as we are born and bred Aberdonians we got the car for nothing! With the car suitably 'prepared', Gordon and I started the event on Wednesday, July 10, 2013 and immediately headed off on a 600 mile trip to the Euro Tunnel before arriving in Saint Quentin in France for the official start.

The route took us to Dijon, a further 250 miles away, and then round a loop of 300 miles which saw us reach Switzerland. Then we headed down into Turin in Italy on the Saturday for the final push, and we were certainly hoping that it would *not* be a push. That was the 165 mile jaunt to the finish of the event in Monte Carlo on July 14.

I'll let Gordon take up the story:

'David and I were each having a cup of coffee in the Malmaison Hotel on Queen's Road one morning, when he asked:

'Have you read "The Press and Journal" today?'

'No. Why?'

'It mentions a charity drive to Monte Carlo.'

'I'd love to do that.'

So Gordon went home and entered right away, then said:

'The next time we met, David asked my thoughts on the forthcoming event:

'Well, I've signed up for it.'

'Never!'

'He couldn't believe it; neither could Meldrew....

'The next challenge was to get a car, so we initially shopped around on the internet, but David knew someone who knew someone, who knew someone else, and the end result was that he found a 17-year old Nissan Micra. It was a funny, faded, terrible colour of red, but through David's motor trade connections we re-sprayed it matt black with the Saltire, the national flag of Scotland, painted on the roof.

'Because our competition number was 007 we really had to call it something James Bond-like, and since a car is usually a girl, (for us boys, anyway) we decided that we had to call her 'Miss Moneypenny'.

'We did absolutely nothing to the engine; we were a bit frightened to touch it because it was so old, but we got all the nice-to-have gadgets and also bought some fancy black clip-on things (dust caps) for the wheels.

'However, as David mentioned earlier, this was for the Linn Moor Residential School for autistic children, and so we went to Peterculter beforehand to show the kids the car, which they absolutely loved. Some of them couldn't access it, but others were able to, and one even managed to get in and start waving his hands through the open sunroof. They thoroughly enjoyed it.

'But after that interlude we had to get down to the serious business of the event itself. Before the actual 'off', we had a lovely soirée which included a barbeque in the Malmaison Hotel. After this we hit the road in our purpose-designed shirts. We had trousers on as well, but we had different coloured tops for different days because I'm a bit of a freak with that sort of thing. Everything had to look right, and be right.'

'Autosport' used this photograph of me and Ken Rees - 1987.

Photograph: Courtesy of 'Autosport'.

It was most definitely a case of 'super performance' in the MG Metro 6R4 (on the previous page) and 'super fun' in the Nissan Micra (below right).

Outside the Malmaison Hotel with Gordon and 'Miss Moneypenny'. Photograph: Courtesy of the "Deeside Piper".

Gordon continued:

'Everybody waved their goodbyes to us on July 10, and we headed west along Queen's Road and then south onto Anderson Drive and over the 16th century Bridge of Dee, then onwards to the Channel Tunnel. We had only gone 30 miles or so when we found that we had a wobble which appeared to be from the front wheels. It was an indication that something was wrong with 'Miss Moneypenny'. That didn't auger too well as we'd another 1,300 miles to go and we had only driven as far as the town of Laurencekirk in the Howe o' the Mearns.

Friendly faces in the garage in Laurencekirk. Photograph: David Gillanders.

'We found a wee garage in the town and the friendly mechanics took the wheels off and checked them. They were found to be alright so they put them back on with these plastic things we'd bought, and we duly continued on our merry way, down the A90 towards Dundee and beyond. We crossed into England and then dropped in past M-Sport at Dovenby Hall near Cockermouth at the edge of the Lake District.

'It was a bit of fun to see 'Miss Moneypenny' beside all of Malcolm Wilson's valuable rally cars, and there was us in our old banger. But, we were there for a service halt as we'd an electrical problem with the lights.

Low Tech meets High Tech

Malcolm Wilson (left) couldn't believe it either! Here, the low-tech Nissan nestles nicely in beside the high-tech M-Sport WRC workshop.   Photograph: Courtesy of M-Sport.

'We stayed overnight in Cumbria whilst the M-Sport technicians fixed the electrics to enable us to continue on the Banger Challenge the very next day, and I have to thank Malcolm's Men for all the care and attention they afforded to 'Miss Moneypenny'.

'We were about halfway towards the Tunnel, with something like 300 miles to go when we found that it was the fancy black plastic things, the wheel trims, that had been causing *the wheel imbalance, so we simply ripped them off there and then and from that point onwards, 'Miss Moneypenny' ran faultlessly to the finish.*

'Through the Euro Tunnel we went, into France and then up into Switzerland and down into Italy. It really was 'something else'. We went back into France again, before we arrived in the Principality of Monaco. We did a quick tour (well, it wasn't that quick) of Monte Carlo and also devoured yet another of the fantastic lunches we enjoyed en route.

'It was a tough job, but somebody had to do it!

'I've had a lot of fast cars and driven quickly in my time and I've also been a passenger at speed too, so I was quite comfortable and relaxed sitting in the passenger seat with a champion rally driver at the wheel.

Monte Rosa, the second highest mountain in the Alps, is located between Switzerland and Italy, and at 4,634 metres (15,203 feet), I think that 'Miss Moneypenny' would have really struggled there.   Photograph: Jack Davidson.

'But, to put this all into perspective, there we were, flat out in this old Nissan, going up and over the Col du Grand-Saint-Bernard at 2,469 metres high (8,100 feet). It's actually

the third highest road pass in Switzerland but conversely, it's actually the lowest pass lying on a ridge between the two highest summits of Mont Blanc and Monte Rosa and is the main road into Italy.

'To prove that we went over the top of the pass, the organisers stipulated that we **had** to get our photograph taken with a St. Bernard dog, which we duly did.....'

*They didn't say it had to be a **REAL** St. Bernard dog!*

*We had a great laugh with this until we did realise that we really **had** to obtain a photo with a **REAL** St. Bernard dog!*

I had been enjoying myself in 'Miss Moneypenny', but I sensed that Gordon was beginning to get a little bit concerned, so I'll let him expand on that:

'I had realised that what goes up, also comes down... David, though, would have said that this was definitely not Bennachie! On a flat road it wouldn't have bothered me but some of the drops were on my side of the car and we were going downhill at a fair old rate of knots in a pretty old Nissan, and all I said was:

'David, I'm uncomfortable.'

'Give him his due, he did slow down, but by this time, we'd also run out of brakes! The thing had nae brakes! It was really funny... (afterwards).'

I thought Gordon was a really great co-driver. He did everything he needed to, but here's an absolute 'belter': we were in Turin and had come in from the back side of the city and, frankly, I have never seen such a dump of a town in all my life. Gordon had his iPhone out and he guided me through the place on his mobile, with:

'Left, right, left, right, and so forth.'

As I said earlier, he was good at navigating, but then something went wrong and it looked as though we'd ended up in a mart. We actually drove through an area where people were being served food; we simply cruised past them. There were other folk selling fish, butcher meat, and so on, and in fact, we *had* driven right through a market! It was like a scene out of the Michael Caine film, *"The Italian Job"*.

We ended up driving alongside a tramline and you've guessed it, yes, on either side of us were platforms... and there, right in front of us... was a train! We'd to wait for the locomotive to go away before we continued, but at least it was going in the same direction as we were!

Honestly, we found the Monte Carlo or Bust Banger Challenge to be absolutely fabulous. The car was good, the route was brilliant, and the people we met were truly fantastic.

As I said, Gordon was excellent with the navigation: he guided me to Rheims and found the MUMM winery where he bought two magnums of Cordon Rouge. Maybe it should now be renamed Gordon Blue...

BEFORE ....AFTER

I'll let Gordon conclude the story:

'Eventually we reached Monte Carlo and then on to Nice where we had the end of the rally party, although David had to leave early the next morning because he was an expert witness in a four wheel drive court case back home.

'Paul, my son, lives in a town by the name of Bourg-Saint-Maurice, or Bourg, the last large settlement along the Tarentaise valley in the heart of the French Alps, so I decided to take 'Miss Moneypenny', the money-spinner, back to his house after our fund raising challenge. The idea was to leave the car with him to sell it. He got €350 for the Micra and this was duly added to the charity fund. Two years later, Paul saw the old dear still going strong in Bourg. A total of £18,000 (three times our goal) was raised for the VSA and the Linn Moor Residential School. That was very satisfying.'

Gordon Hutcheon.

The Fool Monte

Not such a fool, because we raised so much money!

G'Day, Sport!'

Monte Postscript

When Gordon and I stopped off at the small garage in Laurencekirk to investigate the wheel imbalance of the Micra, the mechanics were blown away by *'Miss Moneypenny'* and what we were then about to undertake. I don't think they could believe it either... They were a great bunch of guys, but the problem was that the judder was still there even after we left. I actually thought it was a wheel bearing, but we didn't have the heart to go back to the mechanics again, so we continued on our adventure.

Rolls Royce

That same year I received an Ambassadorship from Rolls Royce, and one day I happened to be driving the new Wraith model, of which the Goodwood manufacturer said was:
"The most technologically advanced and potent Rolls - Royce in history."
Anyway, Gordon was my passenger that day, and as we spirited our way south we made the decision to drop in past Laurencekirk, to the same wee garage where we just had to ask the very same mechanics:
'Would you balance the wheels, please?'
It was like chalk and cheese, one car cost nothing and the other well over £250,000. The mechanics' jaws collectively dropped. They couldn't believe it, but they got some pictures of us with them and the Rolls in the forecourt. That was great fun!

Court Case

Gordon mentioned earlier that I had to leave Monte Carlo almost as soon as the event finished. This was because I had been cited as an expert witness in a court case, and as I was a qualified off-road instructor with Land Rover, the court valued my opinion.

The case involved the Land Rover Experience in Dunkeld, where, allegedly, one of their instructors fell out of his car and subsequently claimed that the organisers should have 'salted' the off-road track. My eyebrows went up at that point too. Anyway, I became the expert witness for the defence, and because I was in court in an official capacity, I had to read every single page of the report – and there were yards and yards of material. I also had to listen to all of the witnesses before presenting my 'expert opinion'.

There were two expert witnesses present: one for the prosecution, and one for the defence – that was me. I talked on behalf of the Land Rover Experience and the worry was that if the claimant won the case it would set a very unwanted precedent for all businesses who provide such experiences.

I was in the court building, waiting to be 'called' to present my expert opinion, but I really couldn't wait any longer; I simply *had* to answer a call of nature. Inevitably, I found that I *had* been 'called' during my absence, and I was therefore a little bit late when I burst into the courtroom. I planned to say:

'I'm really sorry, My Lady, but I was indisposed at the time I was called.'

Then I looked up and saw that 'My Lady' was really quite a 'good-looker' and I instantly started to stutter:

'My, My, My Lady....,'
'Are you alright, Mr. Gillanders?'
'I'm very well, thank you.'

I responded as though we were having a wee chat before the actual proceedings! The outcome was that the Defence won. 'My Lady' believed my 'expert witness' account instead of the claimant's expert witness account.

Allegedly, what happened was this: the student driver managed to get stuck on an incline, and what the instructor *should* have done was get on the radio and call for back-up, but he failed to do that. Had he done so the back-up vehicle could have roped up the stranded vehicle and winched it back onto level ground. Instead of doing this, however, the instructor, again allegedly, opened his door because he wanted to swap seats with the lady driver. His intention was to free up the car, but when he opened the door and stepped out, he fell.....

A HOLE-IN-ONE

I would say that golf is a passion of mine these days – my handicap is 16, but it has been as low as 14. I am unlikely to improve on that because of my left hand, as I don't have total control of the club. That's not an excuse, but a fact. However, I do like the competition of it, and I like playing a round of golf with Gordon Hutcheon.

The Deeside Golf Club, which is located above the River Dee on the western approaches to Aberdeen, has an 18 hole, par 70 course, and a nine hole short course. I've been a member there since 1995 and a nice bunch of guys play and work there. I go to Gleneagles on occasions, and also to Skibo Castle, of course. I have played a lot of courses, including some abroad, and I like the exercise because it's good for me, but it is very frustrating, I'd like to play golf a lot better than I actually do.

After I retired, I found that I had to either become a little bit special on my own or just wither away, and as I'm not the type to wither away I found that this, the third main phase (the current period) of my life, has been the most difficult to maintain. My life *has* been remarkable, and one of the reasons I decided to write this book was to let my grandchildren know of my life of fun, adventure and achievement.

I felt a little 'special' when I scored a 'Hole-in-One' at my home course on Deeside because I saw it happen. I was playing a round of golf in 2013 with my playing partners, Ronald Herd, Graham Yule and Drummond Whiteford. It *was* very special because a golfer doesn't always witness his or her own 'Hole-in-One' shot, even if lucky enough to achieve one in the first instance. Such successes are usually at par three holes of between 150 and 170 yards, with the hole on the green at an angle or just over a brow out of immediate sight.

The first tee at Deeside is an elevated one, about 100 yards above the green, and it's easy to follow the flight of the ball all the way. I was there with my three pals, and when after I hit the ball, I immediately thought:

'Oh, this looks pretty handy.'

I saw it drop and I thought:
'That's very close.'
Then the ball disappeared altogether.
It *was* a Hole in One!

The Deeside Golf Club's "Hall of Fame" now sports this particular photograph, taken on the day of my 'ace'.

Photograph: courtesy of the Deeside Golf Club.

This little piece has some good news and bad news:

First the Good News: Early in March, 2016, my good friend and Monte Carlo co-driver, Gordon Hutcheon, played a round of golf with me at Royal Aberdeen at the Balgownie Links, Bridge of Don; it was a marvellous statement of his return to health. Gordon had not been well for almost the full year and in fact he only found out that he was really ill after he kept falling uncontrollably. Thankfully, he appears to have made a remarkable recovery from a very serious illness, and much of his recovery, I believe, has been down to ANCHOR, and I make no apology for copying the following text from one of the many websites online:

"The Aberdeen and North Centre for Haematology, Oncology and Radiotherapy (ANCHOR) unit is an NHS department at Aberdeen Royal Infirmary which treats patients with all forms of cancer, leukaemia and benign blood disorders throughout the North-East of Scotland including Orkney and Shetland. The Friends of ANCHOR was set up to directly support the ANCHOR unit by committing long-term funding to the following three areas: Medical Equipment, Patient Wellbeing, and Ground-breaking Research."

About the same time as our round of golf, Gordon thanked the ANCHOR charity which helped him through his battle with the disease and, with the help of Friends of ANCHOR's specialist cyclotron machine, he is now *"as all-clear as is possible"*. I'd say he was probably about 99% fit again.

Now the Bad News:
'He beat me!'

In July, 2017, Gordon and I played in a foursome at the 3,192 yard Queen's Course at Gleneagles, but we got absolutely stuffed by two friends from St.Andrews and Edinburgh.

CHANNEL OF DISCOVERY

Having met an award winning producer of a number of documentaries and reality shows, my thought was to introduce him to M-Sport to see if we could maybe persuade the popular *"Discovery"* Channel to create a series of programmes which we planned to entitle, *"Engineering with M-Sport"*.

Malcolm Wilson kindly agreed to facilitate a meeting to discuss the proposal, so I made the necessary arrangements before I headed south to stay overnight in the Trout Hotel by the River Derwent in Cockermouth.

It was quite late when I arrived in Cumbria, but I still had time to meet the others involved in the proposal; I started the introductions along with some general chat, but, at around 10 o'clock in the evening, just as we had begun to get to know each other, by saying who we were, what we did, and also generally relax in each others' company, I noticed a man approach from across the dining room. This gent stopped at our table and politely asked me:

'Are you David Gillanders?'

'Yes, I am.'

'Could I have your autograph please?'

I looked at him, and because I thought that this was a set-up by the people round the table, I said:

'No!'

You can imagine that my response didn't go down very well with anybody in the room, including the guy himself. But then I realised he was a bit hurt, so I said:

'Come on then, give me your business card!'

I signed it and then basically dismissed him.

He walked away and the guys at the table said to me:

'You know, David, what you said was very rude.'

So I asked them:

'Well, which one of you set that up?'

'None of us set it up.'

I had put two and two together and, on this occasion, got five, but afterwards, I have to admit, I felt really bad about it. Unfortunately, the gentleman had left the dining room by then and so I retired to my room. I had rather a restless night and woke up around 2 o'clock in the morning and thought long and hard about what I had actually done because fans at my age are few and far between.

I muttered to myself:

'My God, what an ass I've been.'

I went for breakfast in the morning to see if I could find the autograph hunter, and lo and behold, just as we were all about to check out, I saw him sitting in the lounge. I then approached and offered him my sincere apologies:

'Look, I am extremely sorry about last night. I have to apologise to you because I am not like that. I thought my colleagues at the table had been winding me up. I'm a really nice guy and I'm touched that you asked me for my autograph. Are you sure you've got the right person?'

'Oh yes, you made my night although you were a bit rude. I phoned my wife to say I'd met David Gillanders.'

I asked him why he wanted my autograph and he told me all about the stages he'd been to as a spectator; stages like Keilder, Otterburn, the Forest of Ae, and all the rest of it. He'd seen me in my Escorts, my Volvo and also my Metro 6R4. This chap, Brian, was a complete and utter nutter of a rally fan! I sat and spoke with him for a good ten minutes and then I synched his iPhone with mine and then swapped some photographs back to back with his. I gave him three or four pictures of my cars, and then I took one of my business cards and signed it properly:

'To Brian, many thanks, this is me, David Gillanders, the nice guy!'

I handed it to him, but unknown to me, one of the guys on the way out had stayed within earshot and had listened to the entire episode. He then spoke to me privately:

'You know something, David? That was really nice.'

327

'You know something, chum? I hardly slept a wink all night thinking about it, because there was a guy who wanted to meet me, me of all people! He actually made my night by asking for my autograph at the age of 65. I felt really bad about it, but I think we're friends now.'

I think that could be another one of several reasons why somebody might want to read this book; it is just possible that there *are* people out there who maybe *do* want to know about David Gillanders and what I have done with my life.

After that interlude we arrived at M-Sport for our meeting at 9 o'clock to meet up with Malcolm Wilson, who spent two or three hours with us. He then walked us round the premises and showed us the racing Bentleys being assembled and also the rally cars in the process of being prepared for Rally Finland (although I much prefer to know that event by its original name, *"The Rally of a Thousand Lakes"*).

The M-Sport organisation was on its 'high-alert' status, ready to ship both of their cars, plus loads of spares and equipment to Scandinavia. Their plan was to test the cars first, near Jyväskylä, the largest town in central Finland, because their (then) new driver, an Estonian by the name of Ott Tänak, had started to show a bit of pace (speed) and Malcolm had reckoned that M-Sport should give him all the help they could at this stage of his career.

"Rally Finland" is often (unofficially) called *"The Grand Prix of Rallying"* because of the high speeds that can be achieved by the rally cars. In fact, the (then) new breed of World Rally Championship cars were able to reach speeds of over 200 kph (almost 125 mph) on the very smooth, loose surface forest tracks which are regularly punctuated by really enormous jumps. It remains the fastest rally in the world and the driver *does* need to know where he's going, and with a car that will handle the crests, the short flight, and the subsequent landings…. Because of this, M-Sport planned to go early to conduct a lengthy test session.

To digress, but to provide an element of perspective, I have to tell you about 2017 Rally Finland and its famous Ouninpohja jump. The Norwegian Ford Fiesta driver, Mads Østberg took off over the crest and landed an incredible 164 feet away! That really was impressive, and quite a motorised flight too, but hark back to 1903 (according to records, not personal experience…), the Wright Brothers, with Orville at the controls, was airborne for only 120 feet…

After we finished our tour of M-Sport's facilities the *"Discovery"* people and I sat down with Malcolm, and at that point the producer asked:

'Would it be possible to film you and your team over the period of one year, Malcolm? We would 'ghost' you, and by that we mean we'd have the cameraman figuratively sit on your 'shoulder' and watch what you do, record what you say, meet your wife, your family, and go on events with the entire team. What we'd like to do is concentrate more on the logistics and engineering pertaining to each of the rallies – that's the building, the testing, and also the shipping of them – because the rally itself would be filmed by others. The event is not what is important to the "Discovery" programme, although we would want to be in the team hut to film you and watch the cars coming in for service.'

The conversation moved on:

'We'd also record the mechanics when they change a clutch, a front suspension unit, or rebuild an entire car in record time if need be. At the Service Halt, I'd have the cameraman film the interaction between all of the team members, but especially with you, Malcolm, and your drivers, because we understand that you know exactly how to handle the skills required, the pressures, and the actions needed to secure a good performance.

'The end of the rally would be filmed, hopefully with the team getting a result, maybe even a podium, but who knows? Then, after this, the cameraman would record the cars being packed up, loaded into the aircraft and then being shipped back to Dovenby Hall. Upon arrival, we would film them being stripped down and then prepared for the next event, with the cycle continuing throughout the year.

'We'd also like to film the testing of the cars between the events along with the general work of putting a rally car into its operating environment.'

The manufacturers in the World Rally Championship in 2017 had a chance to build a new version of the old Group 'B' rally cars (that's my terminology), except they were lighter, and had no carry-over from the cars of 2016 (or even from the 1980s after Group 'B' was banned). These cars were in effect brand new vehicles.

The engines were certainly more powerful, the transmissions further improved and the drivers had a new sixth gear to play with instead of five. The brakes, too, had been greatly improved, and the overall balance of the car was much enhanced. They also made more noise, and flames spat out from the exhaust on the overrun, reminiscent of my old 'Pop, Bang, Whiz' Ford Escort RS Cosworth, so the spectacle became huge, and really spectacular. A bit like an old Group 'B' rally car, in other words, but safer.

Safety is always a top consideration, obviously, but the top Group 'B' cars of the 1980s pushed out over 500 brake horsepower! The baby Quattro, officially launched as the Audi Quattro Sport S1 E2, was insanely quick, but nevertheless was admirably handled by the double World Rally Champion, Walter Röhrl.

The roll cages in the cabins were much inferior in the early days compared to what they are today, as were the suspension and brakes. I also think that the drivers, co-drivers and mechanics perhaps weren't as professional then as they are nowadays, but to be fair to them, the vast majority of competitors didn't have the money to splash out on the best of equipment either.

Take the suspension in a modern rally car as an example: I could easily drive a 30 kilometre forest stage and find that the suspension I started out with would still be in exactly the same condition by the end of that section. But, if I took out an older Group 'B' rally car – the kind that I knew and loved – I'd find it a very hard car to manage because it was everything a driver didn't really want. For instance, if I took that Group 'B' rally car out into the forest, I'd find that by the time I had done 10 kilometres, I'd hazard a guess and say that the front suspension would be getting soft, and by the time I had done 20 kilometres, I'd find that the rear suspension would be getting soft. And by the time I'd done 30 kilometres, the car would have been pretty much impossible to drive because the brakes would have been totally knackered, the suspension would have overheated, and it would be tantamount to driving a sponge without brakes, but still with oodles and oodles of horsepower!

The intention was for the producer and me to persuade the *"Discovery"* Channel to commission a film series to record the efforts of M-Sport and their engineering and logistics personnel during the 2016 season. And, (at the time) under embargo, also film the 2017 car. We would all have had a chance to watch it being built from the computer-aided design (CAD) systems through to the physical build in Dovenby Hall, and thence into the forests for testing and eventual competition.

The plan was to record all of that, as well as all of the ongoing development of the car right up to and including its debut on the Monte Carlo Rally at the end of January, 2017. The hope (at the time) was that the *"Discovery"* Channel would kick off a year-long series which could have been introduced by stating:

'Here is the new generation M-Sport Ford Fiesta rally car; we shall record the entire year of the car's development and testing as part of the series.'

I was going to be one of several people to 'front' the programme although the producer's intention was to also interview the personnel within M-Sport and talk with the drivers, the test engineers, the gearbox engineers, the engine engineers and of course, Malcolm Wilson. My role would have been the question and answer man, but would you have seen me in it?

'Yes, but you would have also heard me talking…'

The star of the series would have been M-Sport itself because it wasn't intended to be presenter-dominated like the *"Discovery"* Channel series, *"Idris Elba: no limits"*. Elba, the Hackney-born Londoner who played Nelson Mandela in the film, *"Mandela: Long Walk to Freedom",* attempted to beat Sir Malcolm Campbell's world land speed record, as well as try his hand at dragster racing, rally car driving, and flying a stunt plane. He 'sold' the whole idea to the *"Discovery"* Channel.

I viewed the one about rallying, but I really didn't like it! He had Jimmy McRae as his instructor, and I don't mean this as a slight against Jimmy, but I thought that the programme was awful! My personal opinion was that the whole thing wasn't very professional from a rallyman's point of view and I thought it made my sport look amateurish.

Elba's attempt at breaking the World Land Speed Record that Donald Campbell had set in 'Bluebird' at Pendine Sands in Wales on February 4, 1927, was just short of 175 miles per hour over the flying kilometre – the average speed over two runs.

They gave Elba a 7-litre Bentley – the very latest model – and on the same sands in Wales, and he did it! But the thing that annoyed me about the whole programme was that *he* was the star, when, in my opinion, the star throughout the whole attempt was the Bentley!

In conjunction with the *"Discovery"* Channel, the producer planned to record much more than the just the M-Sport drivers and their cars on the WRC events. The film crew planned to cover the 'behind the scenes' elements, as well as the development of the then new generation WRC Ford Fiesta, which I thought, looked fabulous with its big wings, big tail, big spoilers, and all that. To me, it looked and sounded just like the Group 'B' Rally Cars of the 1980s.

Apparently, all the drivers loved the idea of having something that would force them to 'think' a bit more, because although the 2016 cars had been quick, the drivers always seemed to be looking for an extra gear to change up to. For example, on Rally Finland, they would be in fifth gear for a lot of the time and, having looked at the onboard action, I got the distinct feeling that all of the drivers had indeed been searching for yet another gear.

I'd even hazard a guess that the 2017 and 2018 World Rally cars, and of course the more recent 2019 machines, probably had the drivers think a little bit less about going into top gear because the latest WRC models have an extra 20 mph top speed!

However, despite our best endeavours, the *"Discovery Channel"* project with M-Sport stalled.

I still think it's a great idea.

M-SPORT

I've known Malcolm Wilson for a very long time, initially as a fellow competitor when he was a Works driver for Ford, and then when we were team-mates at Austin Rover in our MG Metro 6R4s. He was more of a colleague back then, but I'd say we became really firm friends around the time he began to look after my Ford Escort RS Cosworth in the 1990s.

We've kept in touch ever since, and in 2011 he presented an opportunity for me to get involved in 'his' rally, the Malcolm Wilson Stages, the event he sponsors on his doorstep in Cumbria. I didn't need much convincing, and I jumped at the chance to drive one of the last Ford Focus WRC cars as Course Car. Honestly, I didn't need much persuasion.

I thought I'd ask Tommy Dreelan, a good friend and a former oil industry executive in Aberdeen, to co-drive for me because, quite often, Tommy has said to me:

'You know, David, I'd like to go in a rally car.'

Malcolm's offer allowed me to extend an invitation to Tommy, just as Jerry Weintraub granted me my wish of a flight in an F-15. I was now able to give Tommy his wish of a run in a rally car, and so I said to him:

'Malcolm has given me an opportunity to drive the Course Car on the Malcolm Wilson Rally, so why don't you come along and co-drive for me?'

He didn't take long to answer:

'You're on!'

At the time, Tommy was the Team Principal of Celtic Speed, located in St. Cyrus, near Montrose on the east coast of Scotland. He'd previously done a bit of motor sport himself and had become involved in some historic events that year when Celtic Speed expanded into Group C racing, initially with a Spice C2 Group C car. Then he acquired a couple of Formula One cars (as you do…). The first was the March 761 raced by Arturo Merzario in 1976; then he bought the Williams FW08 that took Keke Rosberg to the Formula 1 World Title in 1982.

Course Car duties on the Malcolm Wilson Stages in 2011 with Tommy Dreelan in the hot seat of the Stobart-sponsored M-Sport Ford Focus RS WRC 09.
Photograph: Chris West (www.chriswestphotography.net)

The M-Sport Ford Focus RS WRC09, registration number 'AG57 CKA' was what was called an 'active', fully hydraulic ex-Stobart sponsored, and very quick car. I put Tommy in the driving seat for a couple of stages and coached him too, although I did the majority of the driving. I have to say that on the first couple of stages I was extremely rusty and I couldn't grasp the car at all, but slowly, and surely, it all came back to me and by the last stage I (unofficially) set a top five time and this was pretty much without a co-driver, because, with all due respect to Tommy, he just laughed the entire time!

On test with Matthew Wilson, M-Sport Ford Focus RS.
Photograph: Gladys Gillanders.

Motor Sport History in the Making

I was privileged to witness one of the greatest feats of motor sport on Sunday, October 29, 2017, when Malcolm Wilson's M-Sport World Rally Team beat three of the biggest car manufacturers on the planet to win:

a) The World Rally Championship (Manufacturers);
b) The World Rally Championship (Drivers); and
c) Wales Rally GB (with Welshman, Elfyn Evans).

The reigning World Champion was Sébastien Ogier who secured his fifth consecutive title, and Ott Tänak was sufficiently well placed on the rally to secure the manufacturers' title for the Cumbrian outfit. The icing on the cake for the team was when Elfyn Evans scored his maiden WRC win on his home event! All had been driving M-Sport Ford Fiestas, but the team's success was even more remarkable given that there was, at the time, still one round of the series left to run.

I was there, but I can't remember everything about the celebrations that day, so I later checked the M-Sport website after the elation had eventually abated to find out exactly what Malcolm had said:

"It's been a very emotional day and I have to say that there were a few tears during the last stage – firstly when Ott crossed the line to take the manufacturers' championship, then when Sébastien took the drivers' and finally when Elfyn crossed the line to the win on our home event, it really was the Triple Crown, and a very emotional day for all of us."

Malcolm continued by stating:

"We have a great team of people and their hard work has resulted in something truly amazing. We've been on the podium at every event and we're the only team to have had all three drivers secure a win this year. The Fiesta has proven itself to have the performance and the strength, and that is down to the tireless hours that every single member of the team has put into this incredible achievement."

I'd call that a legendary season, without a doubt, and I felt it was quite fitting because, to me, and I suspect many others, Malcolm Wilson is most definitely a rally legend – although not a 'Granite Legend' like me – despite his 1979 win on my home rally. His record as a driver is impressive with two British National titles and the British International title to his name. He also drove for three different teams in the World Rally Championship and, as Managing Director of M-Sport, he has guided Ford to two FIA World Rally Titles in 2006 and 2007. Then, in 2017, M-Sport became World Rally Champions in their own right.

The 2017 WRC model was based on the then 'new-for-2017' road going Ford Fiesta, but just about the only thing 'Ford' about it was the blue oval badge and the basic outline of the body shape. It shared the same platform with the best-selling small car in Europe, but M-Sport took that base car and designed it from scratch to adhere to the next generation technical regulations implemented by the FIA.

The result was such that the car, in so many ways, actually resembled the 'flying' machines of the old Group 'B' days, sporting huge wheel arches, spoilers, wings and fins all over the place, so much so that it looked sensational and sounded absolutely phenomenal! Apparently, Malcolm's team started with a clean sheet of paper – just like I did with this book of mine – and designed it from the ground up, along with some technical support from Ford.

Before the start of the 2017 season, the M-Sport team had high hopes of securing some podium places, especially after they had captured the services of Sébastien Ogier, the winner of 38 rally victories from 2013 through to 2016. Once he joined Malcolm's team, the Frenchman added to that tally.

It was a perfect start to 2017: Ogier won the fabled Monte Carlo Rally and all of a sudden there was a huge dose of optimism in the M-Sport camp. Another win for Ogier in Portugal was followed by a win for Ott Tänak in Sardinia. The Estonian took his second WRC win in Germany and of course, Elfyn Evans had his maiden WRC victory on Wales Rally GB.

The Ford Fiesta WRC, with its M-Sport designed and built 1,600cc engine, had been coupled up to a brand new design six-speed sequential gearbox with an hydraulic gear change. It was all very technical, and all very costly, but Malcolm himself drove the car and said:

"The 2017 Ford Fiesta WRC is one of the most imp-ressive cars M-Sport has ever produced. It's exciting to drive, it sounds fantastic, and looks sensational."

I was in M-Sport's control room on that Wales Rally GB, waiting for the results to come through at the finish when I bumped into one of my former co-drivers, the larger-than-life Welshman, Howard Davies. I called him on the phone a few weeks afterwards and we reminisced about the fantastic result that M-Sport achieved and also about the three events we did together many years ago. Howard exclaimed:

'The really great thing has been the incredible success of M-Sport, especially in the latter period of 2017, winning both championships and the Wales Rally GB.'

I felt as though I was interviewing him, so I asked:

'Yes, I was just going to ask you about that and also how Wales took to Elfyn winning the Wales Rally GB?'

And, being from the Principality, he replied:

'To be fair, Wales erupted, didn't it? You know, the lad is a national hero, and he was so modest about it. He was so confident, wasn't fazed at all, and was incredibly relaxed! All

the way through the rally, and right up to the last stage I interviewed him for Welsh TV. He was extremely cool. In fact, I think actually, Gwyndaf was more excited!'

He was, I had met Gwyndaf (Elfyn's father) at the end too and he had tears in his eyes. He couldn't speak with emotion.

Howard reflected on that:

'It was a big moment for Gwyndaf because he (and I) never got the opportunity to compete at the top level in a proper car; we always had second class opportunities and second class cars. You need to be competing and be game fit, and I have to say that once Elfyn got out in front on the Friday he was confident he would keep the lead. I think it was no problem for him at all. The others had to play catch-up.'

I summed it up:

'I think I was lucky to be there and in the 'control tower' the whole time with Malcolm and the others in the team – some said that his tyres were better but I pointed out to the guys that he still had to drive the car!'

Howard, too, had been asking that question:

'Would Elfyn have won if he'd had Michelins?'

Howard commented on the fact that nobody actually said to 'no' to that question. They all said it was Elfyn's rally, and he drove it brilliantly; it was *his* rally and he did drive exceptionally well. Howard continued:

'Even with Michelins he would have won it. Yes, I think it would have been the same result, but I definitely feel that the D-Mack tyres held him back on other rallies this year. Of course, what Michelin had was the durability, longevity and reliability; the D-Mack tyres could perform, but its window of performance was a little more restrictive, whereas the French company's product was all encompassing.'

Once Howard starts talking it's pretty difficult to get him to stop (a bit like me, I suppose), but his conversation is usually witty and informative. He added:

'Before I go, I have to say a word about M-Sport and what Malcolm Wilson has done with that team. The team is led by a fantastic guy whom I have a lot of admiration for, and what they have done this year (2017), to win the world championship for manufacturers, for drivers, and also win Rally Wales

GB, has been absolutely fantastic. It'll never happen again. History has been made.'

I agreed, but then Howard started talking again.....

'I have to take my hat off to Malcolm, not because I received an invitation from the gaffer to go up and say a few words (well, maybe a few more than a few) and do a question and answer session with the drivers. I was actually quite choked (and lost for words.....) when the invitation came through.

'Accordingly, I ended up in M-Sport's headquarters on November 28, 2017, and thoroughly enjoyed the event which was made even more special when Sébastien Ogier and Elfyn Evans both stepped up and signed new contracts to be the company's main drivers for the 2018 season and also drive the M-Sport Ford World Rally Team Ford Fiestas.'

As I mentioned earlier in this chapter, I had been invited to join Malcolm's team at Ruthin in North Wales where I witnessed first the expectation, then the euphoria. I think it is fair to say that the atmosphere at the time was electric.

However, I think I must have overdone the celebrations, because a week or so afterwards I ended up in the hospital following a very bad heart attack! After a few days of receiving some more quality NHS treatment I found myself still standing and still hoping that I live long enough to see the publication of this book!

The motor car has been an integral part of my life, even now, long after my retirement from competition. I particularly enjoy my relationship with M-Sport in my role as their Manufacturer Liaison – that means that I'm the first port of call when a Manufacturer (such as Jaguar Land Rover) comes along, especially in respect of new opportunities where it could involve Malcolm Wilson's business interests.

At the end of 2018, Malcolm announced that he would stand down as the WRC Team Principal and that his role would be taken over by Richard Millener. Malcolm, however, remains as Managing Director of M-Sport, but his plan now is to remain in charge and oversee all areas of the company as a whole.

CHAPTER TWENTYSIX

A DIFFERENT PERSON

Nowadays, I like to think that I'm a totally different person. I'm no longer the arrogant, bumptious character that I used to be. I think I'm a much nicer individual to talk to, and people can be drawn to me, and want to talk with me. It seems that people like being around me, and are interested to know what I am currently doing. I find that really quite flattering.

I also understand things a bit more as well, and I'll tell you something, although you might find this really strange. You'll hardly believe it, but I actually *understand* more about cars now, right now, today, than I've done in all my life previously. I've been driving fast cars and also handled some extremely interesting cars over the past 50 years, but latterly, I've been working very closely with top class engineers, and talking with them.

But, in the days when I was a rally driver, I really didn't know very much at the time. Back then, I actually pretended that I knew what the engineers had been saying to me. For example, someone would say:

'Let's stiffen up the roll bar.'

I'd not a clue what that meant, but I'd say:

'Let's stiffen it up'.

I'd also hear someone else say:

'Let's have a bit more negative camber on the front.'

And I'd say:

'By Christ, we'll have some of that!'

Then another person might ask:

'How does it handle?'

And of course, I'd simply answer:

'Brilliant!'

I told this to Malcolm Wilson not that long ago over dinner one evening:

'You know something, Malcolm, I honestly and truly wish that I'd understood the engineering better during my rally days. I think I'd have been a much better driver, because now I can actually get into a car and say to the engineers:

'Right, we'll soften the anti-roll bar, and we'll do this and that, and by making these alterations I can actually make the car's handling characteristics totally change.'

That's me today. I *am* more methodical.

I *am* more understanding *and....*

I *listen* better.

It's not *my* way any more, it's *everybody's* way now.

Jim Robson

I have to go back to my Mini days to tell you about Jim Robson who lived in Aberdeen at the time. As I mentioned earlier, he was my Best Man at my wedding to Gladys, and he and I became extremely close. I have to say if it hadn't been for Jim I don't think I'd have been half as competent as I was in motor sport because he showed me how to take a Mini gearbox apart and put it back together again.

In those days there were no special outlets that stripped engines or gearboxes, so we had to do absolutely everything ourselves if we wanted to tune our Minis. If I wanted to fit idler gears in my Mini I had to do it myself because there was no local Mini garage. With Graham Neish, I would take my car to bits, as would Jim Robson, Simon Cobb, Derry Taylor, Jim Milne and John Whyte, all of them really good chums. Irrespective of whose garage I would go to, there would be a Mini there, in component form. Nobody taught us how to take it apart or put it back together again, we just hoped that when we reassembled it there was nothing left over! Simon, though, often put the bits in back to front!

Anyway, Jim and I became very close. We rallied together (albeit not in the same car); we raced on hill climbs and sprints together; and eventually he came to work for me at Gillanders Motors. He was a self-taught electrician and very good at fitting and taking out radios. Jim was a great guy, but he ended up with a lot of problems. I hope he is alright, because I haven't seen or heard from him for years.

I do miss him, because he has been a huge part of my life, certainly in the first period, and I have to say that I miss my chums and my time with them because as I grow older I generally don't have any new chums any more – I have friends and acquaintances. Take Gordon Hutcheon, for example; he's a very close friend, but I didn't grow up with him. I sort of grew up with Neish, Robson, Cobb, Taylor, Milne and Whyte.

Most of my current friends are people that I have met more recently and enjoy their company, but my chums are the ones I grew up with from the age of 17, when I got my driving licence. That's the difference.

My memory of some of my friends, and things that have happened in the past, are beginning to get a little bit fuzzy, and that's another of my reasons for writing this book – before my memory goes completely.

However, I do remember one such friend, Donald Milne, and I'm sorry to say it was when he started to compete in his Nissan-engined MG Metro 6R4 that our friendship cooled somewhat. Nevertheless, I respected Donald for his rallying exploits, especially the time he won the Scottish Rally Championship in 1991 (with Bob Wilson).

I was shocked, though, when I heard of his passing following a tragic flying accident at the small Mutxamel airstrip near Alicante, close to his retirement home at Dénia, in Spain, where he had lived for the past 20 odd years. Donald, apparently, had been flying his ultra-light biplane, a replica Bü-131 Bücker Jungmann, and by all accounts, he really enjoyed it.

Donald was a wee bit like me and had a real passion for flight, but I have to say, in my humble opinion, he wasn't born to fly – his record, sadly, was actually controversial: he once landed at Dyce (Aberdeen Airport) without lowering his undercarriage and his subsequent crash-landing caused an Aberdeen-bound Royal Flight to be diverted elsewhere!

Donald also wrote off his helicopter whilst trying to land at his house at Auchattie, by Banchory, and then he wrote off another helicopter in the Republic of Ireland while out on a "test flight" in July, 2015. Allegedly, in this incident, he had attempted to land at a Pub called the Rustic Inn in Abbey-shrule, Co. Longford.

Miraculously, nobody had been injured in any of Donald's earlier flying incidents, but his luck ran out on Saturday, December, 30, 2017. Ironically, it seemed that his fourth accident involving flight was *not* caused by him. Allegedly, he was on 'final approach', only 100 feet off landing when he was involved in a mid-air collision with a fire-fighting helicopter. It would have been impossible for him to see what was immediately ahead and below, and his biplane hit the unsighted tail rotor of the helicopter. Following the crash, Donald was taken by ambulance to Alicante General Hospital where his condition was described as critical, but despite the valiant efforts of the medical personnel, he died later that day. The helicopter pilot and the six fire fighters onboard had a miraculous escape.

Although we had our differences, I do have to admire how Donald became a mentor and sponsor of Colin McRae in his early rally career. He actually loaned Colin his Nissan 240RS to use on some events during his 1988 Scottish Rally Championship winning year.

Humbling

One of the most humbling occasions that I have ever experienced was the time when Gordon Hutcheon and I went to meet the autistic children in the Linn Moor Residential School. I had to spend, well no, I *wanted* to spend, and I *did* spend, a few hours with them all. The whole encounter completely floored me and I found that there is an incredible amount of work and care that goes into looking after the children. The employees are absolutely fantastic; they are immense, and honestly, I found it a very humbling visit.

It looked as though the staff-to-pupil ratio was in the region of five-to-one, but whatever it is I applaud all the hard work and dedication of all of the staff. I feel that the unselfish care that these people give in helping the children of all ages from 5 years of age through to 18, (and each with varying degrees of learning difficulties) is truly amazing. Their efforts have to be seen to be appreciated and I was proud that Gordon and I managed to raise the sum of £18,000 – three times our goal – for such a good cause. I take my hat off to the staff for the way they look after the children. I left, totally blown away by the whole episode. That visit has really stuck in my mind.

Fortunate

I've been extremely fortunate to know a lot of people in my lifetime: my father, obviously, had a really huge influence in my life, as had my mother, but it was another gentleman, the Late Dr. Francis Clark, who became my inspiration. When my father passed away, Francis Clark became a father-figure to me. I looked up to him because he had 'done everything', had 'been everywhere', and had 'talked to everybody'. He gave me a yardstick on how to do things, so I'd certainly state that he was very influential in my early life.

Francis Clark was actually a medical doctor, but he also founded 'Claben', a hugely successful company in the fish processing and transport industries, prior to being bought over by Christian Salvesen Plc. in the mid 1970s. However, he continued to play a large part in the management of this company in Edinburgh. He was, undoubtedly, a giant in the fishing industry and it was he who helped to make Peterhead the busiest white fish port in the UK.

Another man whom I hold in high esteem is Stewart Spence, a well known hotelier in Aberdeen who has been of great help and support over many years.

I've had help from many people in my time, but *how* have they helped? Often, they've helped by just being there for me, because as I get older and more on my own, other than with Gladys, I feel I need people who understand me and to be by my side.

Certain people, like Gordon Hutcheon, Brian Lyall, Bill Cruickshank and Martin Whitaker, all of whom I can rely on, are crucial to have around me because if I have a problem with my life, and wish to share it, then I'd share it with folk that I know, trust, admire and respect.

Regrets

Regrets? Yes, I have a few. For example, I should not have sold the garage, Gillanders Motors, but I feel I was almost coerced into selling it when actually there was no real need to. If I'd been stronger at the time and a bit more savvy, I probably would have kept it, but nevertheless, I have to admit that I had lost interest in the motor trade.

The company had grown, my father had passed away, and I had become the sole owner of the garage; I ran it without any family support. I also had squeezes on the business from various financial institutions, and some of the manufacturers were less than helpful. I could see that the business needed to move in a different direction and in that respect I felt I had to get rid of some of the franchises, or grow the business, but to grow it would have meant putting a vast amount of money into it.

The motor trade had started to become very big with the likes of Arnold Clark and John Clark and the idea of a family business surviving was pretty much a pipe dream. John Clark, though, has done a great job with his because he was certainly much more focused on his business than I was with mine. My motor sport career had distracted me; I had taken my eye off the ball and I let other people run the business, much to the detriment of Gillanders Motors in Aberdeen. It became rather obvious when people used to come into the showroom and ask for David Gillanders, because the answer they would often receive was:

'Oh, he's away on a rally.'

And the thought was:

'Oh well, he doesn't care about customers.'

In business, the hands-on approach is important, vital even, especially when a person's own name is over the door. Anyway, Brian Lyall and Anderson Cars came along with a deal that seemed to be the right one at the right time. He represented Nissan (South) with Anderson Cars whereas I, in Gillanders Motors represented Nissan (North), but Brian wanted both Nissan outlets, and so he made me an offer I couldn't refuse! I wasn't a threat, but Anderson Cars simply wanted to take me out of the competition.

His acquisition of my Gillanders Motors business gave Anderson Cars the Nissan agency on both sides of Aberdeen, but they were much more into selling used cars than they were into new vehicles. Nevertheless, the deal subsequently went through and I retired late in 1995.

It had got to the stage where I had been selling new Nissans for a mere £50 profit. Not only that, there was the rise of the German marques such as BMW, Audi, and also Volkswagen. They were all rising stars in the trade and the prices of the German cars were coming down, but I wouldn't say they were any better built than the Swedish or French ones. But there *was* something about them: perhaps it was a triumph of Marketing over Engineering?

Not long afterwards, Brian Lyall left Anderson Cars and went to live in Spain, but the business was never the same; I got the feeling that the new owners were not really 'car' people, and from the outside (to me anyway) the whole set-up just seemed to implode and Anderson Cars collapsed soon after the Nissan marque dropped in popularity in Aberdeen and the surrounding area. I suppose the additional wealth from the prosperous days of Oil and Gas industry meant that people could afford more expensive cars, such as the BMW and Audi marques.

Fintray at Fifty

A few of my old pals met again up at a Fintray Hill Climb in May, 2015. That was when the Grampian Automobile Club (GAC) celebrated the 50th anniversary of sealed surface (asphalt) events there. The GAC took over the running of the venue, a working farm, from the Aberdeen and District Motor Club in 1985.

One of my old road rally navigators, Roger Reed, was there as the MSA Steward, and Brian Sim, the former Stonehaven and District Motor Club Secretary, was acting as the Club Steward. John Whyte was also there, as Treasurer and as a saviour of the track, and Jack Davidson arrived to promote the club's celebratory publication, *"Fintray at Fifty"*, which he happened to produce on the club's behalf. It was when I saw the magazine my thought process sped into overdrive, and I said to him:

'I've often been asked if I'd ever written a book, and of course the answer up to now has always been 'no', but since you're standing there in front of me, I'll do the talking – you do the writing!'

Some of my old chums (some older than others) at the Fintray Hill Climb in May, 2015; Left to Right: Trevor Park (who was too busy talking to look at the camera), me, not talking for a change... then Jack Davidson, Brian Sim and John Whyte. Photograph: Alan Banks.

I was saddened to learn that Roger Reed had passed away after an illness on Friday, April, 29, 2016, but what a marvellous send-off he got at the Aberdeen Crematorium on May 5, 2016. In addition to motor sport, Roger had also been involved with the local Lyric Society and Amateur Dramatics Group along with wife, Pat, and that was extremely obvious at the crematorium because the singing was incredible. I had never, ever, heard anything quite like it, so much so, that I later said to Pat:

'I'd like them at my funeral! I only need their names and addresses....'

A Great Life

I was asked to identify the most important thing in my life and I had to think long and hard before I gave an answer because that was a really good question. It has to be 'Family'; it's not motor sport, it's not driving cars, it's not making deals, it's not flying helicopters, it's not going on holiday, it's not fishing, it's not going out for dinners, it's not meeting people, and it's not golf. It's actually going home and sitting at the fireside with Gladys, and discussing what we have done that day.

You've probably figured this out all by yourself by now, but the fact is that I talk a lot. You might also understand why a particular journalist turned round to me one day and asked:

'Why say a word when a paragraph will suffice?'

'I can't help it. I just like to explain myself, and the more I talk about the particular things I might be talking about, the more it seems to make sense to talk more, so maybe I do use a paragraph when a word would suffice.'

But I'm still not finished although I am close to the end of the 'stage', I am not yet out of the woods.

Have I had a good life?

*'Yes. In fact I'd say that I have had a **great** life.'*

The Horizon

So, what's on the horizon now for David Gillanders? Well, I'd like to think that after publishing this book there could be some longevity left in me. I'd like to grow old gracefully with Gladys, but I don't want to end up with auldtimer's disease, cancers, or anything that would turn me into a vegetable. I'd rather jump off a window ledge.

However, I very much doubt if I'll get to see all of my hopes come to fruition, because of my faulty 'pump' and 'electrical system' and that's one of my main reasons for writing this book. I fear, I genuinely fear, that I won't have that luxury. I really do.

David (Dave) Edgar Bignald of Gartrac didn't have that luxury. I would have loved to have had his input to this book given his influence on my motor sport career, and I would have been proud to have given him one of the first copies, but I learned that he had passed away after an illness on Sunday, November, 8, 2015. To his family, and of course, all at Gartrac, I offer my profound condolences. Dave knew I was writing this book, and he knew that I respected and appreciated all he had done for me, but unfortunately, he did not have the health to be able to contribute.

You might just have noticed in the earlier pages that there's been a lot of high flying rally cars in my life but it's not so much the flight that's the problem but what happens immediately afterwards…. and I think that years and years of heavy landings have actually taken their toll on me.

I have been suffering quite a lot from what is known as 'Decompression of the Spine', and I subsequently underwent an operation on my back on June 23, 2016 to avoid the horrendous possibility of becoming a paraplegic! It was *that* serious, and it was also mentioned to me that this particular operation was the one which carried the greatest risk of litigation to the NHS because it happens to be one of the most difficult conditions to diagnose.

The cars in the 1970s and 1980s were not exactly famed for having much in the way of creature comforts and suspension travel. It was as though the seats, shock absorbers, springs and dampers were added almost as an afterthought to the continuing quest for an increase in power, improved braking and better handling.

I literally took all of the bumps and compressions in my stride, but, in hindsight, I believe that it has been the years of traversing the rough special stages, and flying over hundreds of crests at speeds, often well in excess of 100 mph, that have caused my back problems. Although, as I said, it wasn't so much the flying but the landing!

I mentioned Sir Isaac Newton and his famous saying of: *"What goes up must come down"* earlier in my book, but what the eminent physicist and mathematician did not and obviously could not consider in his lifetime, was just how high a rally car would reach and how fast and heavy it would crash land when it returned from orbit.

Given the pounding my body has had over the years I began to find myself to be in constant pain. It became quite intolerable and it felt as though I'd been sticking three fingers into a live socket (not that I have done that of course, and neither for one second do I recommend doing that either). I felt each and every sharp pain from the electrical pulses which ranged from one second to ten, and it was extremely frustrating not being able to do a damn thing about it.

Here's another example of me flying high – this time in my Ford Escort RS1800 during an Autocross event in 1980 at fellow rally driver, James Ingleby's farm at Westhall, Oyne, Aberdeenshire. *Photograph: Jack Davidson.*

On September, 8, 2016, I endured a second back operation, but following this the pain remained excruciating. Even with my extensive vocabulary at my disposal, I simply could not find words suitable enough to describe how I felt, and it really didn't help when the surgeon told me that if this latest operation didn't work then I would have one option left: this, he called a 'Nuts and Bolts' option, and by the sound of it. I really didn't want that!

I was discharged from the hospital but in less than a fortnight I was re-admitted, but this time with a *'leak from my dura mater'*, basically the protective fluid of my brain. This had formed a large lump which had to be drained several times! I hadn't a clue if it was connected to the back surgery, but it was all a big concern. However, after only three days I was discharged, despite the fact that I had a blinding headache, so I wasn't too sure if that last stay in the ARI actually helped me much at all. Then, to cap it all, I was again re-admitted the very next day with, I believe, a bleed in my back which was, allegedly, a legacy from my first back operation.

I fell out with a Registrar when my patience began to wear thin, but after this, though, I met with a Senior NHS Manager and following our discussion I underwent a CT scan to rule out a tumour in the pelvic area. A third back operation was planned for October 6, 2016 but I didn't have to go through with it as the medical staff decided instead to release the excess fluid through an alternative and less invasive process.

It was a huge relief to me that this solution appeared to work; and I was heartened to learn that the medical personnel were of the opinion that the procedure would, over time, clear up all of my back problems. At the same time I was also advised that the MRI scan of my lower body produced an 'all clear' with no sign of anything sinister, so that too was a huge relief.

Mind you, it's no wonder that Gladys said to me:

'You are an impossible patient!'

Since then I have been in and out of Aberdeen Royal Infirmary a number of times in connection with my ongoing health concerns, and I fear that I might not have the luxury of seeing all of my hopes come true. These thoughts intensified somewhat on September 17, 2018, when I was admitted to the stroke ward! I had actually gone to the A&E Department because I had a problem with my water works but, apparently, when I arrived at the reception, I started to speak a whole lot of gibberish and the receptionist thought that I was having a stroke, and she triggered an emergency. In hindsight, it's nice to know that the NHS staff reacted so quickly, but apparently a urinary infection can sometimes have that effect.

I thought I had been making perfect sense.

Mind you, one of the tests they gave me in the stroke ward was to set the time on a clock face to 2.35pm and try as I might, for some reason, I could only manage to set it to 2.25pm! However, I was discharged the following day, and all was well until early in November, 2018 when, I believe, I did have a couple of minor strokes, and when Ross Baird visited me on Tuesday, November 13, he told me that I really looked awful!

That didn't exactly cheer me up, but if I do nothing further with my life….

'I'll keep on going flat out and….

*…. **still** do all the talking!'*

APPENDIX
MAIN RESULTS

The following is a record of my known competition results; it is definitely incomplete, and may not even be in the correct chronological order. When I moved house I lost a lot of my motor sport records, but every effort (from many people) has been made to try and make the list as comprehensive as possible. Any errors and/or omissions will be corrected in any subsequent reprint(s).

CHAMPIONSHIP RESULTS:
1987:   **British National Rally Champion (MG Metro 6R4)**
1995:   **Scottish Rally Champion (Ford Escort RS Cosworth)**

EVENT RESULTS:
1970

Crimond Sprint

Co-Driver:	N/A	Mini Cooper S	ERG574D	3rd	In Class

1971

Fonthill Barracks Autotests

Co-Driver:	N/A	Mini Cooper S	ERG574D	3rd	In Class

Blairydrine Autotests

Co-Driver:	N/A	Mini Cooper S	ERG574D	3rd	In Class

Blairydrine Autotests

Co-Driver:	N/A	Mini Pick-Up	Unknown	5th	In Class

Garioch Autotests

Co-Driver:	N/A	Mini Cooper S	ERG574D	2nd	In Class

1972

Kinkell Hill Climb

Co-Driver:	N/A	Mini Cooper S	ERG574D	1st	In Class

Rumster Hill Climb

Co-Driver:	N/A	Mini Cooper S	ERG574D	1st	In Class*

1973

Peter Plastics (Scotland) Granite City Rally

Co-Driver:	Nige Cumming	Mini Cooper S	ERG574D	35th	Overall

Blairydrine Quarry Autotests

N/A	N/A	Renault 4L	Unknown	2nd	In Class

Pitcaple Quarry Autotests

N/A	N/A	Mini Cooper S	ERG574D	1st	FTD

Heelantoe Rally

Co-Driver:	Malcolm Lamont	Mini Cooper S	ERG574D	1st	Overall

1974

Rothmans Fintray Hill Climb

Co-Driver:	N/A	Volvo 142S	PRG1M	2nd	In Class

Aberdeen Stages Rally *(No Granite City Rally due to Foot and Mouth Epidemic)*

Co-Driver:	Graham Neish	Mini Cooper S	ERG 574D	48th	Overall

Lombard RAC Rally

Co-Driver:	Ross Baird	Volvo 142S	PRG1M	Rtd	Accident

1975
Granite City Rally

Co-Driver:	Ross Baird	Volvo 142S	PRG1M	51st	Overall

1977
Snowman Rally

Co-Driver:	Ross Baird	Ford Escort RS2000	RFX300R	16th	Overall

CP Granite City Rally

Co-Driver:	Ross Baird	Ford Escort RS2000	RFX300R	34th	Overall

Blane Stages Rally

Co-Driver:	Ross Baird	Ford Escort RS2000	RFX300R	1st	In Class

D&A Arbroath Stages Rally

Co-Driver:	Ross Baird	Ford Escort RS2000	RFX300R	8th	Overall

Robertson Stone Centre Autocross

Co-Driver:	N/A	Ford Escort RS2000	RFX300R	1st	In Class

1978
Snowman Rally

Co-Driver:	Ross Baird	Ford Escort RS2000	RFX300R	8th	Overall

CP Granite City Rally

Co-Driver:	Ross Baird	Ford Escort RS2000	RFX300R	24th	Overall

Burmah International Rally

Co-Driver:	Ross Baird	Ford Escort RS2000	RFX300R	19th	Overall

Border Counties Rally

Co-Driver:	Ross Baird	Ford Escort RS2000	RFX300R	7th	Overall

1979
Snowman Rally

Co-Driver:	Ross Baird	Ford Escort RS1800	LBO2P	3rd	Overall

CP Granite City Rally

Co-Driver:	Ross Baird	Ford Escort RS1800	LBO2P	11th	Overall

Bowmaker Rally

Co-Driver:	Ross Baird	Ford Escort RS1800	LBO2P	19th	Overall

Fintray Hill Climb

Co-Driver:	N/A	Ford Escort RS1800	LBO2P	1st	In Class*

Fintray Hill Climb

Co-Driver:	N/A	Ford Escort RS1800	LBO2P	1st	In Class

1980
CP Granite City Rally

Co-Driver:	Ross Baird	Ford Escort RS1800	LBO2P	Rtd	Unknown

Fintray Hill Climb

Co-Driver:	N/A	Ford Escort RS1800	LBO2P	1st	In Class*

Fintray Hill Climb

Co-Driver:	N/A	Ford Escort RS1800	LBO2P	1st	In Class

1981
Fintray Hill Climb

Co-Driver:	N/A	Ford Escort RS1800	LBO2P	1st	In Class

Fintray Hill Climb

Co-Driver:	N/A	Ford Escort RS1800	LBO2P	1st	In Class

1982
John Clark BMW Granite City Rally

Co-Driver:	Graham Neish	Ford Escort RS1800	OSO151W	12th	Overall

Fintray Hill Climb

Co-Driver:	N/A	Ford Escort RS1800	OSO151W	1st	In Class*

1983

Ladbroke Snowman Rally					
Co-Driver:	Graham Neish	Ford Escort RS1800	OSO151W	8th	Overall

John Clark BMW Granite City Rally					
Co-Driver:	Graham Neish	Ford Escort RS1800	OSO151W	Rtd	Unknown

D&A Arbroath Stages Rally					
Co-Driver:	Graham Neish	Ford Escort RS1800	OSO151W	Rtd	Hd.Gskt

Sprint Tyres Trossachs Rally					
Co-Driver:	Graham Neish	Ford Escort RS1800	OSO151W	5th	Overall

1984

Ladbroke Snowman Rally					
Co-Driver:	Graham Neish	Ford Escort G3	KSR896X	6th	Overall

Hackle Rally					
Co-Driver:	Graham Neish	Ford Escort G3	KSR896X	4th	Overall

John Wilson's Bedroom Stages Rally					
Co-Driver:	Graham Neish	Ford Escort G3	KSR896X	4th	Overall

John Clark BMW Granite City Rally					
Co-Driver:	Graham Neish	Ford Escort G3	KSR896X	Rtd	OTL

Forth Electrical Stages Rally					
Co-Driver:	Graham Neish	Ford Escort G3	KSR896X	5th	Overall

Fintray Hill Climb					
Co-Driver:	N/A	Ford Escort G3	609SR	2nd	In Class

Fintray Hill Climb					
Co-Driver:	N/A	Ford Escort G3	609SR	1st	In Class

Andrews Air Conditioning Border Rally					
Co-Driver:	Graham Neish	Ford Escort G3	609SR	Rtd	Unknown

Sprint Tyres Trossachs Rally					
Co-Driver:	Graham Neish	Ford Escort G3	609SR	Rtd	Unknown

1985

Ladbroke Snowman Rally					
Co-Driver:	Graham Neish	Volvo 240 Turbo	609 SR	13th	Overall

Hackle Rally					
Co-Driver:	Graham Neish	Volvo 240 Turbo	609 SR	13th	Overall

John Wilson's Bedroom Stages Rally					
Co-Driver:	Graham Neish	Volvo 240 Turbo	609 SR	10th	Overall

Sonat Granite City Rally					
Co-Driver:	Graham Neish	Volvo 240 Turbo	609 SR	13th	Overall

Autofit Stages Rally					
Co-Driver:	Graham Neish	Volvo 240 Turbo	609 SR	6th	Overall

Marlboro Russek Rally					
Co-Driver:	Frank Lorasio	Volvo 240 Turbo	609 SR	Rtd	Turbo

Andrews Air Conditioning Border Rally					
Co-Driver:	Graham Neish	Volvo 240 Turbo	609 SR	9th	Overall

Tweedies Daihatsu Autumn Stages Rally					
Co-Driver:	Graham Neish	Volvo 240 Turbo	609 SR	1st	Overall

Sprint Tyres Trossachs Rally					
Co-Driver:	Graham Neish	Volvo 240 Turbo	609 SR	3rd	Overall

1986

Ladbroke Snowman Rally					
Co-Driver:	Graham Neish	MG Metro 6R4	C670 JSU	2nd	Overall

Datamart Valentine Rally					
Co-Driver:	Graham Neish	MG Metro 6R4	C670 JSU	4th	Overall

Sonat Granite City Rally					
Co-Driver:	Graham Neish	MG Metro 6R4	C670 JSU	Rtd	Tim'g blt

Autofit Stages Rally					
Co-Driver:	Graham Neish	MG Metro 6R4	C670 JSU	2nd	Overall

Lloyds Bowmaker RSAC Scottish Rally

Co-Driver:	Graham Neish	MG Metro 6R4	C670 JSU	4th	Overall

Fintray Hill Climb

Co-Driver:	N/A	MG Metro 6R4	C670 JSU	1st	In Class

Border Rally

Co-Driver:	Graham Neish	MG Metro 6R4	C670 JSU	Rtd	Unknown

Marlboro Port Talbot Rally

Co-Driver:	Graham Neish	Volvo 240 Turbo	609 SR	Rtd	Fuel Pipe

Marlboro Lindisfarne Rally

Co-Driver:	Graham Neish	MG Metro 6R4	C670 JSU	10th	Overall

KARS Kingdom Stages Rally

Co-Driver:	Graham Neish	MG Metro 6R4	C670 JSU	2nd	Overall

Sprint Tyres Trossachs Rally

Co-Driver:	Graham Neish	MG Metro 6R4	C670 JSU	2nd	Overall

Lombard RAC Rally

Co-Driver:	Ken Rees	MG Metro 6R4	C670 JSU	Rtd	Engine

1987

Autofit Stages Rally

Co-Driver:	Bob Wilson	MG Metro 6R4	C670 JSU	1st	Overall

Citroën National Winter Rally

Co-Driver:	Ken Rees	MG Metro 6R4	C670 JSU	4th	Overall

Ladbroke Snowman Rally

Co-Driver:	Ken Rees	MG Metro 6R4	C670 JSU	Rtd	Cambelt

Skip Brown Rally

Co-Driver:	Ken Rees	MG Metro 6R4	C670 JSU	2nd	Overall

Valentine Rally

Co-Driver:	Ken Rees	MG Metro 6R4	C670 JSU	2nd	Overall

Northsound Radio Granite City Rally

Co-Driver:	Ken Rees	MG Metro 6R4	C670 JSU	1st	Overall

Hackle Rally

Co-Driver:	Ken Rees	MG Metro 6R4	C670 JSU	1st	Overall

Manx National Rally

Co-Driver:	Ken Rees	MG Metro 6R4	C670 JSU	Rtd	Camshaft

British Midland RSAC Scottish Rally

Co-Driver:	Ken Rees	Subaru RX Turbo	NA5166	40th	Overall

Kayel Graphics National Rally

Co-Driver:	Ken Rees	MG Metro 6R4	C670 JSU	1st	Overall

Shell Oils Cumbria Rally

Co-Driver:	Ken Rees	MG Metro 6R4	C670 JSU	8th	Overall

Kingdom Stages Rally

Co-Driver:	Ken Rees	MG Metro 6R4	C670 JSU	1st	Overall

Quip Forest Stages Rally

Co-Driver:	Wayne Goble	MG Metro 6R4	C670 JSU	4th	Overall

Audi Sport Rally

Co-Driver:	Ken Rees	MG Metro 6R4	C670 JSU	1st	Overall

1988

Snowman Rally

Co-Driver:	Ken Rees	MG Metro 6R4	C670 JSU	1st	Overall

Cordiners Granite City Rally

Co-Driver:	Ken Rees	MG Montego	E666UOM	54th	Overall

Shell Oils Cumbria Rally

Co-Driver:	Ken Rees	MG Montego	E666UOM	9th	Overall

Excell Valentine Rally

Co-Driver:	Bob Wilson	MG Metro 6R4	C670 JSU	1st	Overall

Autofit Stages Rally

Co-Driver:	Bob Wilson	MG Metro 6R4	C670 JSU	1st	Overall

British Midland RSAC Scottish Rally

Co-Driver:	Bob Wilson	Volvo 240 Turbo	609 SR	Rtd	H/Gasket

Fintray Hill Climb

Co-Driver:	N/A	MG Metro 6R4	C99KOG	1st	In Class*

Croall Bryson Jim Clark Memorial Stages Rally

Co-Driver:	Bob Wilson	MG Metro 6R4	C670 JSU	3rd	Overall

Quip Forest Rally

Co-Driver:	Ken Rees	MG Montego	E666UOM	25th	Overall

Border Auto Developments Rally

Co-Driver:	Bob Wilson	MG Metro 6R4	C670 JSU	3rd	Overall

Artigraf Kingdom Stages Rally

Co-Driver:	Bob Wilson	MG Metro 6R4	C670 JSU	1st	Overall

Chesterton Hackle Rally

Co-Driver:	Bob Wilson	MG Metro 6R4	C670 JSU	Rtd	Accident

Audi Sport Rally

Co-Driver:	Ken Rees	MG Montego	E666UOM	Rtd	Unknown

Park Systems Furniture Trossachs Rally

Co-Driver:	Bob Wilson	MG Metro 6R4	C670 JSU	Rtd	Accident

Castrol International Rally (South Africa)

Co-Driver:	Leon Joubert	Toyota Corolla	LPW 656T	?	Unknown

1989

Mercury Snowman Rally

Co-Driver:	Bob Wilson	Ford Sierra RS Cos.	B192BUH	19th	Overall

Skip Brown Rally

Co-Driver:	Ken Rees	Ford Sierra RS Cos.	B192BUH	11th	Overall

Cordiners Granite City Rally

Co-Driver:	Ken Rees	Ford Sierra RS Cos.	B192BUH	Rtd	Engine

RSAC Scottish Rally

Co-Driver:	Ken Rees	Toyota Celica GT-4	E889DPJ	Rtd	Driveshaft

Autoglass Tour of Britain

Co-Driver:	Ken Rees	Ford Sierra RS Cos.	Unknown	2nd	Overall

1990

Cordiners Granite City Rally

Co-Driver:	Ken Rees	Ford Sierra RS Cos.	D456RVW	18th	Overall

CHI Scottish Rally

Co-Driver:	John Davenport	Subaru Legacy RS	G330TUE	12th	Overall

1991

Fram International Welsh Rally

Co-Driver:	Ken Rees	Ford Sierra RS 4x4	609SR	8th	Overall

Perth & Kinross Scottish Rally

Co-Driver:	Ken Rees	Ford Sierra RS 4x4	609SR	Rtd	Accident

Audi Sport Rally

Co-Driver:	Nicky Grist	Ford Sierra RS 4x4	609SR	5th	Overall

1992

Granite City Rally

Co-Driver:	Howard Davies	Ford Sierra RS 4x4	609SR	4th	Overall

Cop-Y-Cat Manx National Rally

Co-Driver:	Howard Davies	Ford Sierra RS 4x4	609SR	Rtd	Gearbox

1993

Snowman Rally

Co-Driver:	Campbell Roy	Ford Sierra RS4x4	609SR	?	Overall

Grampian Business Products Granite City Rally

Co-Driver:	Campbell Roy	Ford Sierra RS4x4	609SR	2nd	Overall

Perth Scottish Rally

Co-Driver:	Dougie Redpath	Ford Escort RS Cos.	609SR	?	Overall

1994

Snowman Rally

Co-Driver:	John Bennie	Ford Escort RS Cos.	609SR	19th	Crossmbr.

Bournemouth Winter Rally

Co-Driver:	John Bennie	Ford Escort RS Cos.	609SR	1st	Overall

Scotphone Stages Rally

Co-Driver:	John Bennie	Ford Escort RS Cos.	609SR	8th	Overall

Granite City Rally

Co-Driver:	John Bennie	Ford Escort RS Cos.	609SR	2nd	Overall

Manx National Rally

Co-Driver:	John Bennie	Ford Escort RS Cos.	609SR	11th	Overall

Kerridge Severn Valley Stages Rally

Co-Driver:	John Bennie	Ford Escort RS Cos.	609SR	3rd	Overall

Kayel Graphics Rally

Co-Driver:	John Bennie	Ford Escort RS Cos.	609SR	Rtd	Cambelt

Artemis Equipment Stages Rally

Co-Driver:	John Bennie	Ford Escort RS Cos.	609SR	2nd	Overall

1995

Snowman Rally

Co-Driver:	Bob Wilson	Ford Escort RS Cos.	609SR	1st	Overall

Sunseeker Power Boats Winter Rally

Co-Driver:	John Bennie	Ford Escort RS Cos.	609SR	1st	Overall

Anderson Cars Granite City Rally

Co-Driver:	Bryan Thomas	Ford Escort RS Cos.	609SR	3rd	Overall

Valentine Rally

Co-Driver:	Bob Wilson	Ford Escort RS Cos.	609SR	Rtd	Engine

Weldex Rally

Co-Driver:	John Bennie	Ford Escort RS Cos.	609SR	1st	Overall

Steyr Daimler Puch Manx National Rally

Co-Driver:	John Bennie	Ford Escort RS Cos.	609SR	10th	Overall

Perth Scottish National Rally

Co-Driver:	John Bennie	Ford Escort RS Cos.	609SR	1st	Overall

Kerridge National Rally

Co-Driver:	John Bennie	Ford Escort RS Cos.	609SR	3rd	Overall

Jim Clark Memorial Rally

Co-Driver:	John Bennie	Ford Escort RS Cos.	609SR	Rtd	Accident

McRae Stages Rally

Co-Driver:	John Bennie	Ford Escort RS Cos.	609SR	3rd	Overall

Trackrod Forest Stages Rally

Co-Driver:	Steve Harris	Ford Escort RS Cos.	609SR	3rd	Overall

Bulldog Security Products Midland National Rally

Co-Driver:	Howard Davies	Ford Escort RS Cos.	609SR	2nd	Overall

Weir Stages Rally

Co-Driver:	John Bennie	Ford Escort RS Cos.	609SR	3rd	Overall

1996

Anderson Cars Granite City Rally

Co-Driver:	Stewart Merry	Ford Escort RS Cos.	K856DRD	3rd	Overall

2006

Bahrain F1 Pro-Celebrity Saloon Car Race

Shared with	Gavin Green	Chevrolet Lumina	N/A	?	Overall

2011

Malcolm Wilson Rally					
Co-Driver:	Tommy Dreelan	Ford Focus WRC09	AG57CKA	N/A	Course Car

2013

Monte Carlo or Bust Banger Challenge					
Co-Driver:	Gordon Hutcheon	Nissan Micra	N623PCU	£18k	Overall

* denotes New Class Record